GOODWILL'S

LATEST ESSAYS

AF553149

MADAN SOOD

GOODWILL PUBLISHING HOUSE®
B-3 RATTAN JYOTI, 18 RAJENDRA PLACE
NEW DELHI-110008 (INDIA)

Published by

GOODWILL PUBLISHING HOUSE®

B-3 Rattan Jyoti, 18 Rajendra Place
New Delhi–110 008 (INDIA)
Tel: 25820556, 25750801, 25755559
Fax: 91-11-25764396
Email: gph.ylp@goodwillpublishinghouse.com
goodwillpub@gmail.com
Website: www.goodwillpublishinghouse.com

© **Publisher**

No part of this publication may be reproduced in any form or by any means, electronic, mechanical, photocopying or any other method, without the prior written permission of the publisher.

Printed at : Kumar Offset Printers, Delhi-92

CONTENTS

IMPORTANT TIPS FOR ESSAY WRITING

Essay writing is one form of communication and it represents your point of view. We generally come across essay writing assignments in school, college or in a university. Essay writing requires certain skills and a well writing essay will act as a proof of the writer's knowledge towards a certain topic.

Essay writing acts as a valuable tool for monitoring the skills of proper organisation of ideas, good vocabulary and systematic argument. There are various categories of essays. You can write an argumentative essay, comparison-based essay, descriptive essay, or definition-based essay. The seven important tips towards essay writing are as follows:

1. **Make a list of things relating to the topic :** Start with a list of things that are necessary for constructing a good essay. You can do this by jotting down phrases, keywords, definitions, questions or any valid information, relating to the topic.
2. **Build a basic essay structure :** Ensure that your essay is being built on basic essay structure, which consists of title, opening sentence, background, statement of scope, ideas in point form and finally the conclusion summary paragraph.
3. **Write from the readers point of view :** A good essay should be able to attract the eyes of a reader. Make the essay enjoyable for the reader to read and understand your point of view.
4. **Be specific :** You should define your essay in a specific manner. Use definitions in order to help the readers to understand the subject matter. You will be able to write your essay in a far better way if you have been able to

collect the necessary information for your essay. This will help you to write your essay in a more precise manner.

5. **Make it simple :** Avoid using complex words. You should not try to show off by using difficult words. Your essay should consist of simple illustrations which will hold the attention of readers.

6. **Conclude the essay in the right manner :** You should conclude the essay by focusing on the main purpose of the essay. This method will help the readers to have a true understanding of your essay writing topic.

7. **Do proof reading :** To get a good end product, the essay should be read thoroughly. This will ensure that your essay is free from any grammatical errors.

A good essay is based on the ability to formulate and articulate good argument. Always write your essay from the reader's eyes. This will make the essay interesting to the reader.

1

INDIAN NUCLEAR STRATEGY: A PERSPECTIVE FOR 2020

India demonstrated its nuclear capability on May 18, 1974, when it conducted its first nuclear test in Pokhran—a desert area in Rajasthan some 350 miles away from Delhi. However, because of international pressure, particularly from the United States (US) and Canada, Mrs. Indira Gandhi was then believed to have bitten off more than she could chew regarding nuclear weapons. The Central Intelligence Agency (CIA) was caught unawares of the Indian tests. The test was then described as Peaceful Nuclear Explosion (PNE) of India. But few were willing to buy this explanation. It was also considered as being against the spirit of the nuclear Non-Proliferation Treaty (NPT) but since India had not signed the NPT, it was not strictly in violation of any international treaties.

After 24 years, India surprised the world once again by conducting these nuclear tests on Buddha Purnima Day—May 11, 1998. One was a plutonium type similar to the 1974 test. Another was a thermonuclear or hydrogen bomb, and the third one was a low-yield device with a wider application—primarily a tactical weapon. All these devices were triggered by one pull.

Two days later, on May 13, 1998, another two weapons were tested at Pokhran. These tests gave Indian scientists up-to-date knowledge on the latest developments in weaponisation of nuclear technology, including an ability to conduct sub-critical tests or testing by computer simulation in the laboratory.

Western nations in general and the US in particular, had always considered India's nuclear weapons programmes as less advanced. Naturally scientists in the west began to doubt the claims of Indian scientists, particularly the Indian claim of having tested a thermonuclear device, and the level of sophistication and yield of the tests. But Anil Kakodkar, the then Director, Bhabha Atomic Research Centre, said that thermonuclear device was limited in yield to 43 to 45 kilotons, so that seismic disturbance did not affect nearby villages. But the total yield of all the tests was claimed by Indian scientists as 58 kilotons. This claim was also disputed by the American journal *Science* which stated that the total yield of the Indian tests was between 9 to 16 kilotons.

Reaction of Nuclear Weapon States (NWS)

India's declaration of it being a nuclear weapon state was seen by the western powers as an effort on its part to emerge as a major power. The American policy makers were particularly sharp in advising India that there is no linkage between major power status and the possession of nuclear weapons.

On the other hand, the point has not been missed by the observers of international relations that it is the non-possession of nuclear weapons that is responsible for the secondary status of Japan and Germany. As a matter of fact, it is the American fear of the likely nuclear weaponisation by Germany and Japan that made the US in the first instance, react strongly against the Indian nuclear tests. Japan was against the indefinite extension of the NPT in 1995. It wants a rapid end of nuclear weapons under article VI of the NPT.

Indian Compulsions

Then what compelled India to go nuclear against the "International Trend"? First, it was China's growing assertion of power in South and South East Asia. What China claims was the international environment in which it faced a two-pronged threat to its national security in the 1960 which was similar to the national security environment in the 1990s faced by India. China has been a potential security threat ever since its aggression against India in October 1962. But the threat perception has sharpened since the end of the Cold War.

Secondly, Pakistan has been a perennial threat to Indian security under its goal of completing the partition process on the basis of religious identity. Thus, it had launched war thrice against India over Kashmir – once in 1947-48, the second time in 1965 and finally in 1971.The disastrous consequences of the separation of East Pakistan into the independent, sovereign state of Bangladesh, made it think in terms of revenge for its defeat in 1971.

All its decisions in international relations regarding the nuclear bomb have been related to India, the best illustrations are: "If India signs the NPT, it will sign;" or "If India signs the Comprehensive Test Ban Treaty (CTBT), it too will sign." For the first time in 1994, the then interim Prime Minister admitted Pakistan's possessions of nuclear weapons.

Thirdly, Sino-Pakistani collusion and collaboration was not only Pakistan's development of nuclear weapons and missile production, but also their general security and diplomatic cooperation was aimed against India. Pakistan was aided by China in its pursuit of nuclear capability on the principle that an enemy's enemy is a friend. This collaboration between the two nations only increased after the end of the Cold War. The collaboration was also extended for the development of missile technology.

Fourthly, the US—the global policeman—did very little since 1993 to ensure that Pakistan and China adhered to the NPT and, its own creation, the Missile Technology Control Regime (MTCR), under which any nation producing its own missile system was expected to restrain from transferring missile technology to another nation.

Fifthly, in a worst case scenario, the US nuclear weapons in their Indian Ocean base in Diego Garcia are also a serious threat to Indian security. Attending to threats to Indian security, I.K.Gujral, the then Prime Minister, had very elaborately underlined the security environment around India. The US is also mainly responsible for the May 1995 indefinite extension of the NPT. This legitimized the vertical proliferation of nuclear weapons by the five NWS who also are the permanent members of the UN.

Sixthly, there was the need to extricate India from the muddled waters of past rhetoric over the CTBT. The Indian insistence from the beginning was nuclear disarmament. India had joined the US in co-sponsoring the CTBT in the UN General Assembly. But the US officials from the beginning were looking at it as another measure towards nuclear non-proliferation. However, India could have come out of the negotiations in the Conference on Disarmament (CD) as early as in November 1995, if not earlier, instead of waiting till June 20, 1996, because in a speech in Georgetown University in November 1995, the then Director of the US Arms Control and Disarmament Agency (ACDA), John Holum had made very clear that the aim of the CTBT is to prevent India from acquiring nuclear weapons when he said: "In view of the Indian refusal to sign the CTBT as passed by the UN General Assembly as it was discriminatory, non-comprehensive and not a nuclear disarmament measure, India could provided it was keen on retaining the nuclear option—something every prime minister spoke about since Mrs. Indira Gandhi, but which could not be held up indefinitely.

India is not a banana republic which can be moulded to suit international needs as the big powers perceive it. India has its own strength of history and culture and almost a billion people cannot be ordered to forgo their nuclear option, particularly when surrounded by powerful nuclear weapon states.

However, it is pertinent to state that a nation does not act over a potential security threat when it actually materializes—the entire security scenario is built upon the anticipation of threat and being prepared to meet it.

A 2020 Perspective

Some important ingredients of strategic policy can be understood here. To begin with, India will continue to emphasise — in the next twenty years — from a position of strength, global nuclear disarmament. Unlike the US, which till the end of the Cold War believed that a limited nuclear war is thinkable and winnable, India looks at the nuclear weapons as the weapons of ultimate defence. Even after acquisition of nuclear weapons, Indian strategy is not based on the nuclear weapons. On the other hand, India now sees that it can speak on nuclear disarmament more authoritatively. However, in pursuit of global disarmament, we need to change our approach; instead of total disarmament, in the beginning, we need to move only step by step towards the goal.

India has already offered to sign such a treaty with Pakistan which has rejected the proposal by declaring it as "Self-serving". It sees nuclear weapons as a "Credible deterrence in view of India's conventional superiority." Russia's predecessor, the Soviet Union and China had announced during the Cold War their commitment to no-first use of nuclear weapons. But after the end of Cold War, Russia and China have been ambiguous on the issue. Hence, a successful conclusion of a no-first strike treaty will greatly reduce the threat of nuclear war.

The second policy strand relates to halting of production of fissile materials essential for nuclear weapons. India needs to agree on a Fissile Materials Cut-off Tready (FMCT) with certain precautions. Even on the FMCT, the US could take India for a ride by pressurizing it to stop production of fissile materials even before the treaty is negotiated and signed. This again could be a ploy on the part of the US to help Pakistan achieve parity with India on possession of fissile materials.

Thirdly, India needs to concentrate to make its nuclear weapons invulnerable to a first strike with nuclear weapons either by Pakistan or China, or jointly by them. In this respect, not only development of the medium range missile—Agni—is essential but also it needs to focus on its performance to the extent that at least half of the missiles fired will hit the target within a radius of a mile or two. To make nuclear weapons invulnerable to first strike, we have developed nuclear submarine "INS Arihant" in July 2009.

Fourthly, there is the case of deployment versus non-deployment of nuclear weapons to be decided. India will deploy nuclear weapons against China but not against Pakistan. This is because even if China is our potential security threat in the sense of its threatening ambition to be a superpower and make India play second fiddle to it, it is unlikely to use nuclear weapons against India, as a rational decision maker. However, this does preclude it from using them as blackmail which can, of course, be checked because it knows India too has nuclear weapons.

Fifthly, India needs to develop a system of command and control over the nuclear weapons. The ultimate decision to use the nuclear weapons will have to rest with the Prime Minister. But in a worst case scenario, there is a need to clearly lay down the alternative line of control in the event of conflict escalating into a war. Similarly, if New Delhi is made dysfunctional by enemy bombing, from where will the command and control operate? How do you carry nuclear weapons to enemy targets? Will you use aircraft or missiles or submarines or use the tactical nuclear weapons? In other words, it is also necessary to resolve the question of inter-service rivalry over the nuclear weapons. Since all the three services may have to be provided with nuclear weapons, creation of a Chief of Defence Staff assumes additional urgency.

Sixthly, India also will have to develop or acquire, in the next twenty years, necessary protective safety systems for nuclear weapons. There is also a need to take steps to prevent triggering of any accidental war, simultaneously taking confidence building measures between India and its two adversaries on the borders in the north.

Seventhly, in the next twenty years, India will not be able to reduce the size of its armed force because of acquisition of nuclear weapons—though eventually that is a possibility—as the threat to India's security will continue to arise from Pakistan, mainly through low intensity conflict (LIC) in fulfillment of the religiously emotive issue of the incomplete partition process in Kashmir.

Eighthly, Indian strategic policy needs to be backed by a well-conceived diplomatic posture for the future. It will be a prudent policy for India to cultivate cordial relations with countries which feel threatened by the expansionist policies of China. The way in which the US has conducted its policy towards China in the months prior to and after Bill Clinton's summit meeting with Jiang Zemin in June 1998, shows that Japan increasingly might feel threatened. Hence, despite Japan following in the US steps to criticize India for its nuclear tests, India needs to open immediately a strategic dialogue with Japan.

Further, India will have to maintain a steady economic growth to sustain an estimated expenditure of at least ₹ 1000 crore or more in the next ten years to put nuclear deterrence in place. This will need India to continue to maintain its GDP growth at a minimum of 7 to 8 per cent per annum in the next two decades.

India also needs to highlight possibilities of Pakistani nuclear weapons falling into the hands of Islamic terrorists in the Indian subcontinent as well as in the Middle-East. US Senator Patrick Moynihan characterized the Pakistani bomb as an "Islamic Bomb" and apprehended that finally it "will inevitably be pointed at the Middle-East."

Besides, India needs to devise ways and means to secure a stable government, as the political instability that the nation has witnessed ever since 1989 cannot be conducive to peace and stability in the nation's strategic policy. Only then can the political parties develop a non-partisan approach to the nation's foreign policy and security.

Finally, India needs to cultivate different segments of the American ruling elite through public diplomacy. In the highly fragmental system of politics and administration in the US, a large number of politicians and leaders had taken a pro-India stand when India exploded nuclear weapons. We need to remember that their pro-India stand is not because of their acceptance of our compulsions in going nuclear, it is more so because of their internal dynamics of party politics. We need to strengthen our ties with such segments of American politics, including the India caucus in Congress. We need to identify such politicians and develop bipartisan support for India.

When the Democrats have been strong on their advocacy on non-proliferation, the Republicans have been less vigorous on the issue. We need to watch whether a Republican dominated Senate will eventually vote to ratify the CTBT without which the treaty cannot be a binding on the US. If not, it not only provides some more breathing time for Indian policy makers, but also greater hope for being accepted as a NWS.

It is the sovereign right of India to decide whether its security compulsions warrant going in for nuclear weapons as an ultimate shield, notwithstanding the opinions of the Western nations. The opposition of the US and their developed nations appears to be totally self-serving when one looks at the actions of these very powers which advise India to desist from possessing nuclear weapons.

Hence, the pursuit of the above strategic policy will not only make India by 2020 a major power in the global politics and economy, but also a permanent member of the UN Security Council fulfilling Nehru's dream expressed in 1954 in the Lok Sabha, "if nothing goes wrong, like wars—the fourth major power next to US, Russia and China is India." India needs to develop self-confidence and, as A.P.J. Abdul Kalam very aptly observed, begin to think in terms of making India a developed nation in the 21st century. A strong and stable India will be a force for peace not only in South Asia, but in the world as well.

2

FIRST INDIAN WOMAN TO SKI TO SOUTH POLE

Reena Kaushal Dharmshaktu, 38, settled in Delhi, became the first Indian woman to ski to the South Pole. She made the historic ski run as part of an eight-woman Commonwealth team that caused a 900-km Antarctic ice trek to reach the South Pole to mark the 60th anniversary of the founding of the Commonwealth. Grit and a bit of fortune is how Reena skied for seven, eight to ten hours a day, pulling sledges weighing close to sixty kilograms and reached her destination.

Delhi-based Reena did her mountaineering training from the Himalayan Mountaineering Institute in Darjeeling and has been on IMF expedition to Gangotri 1, the first ascent of Argan Kangri, fluted peak stock Kangri, Phawarang, Mt. Num and others. She is currently a freelance instructor with the US-headquartered National Outdoor Leadership School (NOLS) that teaches outdoor skills to people. Her father was an army man. During his posting in Darjeeling, Reena fell in love with the mountains. Being from an army background, she used to go for long walks with her father which set the ground work for her tilt towards mountaineering. Reena got married to mountaineer Raj Singh Dharmshaktu, who had climbed Mt. Everest thrice. Mount Everest is the highest point and South Pole is the lowest point on Earth. She always wanted to challenge herself physically and scale greater peaks. It was a proud moment when she reached the South Pole.

Eight women representing different countries of the Commonwealth went on the expedition to celebrate 60 years of the Commonwealth. They were chosen from among 800 applicants in 2008. After shortlisting a team of 16, she underwent two weeks of conditioning training in Norway and New Zealand. At first, it was hard to stick to the time line with potentially harmful consequences for some of the girls but then they disciplined themselves.

Dharmshaktu has braved temperatures touching 30 degree Celcius for over 40 days in the South Pole. A routine day began for her at 6.30 a.m. when she woke up and melted snow for drinking water for the team. Breakfast was usually a diet rich in carbohydrates like porridge and hot water which is the best source of energy. In that temperature, the body cools down within seven minutes and the extremities are susceptible to frost bite.

Reena said that the charm for her was that she had never skied on snow. She said in an interview, "Something as innocent as skiing can be a big deal when you are surrounded by hidden 20-metre deep crevasses and loose snow. Once, when we were skiing, we narrowly missed a crevasse when the snow beside us fell through."

It was an arduous journey through the incredible cold, all white expanse of the continent. The expedition left behind human waste on 80 kg sledges that each member towed. It is summers in the Antarctica during the expedition, so the team had daylight for 24 hours. "Bewitched by Antarctica", Reena had tweeted four days ago. She was absolutely thrilled to have achieved her goal, and she is the only Indian woman to have been part of an all-woman expedition to the South Pole which made every Indian proud of her.

Reena, who has previously participated in expeditions to Mount Kailash and the Gangotri glaciar, has now set sights on a trip to the North Pole. She lamented the fact that she did not receive any assistance from the government for her path-breaking feat.

3

THE COPENHAGEN CLIMATE CHANGE CONFERENCE

The United Nations Climate Change Conference in Copenhagen, Denmark took place from 7-19 December 2009. It included the fifteenth Conference of the Parties (COP15) to the United Nations Framework Convention on Climate Change (UNFCCC) and the fifth Conference of the Parties Serving as the Meeting of the Parties to the Kyoto Protocol (COP/MOP5). COP15 and COP/MOP5 were held in conjunction with the thirty-first session of the Subsidiary Body for Scientific and Technological Advice (SBSTA31) and the Subsidiary Body for Implementation (SBI31), the tenth session of the Ad Hoc Working Group on Further Commitments for Annex I Parties under the Kyoto Protocol (AWG-KP10) and the eighth session of the Ad Hoc Working Group on Long-term Cooperative Action under the UNFCCC(AWG-LCA8).

The Copenhagen Conference marked the culmination of a two-year negotiating process to enhance international climate change cooperation under the Bali Roadmap, launched by COP13 in December 2007 in Bali, Indonesia—the Bali Roadmap, which included "traces" under the Convention and the Protocol and sets a deadline for concluding the negotiations in Copenhagen. The AWG-KP held four negotiating sessions in 2008: in April in Bangkok, Thailand, in June in Bonn, Germany, in August in Accra, Ghana, and in December in Poznan, Poland. The welcoming ceremony of the high level segment took place on Tuesday, 15th December and opening ceremony on 16th December. Close to 115 world leaders attended the joint COP and COP/MOP high level segment from 16-18 December, marking one of the largest gatherings of world leaders outside of New York. The Conference was subject to unprecedented public and media attention, and more than 40,000 people, representing governments, non-governmental organisations, inter-governmental organisations, faith-based organisations, media and UN agencies applied for the accreditation at the Conference.

Many hoped that the Copenhagen Climate Conference would be able to 'seal the deal' and result in a fair, ambitious and equitable agreement, setting the world towards a path to avoid dangerous climate change. On 7th December, COP14 President Maciej Nowicki (Poland) opened COP15, stressing its critical role in addressing climate change. Parties elected Connie Hedegaard, Minister for the 2009 UN Climate Change Conference in Copenhagen, Denmark, as COP15 President. At the beginning of the high level segment on 16th December, COP President Hedegaard resigned and was replaced by Danish Prime Minister Lars L. Rasmussen. Hedegaard assumed the role of the COP President's Special Representative.

COP President Hedegaard stated that the political will to address climate change had never been stronger. She called for a comprehensive agreement delivering on all building blocks and launching immediate action. Finally, she urged parties to "Mark this meeting in history" and "get it done".

Sudan, for the group of 77 and China (G-77+ China) called upon parties to observe the principles of good faith, transparency, inclusiveness and openness. He emphasized the need for the Copenhagen agreed outcome to ensure full implementation of Developed Country Party Commitments and the Convention.

Algeria, for the African Group, expressed serious concern with the lack of progress at previous meetings and reminded parties that Africans are already impacted by the climate change through increased drought, health hazards, food scarcity and migration. He called for transparent and equitable negotiations during the high level segment.

Lesotho, for the Least Developed Countries (LDCs), urged countries not to betray "the expectations of the anxious global population" and highlighted the importance of adaptation, financing technology and capacity-building support and underlined the need for contributions to the LDC Fund to finance countries' most immediate adaptation needs.

Grenada, for the Alliance of Small Island States (AOSIS), urged an ambitious outcome responding with the urgency needed and guaranteeing the long-term survival of small island developing states (SIDS), LDCs and other vulnerable groups.

Mexico, for the Environmental Integrity Group, supported a legally binding outcome agreed by political leaders in Copenhagen and urged the conclusion of negotiations on both tracks ahead of the high level segment.

Australia, for the Umbrella Group, supported limiting global average temperature increase to 2ºC and a 50% reduction in global emissions by 2050. It suggested that the aim in Copenhagen was to forge a political vision that will guide global actions and lead to a new legally binding treaty—the Copenhagen accord—as soon as possible.

The Copenhagen Accord

In terms of substance, the Copenhagen Accord immediately faced strong criticism. Others, however, argued that the agreement did include a 2ºC target and many other important provisions. Indeed, many saw the Copenhagen Accord as a concise document containing an outline of a future framework to address climate change.

Nevertheless, its provisions on mitigation by developed countries are widely seen as "clearly weak" and "a step backwards from the Kyoto Protocol". Developed countries do not commit themselves to legally binding emission reductions. Similarly, there is no qualification of a long-term global goal for emission reductions, or specific timing for global emissions to peak. Instead, the agreement suggests a bottom-up approach whereby developed and developing countries submit their pledges for information purposes to the Convention, a method advocated most prominently by the US.

With regard to mitigation actions by developing countries, the Accord does not contain any quantified emission reduction objectives and mainly elaborates on the measurement, reporting and verification (MRV) of developing countries actions, one of the major stumbling blocks in the negotiations leading to Copenhagen. MRV of unsupported actions are suggested to be done domestically and reported to the convention through national communications. The Accord, however, does contain some language reportedly a compromise between the US and China, stating that there will be some provisions for "international consultations and analysis", a concept yet to be defined. Those actions supported by international finance, technology transfer and capacity building will, however, be subject to international MRV.

What many characterized as "the most successful part of the Accord" relates to short and long-term financing. Developed countries came to Copenhagen with clear promises to fund mitigation and adaptation actions in developing countries. According to the Copenhagen Accord, US$30 billion for the period 2010-2012 will be provided, and long-term finance of a further US$100 billion a year by 2020 will be mobilized from a variety of sources. The Accord also establishes four new bodies: a mechanism on REDD-plus, a high level panel under the COP to study the implementation of financing provisions, the Copenhagen Green Climate Fund and a technology mechanism. Furthermore, the Accord contains a reference to possibly limiting temperature increase to below 1.5°C as advocated by many SIDS and others, although only with regard to the further assessment of the implementation of the Accord.

"If adopted, the accord would have an important step towards a better and legally binding outcome," commented one delegate before leaving the Bella Centre. After many long nights of tense negotiations, many were, however, reluctant to analyse its legal and operational implications given the "exceptional procedure" through which the Accord was adopted.

In particular, the basis for operationalising the financing provisions in the text is uncertain, which many have pointed out, is very unfortunate and detrimental to those developing countries that really need it.

During the high-level segment, informal negotiations took place in a group consisting of major economies and representatives of regional groups. These talks resulted in political agreement entitled the "Copenhagen Accord", which was not based on the texts developed by either of the AWGS. Details of the agreement were widely reported by the media before the COP closing plenary. While most reports highlighted that heads of the state had been able to "Seal the deal", almost everyone participating in the negotiations openly admitted that it was "far from a perfect agreement".

During the closing COP plenary, which lasted nearly 13 hours long and what many characterized as "acrimonious" discussions it ensued on the transparency of the process that had led to the conclusion of the Copenhagen Accord and on whether the COP should adopt it. Most negotiating groups supported its adoption as a COP decision in order to operationalise it as a step towards "a better" future agreement.

COP Decision

The decisions adopted by the COP that take note of the Copenhagen Accord include the following:

- It identifies climate change as one of "the greatest challenges of our time" and emphasises "strong political will "to urgently combat climate change in accordance with the principle of common but differentiated responsibilities and respective capabilities.
- It agrees that deep cuts in global emissions are required according to science and as documented by the IPCC Fourth Assessment Report, with a view to reducing global emissions and to limit the increase in global temperature to below 2°C.
- It states that parties should cooperate in achieving the peaking of global and national emissions as soon as

possible, recognizing that the timeframe for peaking will be longer in developing countries.

- It states that adaptation to the adverse effects of climate change and the potential impacts of response measures is a challenge faced by all countries, and that enhanced action and international cooperation on adaptation are urgently required in developing countries, especially in the LDCs, SIDs and Africa. They also agree that developed countries shall provide adequate, predicable and sustainable financial resources, technology and capacity building to support adaptation action.
- It decides that the Copenhagen Green Climate shall be established as an operating entity of the financial mechanism of the connection to support projects, programmes, policies and other activities in developing countries related to mitigation including REDD plus, adaptation, capacity building, technology development and transfer.
- It decides to establish a technology mechanism to accelerate technology development and transfer in support of adaptation and mitigation that will be guided by a country-driven approach and be based on national circumstances and priorities.
- It calls for an assessment of the implementation of this accord to be completed by 2015. This would include consideration of strengthening the long-term goal referencing various matters presented by the science, including in relation to temperature rises of 1.5°C.
- The Accord also contains two appendices with blank tables to fill on Annex I parties' quantified economy – wide emission targets for 2020 and NAMAs by developing country parties.

Many recognised the historical significance of the Copenhagen Conference, highlighting the unprecedented success in bringing together the majority of the world's leaders to consider climate change and listing mitigation actions pledged by developed and developing countries as well as provisions on finance and technology. Most delegates, however, left Copenhagen disappointed at what they saw as a "weak agreement" and questioning its practical implications given that the Copenhagen Accord had not been formally adopted as the outcome of the negotiations.

Ultimately, the arrival of 115 heads of state and government in Copenhagen changed the dynamics and routine of the negotiations. On the last day, many well-known negotiators were seen nervously waiting in the corridors with everyone else. Presidents and Prime Ministers, followed by their entourages and journalists, were seen rushing from one meeting to another.

On 18 December, "friends of the chair" consultations at the highest political level resulted in an agreement, which was immediately announced by US President Barack Obama before his quick departure back to Washington and widely reported by the media. In fact, many delegates first learnt about the Copenhagen Accord on the Internet and draft versions of the text were also leaked through the media long before the official UNFCCC document was produced. Most media reports alluded to a deal crafted by a small number of countries. Many close to the process despaired, arguing that announcing an agreement reached by a small group of countries was not democratic or diplomatic. "We are at the United Nations and everyone has to agree before you can report that agreement has been reached," commented one negotiator from a small developing country delegation. Some, however, argued that the only way to "get a real deal" was to get the "big boys" involved and they would inevitably use their own procedure and tactics. They also stressed that most of them are democratically elected leaders and directly accountable to their constituencies.

4

SETHUSAMUDRAM PROJECT: A WHITE ELEPHANT IN THE MAKING

Sethusamudram Ship Channel Project proposes linking the Palk Bay and the Gulf of Mannar between India and Sri Lanka by creating a shipping channel through the shallow sea, sometimes called Sethusamudram and through the island chain of Rama's Bridge, also known as Adam's Bridge. This would provide a continuous navigable sea route around the Indian Peninsula. The project involves digging a 44.9 nautical mile (83 km) long deep water channel linking the shallow water of the Palk Strait with the Gulf of Mannar.

The strategic advantages to India derive from obtaining a navigable sea route close to the coast, with a reduction in travel distance of more than 350 nautical miles (650 km) for larger ships. The project is expected to provide a boost to the economic and industrial development of coastal Tamil Nadu. The project will be of particular significance to Tuticorin harbour, which has the potential to transform itself into a nodal port. The state government has announced its proposal to develop 13 minor ports including Ennore, Cuddalore, Nagapattinam, Thondi, Valinokam, Kolachel and Kanyakumari. Development of the canal and ports is also expected to provide increased maritime security for Tamil Nadu.

The Sethusamudram Project will help Tuticorin Port by allowing ships from the west enter its harbour. Thus, the viability of the existing and planned minor ports in Tamil Nadu will improve. It is also projected that 70 per cent of the traffic through the canal will come from Europe and Africa. It is argued that steering in the proposed canal will be slow and the actual time taken will definitely exceed what is assumed in the project report. With the proposed tariff schedule, ships will find it cheaper to go around Sri Lanka.

Is There Need for the Project?

The issue about Sethusamudram Project is not about whether Lord Rama existed or not. The issue is that this bridge holds great symbolic value for Hindus and one cannot destroy symbols for the sake of economic development just because evidence does not exist. The Sethusamudram project was a dream vision of our national poet Subramania Bharati. He conceived this idea even before India became independent. He has given a hint to the future generation only to strengthen the Sethu which is none other than Ramarsethu, on which points and counterpoints are made.

On the other hand, if the tariff is cut, the rate of return will fall to uneconomic levels, and this could be accompanied by cost overrun on the capital and piling dredging maintenance. This may be one reason why there has been no private participation in the project. Global shipping companies are shifting to bulk carriers and tankers often exceeding 35,000.

The wind and waves bring in a large amount of silt and wash it ashore. The same thing is going to happen to Sethusamudram Canal. Marine scientists have identified five areas on the Indian coast line they call high sinkage pits, and one of them happens to be the Palk Strait. What is left unsaid by the Sethusamudram authorities is that maintaining the 12-metre depth of the channel will entail round the year dredging. Once you establish the channel, you have to maintain it. But this cost is not mentioned anywhere. This is the hidden cost which the authorities will have to pay to the dredging company. It is a high siltation and sedimentation area. So, what you pick up today is going to get filled up the next day.

Also, it is quite true that the 12-metre depth of the canal is not enough for big ships to pass through the canal. If you take global shipping trends today to reduce operating cost, they go in for larger ships of the order of 60,000 dead weight tonnes and above. A 60,000 dead weight tonnes carrier will need anything in excess of 17 metres of draft. And as far as the tankers go, the days of the super tanker are gone and you see only very large crude carriers of the type of 150,000 and 185,000 tonnes. It makes more sense to have such big tankers as in one voyage, you are bringing in more cargo and reduce your operating cost. None of these big ships will ever be able to use the Sethusamudram. So, the question is the for whom are you building the canal? 30,000 tonnes was all right when Sethusamudram was conceived in the early fiftees and the sixties that leaves you with only the coastal bulk carriers that carry coal from Kolkata, Paradeep and Visakhapatnam to Chennai and Tuticorin.

When you go through Sethusamudram, the point to be remembered is that you cannot proceed at the speed at which you are sailing at sea. The reason is the shallow water effect or what we call the "Squat Effect". So, the moment you enter Sethusamudram, you have to reduce the speed by 50 per cent or more depending on the conditions prevailing at that particular time.

The second aspect is that it is not an open seaway; it is like entering a port. A pilot boards the ship, who is a local mariner with greater knowledge of the marine environment. The same thing has to be done at Sethusamudram also.

The Sethusamudram Project from the media reports and the statement given by the finance minister will cost ₹ 2,400 crore, of which ₹ 971 crore is through a special purpose vehicle. The debt portion has been pegged at ₹ 1,465 crore. Assuming an interest burden of 10 per cent, the interest payment on ₹ 1,465 crore is ₹ 146 crore per annum.Twenty to twenty-five years is the time given for repayment.

Assuming 25 years for ₹ 1,465 crore, capital repayment works out about ₹ 56 crore per annum. So, ₹ 146 crore for interest burden and ₹ 56 crore as repayment works out to roughly ₹ 204 crore per annum, which is what the authorities will have to repay to any financial institution.This is only the break-even amount. But the website says it is a profitable industry and is going to make "mammoth profit".

As the earning is going to come only from ships, how many ships are going to transit in a year through the canal? Ships that can use the canal will be coal-carrying bulk carriers as long as the Tuticorin thermal power plant exists.

Therefore, neither are you saving time nor is it viable economically. There are the two aspects that need to be highlighted. So, there is absolutely no advantage to the ships and the shipping industry. So, what are we gaining by spending ₹ 2,400 crore of taxpayers' money? It is a white elephant in the making.

5

RELEVANCE OF RAJYA SABHA

During the last over six decades, Rajya Sabha (Council of States) has emerged as a parliamentary institution of great repute and has contributed immensely to the success of our parliamentary democracy. "It has given representation," as Shri Gopalaswami, Ayyangar, a legal luminary and a member of the Constituent Assembly had aptly said, "to the seasoned people who may not be in the thickest of political fray, but who might be willing to participate in the debate with an amount of learning and importance". Rajya Sabha is a permanent body and is not subject to dissolution. However, one-third of its members retire biennially. A member who is elected for a full term retains his membership for six years.

During the span of over five decades, the Council of States has played a remarkable role as a revisory chamber, deliberative body and legislative apparatus. Compared to many other second chambers in the world, Rajya Sabha has given a good account of its performance. It has succeeded in combining dignity with intense activity. Rajya Sabha's record in initiating legislative measures is a testimony to the fact that while it may be a second chamber, it cannot be treated as a secondary chamber. Numerous legislation have been introduced in Rajaya Sabha, the depth and content of which encompassed the interests of the downtrodden and suffering sections of our society. The Hindu Marriage and Divorce Bill, 1952, The Child Labour (Prohibition and Regulation) Bill, 1986, The Transplantation of Human Organs Bill, 1994, The Marriage Law (Amendment) Bill, 1999, The Prenatal Diagnostic Techniques (Regulation and Prevention of Misuse) Amendment Bill, 2001, etc. speak of the comprehensive vision of Rajya Sabha in taking appropriate measures for the welfare of the underprivileged and the needy.

Over the years, Rajya Sabha has assumed a more dynamic role in deliberating issues of common concern and bringing out legislations of far reaching significance. Active participation of its members in the proceedings of various committees also highlights the expanding role of Rajya Sabha. Occupational background of members of Rajya Sabha has reflected a marked change in the last 60 years. Earlier, lawyers constituted a major chunk of the occupational distribution in the house. Today, maximum number of members have prepared to put their profession as "Political and Social Workers". In 1952, almost all the members were freedom fighters and had participated in the freedom movement, but they preferred to give their chosen profession as either agriculturists or lawyers or medical practitioners or educationists. However, today many members have had previous legislative experience either in the State Assemblies or in the Lok Sabha or have served the Government or judiciary in various capacities. Also, there are members with specialised professional experience in a wide range of fields including editorship of newspapers, magazines, etc., film making to tourism and hotel industry. Thus, we may say that Rajya Sabha members, with their high age profile, varied educational qualifications and diverse professional experience, reflect the changing profile of our nation and to that extent, today they are better equipped to discharge their responsibilities effectively and contribute to the all-round development of the nation.

Public perceptions of the functioning of the democracy is not only based on the quality of governance provided by the executive but also on how far the proceedings in the house are relevant for its welfare and Rajya Sabha has performed this role remarkably well, deliberating fruitfully on numerous socio-economic issues and passing legislations aimed at the welfare of the people. The Rajya Sabha has indeed emerged as a front ranking second chamber translating successfully the principles of bicameralism into practice.

The Case Against

There is an urgent need for redefining and reorienting the role of the upper house of Parliament to make it more relevant and effective in meeting the present and future challenges that confront India as it tries to realise the vision of becoming a frontline nation by 2020. The Council of States has a special role to play in bringing about coherence in national and state development policies. Also, the Rajya Sabha should set high standards for other elected bodies to emulate, particularly the State Legislatures and Zila Parishads. While the Council of States could not bring down a government, it has made a valuable contribution through meaningful deliberations.

Very often, the Rajya Sabha becomes a topic of controversy, generating a debate on the relevance of an "indirectly elected chamber" in this age of democracy and direct elections. In recent years, there seems to be considerable concern over the role money power has come to play in the election of candidates. Almost all political parties are reduced to selecting those candidates who can finance their way into the Rajya Sabha. This is bound to disturb not only the representative character of the upper house but it also defeats the original purpose of having a second chamber.

A second chamber would inevitably tend to act as a "cog in the wheel" of the nation's progress but the dominant leadership of the Constituent Assembly, which packed the all crucial Union Constitution Committee, had no doubts about a second chamber. The inclination was to provide a forum for "elders", "wise men" or "statesmen" from where they could act as speed-breakers, without, of course, doing any great injustice to the principle of direct representation or distracting from the representativeness of the lower house.

What we have really achieved by the existence of this second chamber is only an instrument by which we delay action which might be hastily conceived and we also give an opportunity, perhaps to seasoned people who may not be in the thickest of the political fray, but who might be willing to participate in the debate with an amount of learning and importance which we do not ordinarily associate with a house of people.

In other words, it is "An institutional arrangement designed to provide insurance against legislative tyranny of the popular lower chamber." This original purpose has more than been justified in recent years, especially now that the same political party does not enjoy a majority in both the Lok Sabha and the Rajya Sabha.

Sometimes, even the lack of Rajya Sabha majority acts as an internal check on rash and haughty judgment; in particular, the Centre now seems to be doubly circumspect in wanting to invoke Article 356 against states being ruled by unfriendly parties.

Notwithstanding the unhealthy role money power has come to play in the selection of the Rajya Sabha candidates, it is generally conceded that of late the upper house has been witnessing a higher standard of debate, with rules permitting the members to seek clarifications from the ministers. A good case, all said and done, for the Rajya Sabha priding itself in a bit of institutional history.

6

CONSTITUTIONALITY AND JUDICIAL INTERPRETATION OF BANDH

It is an irony that a bandh professing to protest against anti-people policies becomes anti-people itself, as it inflicts great suffering on hundreds of thousands of people who have no means of protesting against the deprivation of a day's earnings, essential to run their households. It is not as if those organising a bandh do not know of its terrible consequences on the poor. But the bandh is not intended to protect the freedom of the poor or the vulnerable, for example, the Narmada Bachao Andolan. It is a political statement made by one powerful group or another.

Nor, let it be said, is a bandh affected by recourse to the basic freedom guaranteed to citizens by our Constitution; it is affected by coercion and the threats. If nobody works or opens his shop, it is not because they bravely sacrifice a day's earnings to make a political statement, but because they would be punished severely if they did not keep their shops shut or desist from earning that day's wages.

It is necessary for all those parties and unions that resort to this means of inflicting suffering on the poorest in our cities to consider the value of this power they so very clearly have—the power of coercion. The parties have formed governments—the prime source of power—because they were protected by freedoms guaranteed to them as groups and as individuals. Should then they not do all they can to safeguard those rights for all, including the poorest, and not confine their concern only to the urban middle class?

Apex Court and Bandh

The apex court had in 1998 clearly upheld the ruling of a full bench of the Kerala High Court that calling or enforcing a bandh was illegal and unconstitutional. In the recent case of

DMK and its allies calling for a bandh, the apex court observed that the object of the DMK and its constituents was to demonstrate their might rather than doing it for a cause. According to the bench, a bandh call essentially paralyses public life and is violative of the Fundamental Rights guaranteed under Article 19 (Freedom of speech) and Article 21 (Right to liberty) of the Constitution. The media, social activists and the High Court exercise the rights and the freedom guaranteed to all and, by doing so, express in a real sense the value that is collectively placed on the concept of freedom.

Recently, the Supreme Court decided to ban bandh called by Tamil Nadu government. By calling bandh unconstitutional, the court outburst the state government on the basis of what the AIADMK lawyer said, without making any effort to know the other side, was unwarranted, that too on a matter of constitutional importance.

It is true that the state-sponsored bandhs cause tremendous inconvenience to the people. But the highest court of the land cannot speak of recommending the dismissal of a duly elected government. In the context of declining parliamentary values, the rise of judicial intervention may be welcome. But the judiciary cannot undermine other institutions. The subject of making laws and enunciating general principles of public importance should best be left to the legislatures. The function of the courts is to interpret the Constitution, not write it.

In recent years , the judiciary has intervened in many laws passed by the legislature, including the law providing for 27 per cent reservation for the OBCs in elite educational institutions or calling 'illegal' the bandh called by the state governments. Even for small things, the Chief Secretaries of many states have been hauled up. In this context, recent comments of judiciary deserve mention wherein it stated that the court would recommend the dismissal of Tamil Nadu government which is a clear departure from the doctrine of separation of powers. The comments are not consistent with the provision of the Constitution. Nor are they in the interest of a sound and healthy judiciary.

Judges should interpret the law as it exists and as laid down by the representatives of the people. The Constitution clearly says it is the executive's prerogative to recommend the dismissal of a state government when it is convinced that there is a breakdown of the constitutional machinery.

Politically sensitive issues such as the Babri Masjid, Cauvery water dispute, the Mullaiperiyar row and, now, the Sethusamudram issue, which should have been resolved through political acumen and statesmenship, have all been referred to courts for resolution. Any observation or order by courts on the issues generates tremendous heat. Judges should exercise restraint while passing judgements on issues of public concern.

There is a serious concern today over judicial overreach and even highhandedness. Bringing home the point, attention can be drawn to a few of the recent incidents. In a 1998 Supreme Court judgement in CPI(M) versus Bharat Kumar & Ors, which upheld a Kerala High Court ruling of 1997, held all 'bandhs'—as distinct from 'general strikes' and 'hartals'—to be unconstitutional on the ground that they "trempled upon the rights of the citizens of the country protected by the Constitution" and were "not in the interests of the nation", tending to "retard the progress of the nation by leading to national loss of production." Since then, numerous general strikes, hartals and bandhs have taken place across the length and breadth of India, involving a plethora of political players and issues, with nobody in a position to make the fine academic distinctions that the Kerala High Court and the Supreme Court formulated in their judgements.

For example, in recent years, the Bharatiya Janata Party and the saffron brigade have called for, conducted and got away with several attempted bandhs. A case in point is the August 27, 2007 Hyderabad bandh called for to protest against the terror strike at Lumbini Park and Gokul Chat. And what about other forms of protests? Will the Supreme Court rule on what kind of constitutional animal is a *rail roko,* of the kind the BJP state unit staged in Hyderabad in September 2007 against the Sethusamudram project? Does it all fall under the definition of general strike or a hartal or a bandh? Is it constitutional? As political leaders have observed, the logical consequences of the Supreme Court unevenly implemented ban on bandhs will be a ban on protests and the right to strike. If that happens, the highest court in the land will itself be responsible for the trampling on Fundamental Rights that its 1998 judgement warns against.

Even more disturbing is the implications of court's remarks about dismissing a duly elected state government and imposing President's rule, especially in the light of what the Supreme Court has ruled in the Bommai case. In that historic 1994 judgement, a nine-judge bench, reviewing the scandalous misuse of Article 356 of the Constitution largely by the Congress-run Central government over four decades, laid down new guidelines and standards for the constitutional exercise of that power. Thanks to that sagacious judicial intervention, the use of Article 356 has become much more difficult to commit, although still not impossible as is evident in cases of Bihar and Jharkhand in recent years.

Bommai asserted the power of judicial review over Article 356(1) proclamations, that it can be struck down by the higher judiciary if they are found to be mala fide or based on wholly irrelevant or extraneous grounds. Nowhere does the Constitution or the Bommai judgement envisage any role for the Supreme Court in triggering the invocation of Article 356. The court's oral observation that the Supreme Court might "recommend" to the President dismissal of the DMK government, is constitutionally off-track, considering that there would be a flagrant conflict of interest between such pre-emptive, anti-democratic recommendation and the power of judicial review. The Central Government has done well to make it instantly clear that nothing can be further from its mind than unconstitutional courses such as the dismissal of DMK government.

Sufferings Caused

However, the problem in India is that in exercising one

precious right, we often extinguish that right in others, particularly the most vulnerable, those who constitute what is called the unorganised sector of society. When a political party or a trade union, or a group of trade unions, decides to call a bandh, lakhs of people who are in the unorganised sector—labourers, hawkers, tailors, cobblers, roadside barbers, rickshaw pullers, auto and taxi drivers and so on—lose their earnings for that day. Most of them depend on their daily earnings to manage their households and have to do without the means to feed their families.

More often than not, bandhs have no effect on public awareness of the reasons they were organised for except in a vague way. Take the recent bandh called by trade unions, as a result of which West Bengal and Kerala virtually shut down. If one were to ask people in those states if they knew the reason, it is more than likely that most of them would not know. A bandh to protest against "anti-people policies of the United Progressive Alliance government" is seen more correctly for what it is – a demonstration of political power of the trade unions.

No one can deny political leaders the right to call for bandhs or go on a fast to press their demands. But however noble their intentions may be, bandhs provide a chance for anti-social element to impose their writ on unwilling citizens. The right of a party to strike should in no way interfere with the right of a non-concerned citizen to go about his work. The Supreme Court deserves the praise for doing the needful to protect the people's rights. The DMK should have resorted to some other means to draw attention to the Sethusamudram project. Strikes and hartals, which were used as effective means to protest against the British occupation of India, cannot be used in independenat India. But the DMK's bandh call was unjustified as the party is in the power at the Centre and in Tamil Nadu. It is the daily wage earners who suffer the most during bandhs. There is no insurance for their lost wages. A law should be enacted saying the party that calls for a bandh or strike, should bear the economic losses incurred due to strike and bandh.

7

INS ARIHANT: NUCLEAR SUBMARINE

History was created on July 28, 2009 at a brightly-lit, enclosed dry dock called the Ship Building Centre in Visakhapatnam. After 11 years of construction, the Arihant (meaning destroyer of enemies), India's first indigenous nuclear-powered submarine, was finally in the water. The Prime Minister Manmohan Singh's wife Gursharan Kaur broke the auspicious coconut on the hull of the 5000-tonne submarine, following the naval tradition where a lady launches a warship.

The historic launch completed a cycle which began in 1974 with the then Prime Minister Indira Gandhi authorizing the building of a nuclear-powered ballistic submarine under the classified advanced technology vessel (ATV) project. For over three decades, the highly-classified programme has been propelled by political vigour. Carried out under the direct supervision of successive prime ministers, it formed part of the national secrets, including the nuclear weapons programme, which each incumbent bequeathed to his successor. "The launch of the submarine puts us in an exclusive league of five other nations capable of designing and building their own nuclear submarines," says the ATV's first project director Vice-Admiral (retired) M.K. Roy.

Powered by a nuclear reactor, this submarine generates tremendous heat that drives a steam turbine. It is, however, one of the most complex machines on earth, the reason why only five countries have the capability. The last to join this league was China, way back in August 1971. Unlike the conventional diesel-electric submarines which have come to surface to charge their batteries, nuclear submarines have unlimited underwater endurance and their speed is twice that of their conventional counterparts. Armed with nuclear tipped ballistic missiles, they form the third leg of a nation's nuclear 'triad' comprising air and surface-launched nuclear weapons. Over the next five years, the troika of Arihant Class SSBNS, each costing ₹ 3,200 crore, will make the third leg of India's nuclear triad—a strategic underwater platform for launching nuclear weapons.

Completely fitted out submarine, the Arihant, for all practical purposes, is fully functional. After the brief ceremony, the submarine was towed out for the first time across the naval dockyard and moored in an enclosed pier called Site Bravo—"from the maternity ward to the nursery", as one official put it. Over the next few months, it commenced a series of full system harbour trails. The primary system, a nuclear reactor, generates the heat which drives the secondary system, a steam turbine which spins the submarine's propeller, was tested separately. First, the steam turbine was jump-started with shore-based supply. The next significant step was starting up the submarine's nuclear reactor where the zirconium in the core of the submarine's 80 MW pressurized water reactor was slowly raised, allowing the reactor to become critical in slow degrees.

The primary and secondary systems will be mated only after all systems are tested. If all goes well, the submarines will be allowed to sail out to begin sea trials. Weapon trials, including the firing of the arsenal of 12K-15 short range ballistic missiles, are at the last stage of the trials before the submarine is finally commissioned to the navy by 2011. The submarine will carry four of an under-development submarine launched ballistic missile (SLBM) 'K-X' with 3,500 km range, each with several warheads called multiple independently targetable re-entry vehicles (MIRVs). These missiles will enable the submarine to conduct deterrent patrols in proximity to Indian waters. The Indian navy is only responsible for running and maintaining the nuclear submarines. All its tasking and patrols are to be controlled by the Nuclear Command Authority (NCA), headed by the Prime Minister. Orders will be passed to the submarine through a secure communication network.

The launch of the Arihant is a major step forward in India's quest for a minimal but credible nuclear deterrent. Its Asian rival China has 10 nuclear-powered submarines and is building an equal number, giving the Chinese Navy tremendous reach into the Indian Ocean. But India has still a long way to go, says strategic affairs expert Brahma Chellaney. "It will still be some years before an N-sub with SLBMs (Submarine Launched Ballistic Missiles) is deployed. In fact, the gaps in India's nuclear deterrent vis-á-vis China remains glaring. If India's nuclear deterrent was credible, Beijing won't mess with India. But the rising Chinese bellicosity suggests otherwise," he says.

It is the first in a series of nuclear-powered submarines to be built over the next two decades. The long arduous road began in 1967 with a Bhabha Atomic Research Centre (BARC) feasibility report on nuclear propulsion. A more detailed report was presented in 1971. And after the Pokhran nuclear test of 1974, Indira Gandhi authorized a project to build a nuclear submarine which would carry a robust, survivable deterrent. It was always called a naval reactor project for a good reason though. Compacting a nuclear reactor to fit snugly within the submarine's 10-metre diameter steel cylinder was going to be the greatest challenge. The reactor also had to go from full ahead to full astern and also from high speed to low speed.

The BARC derivatives of its civilian power reactors were too large and incapable of meeting the required performance parameters. With the erstwhile Soviet assistance, work on the ATV began only in 1980s.

The first group from the navy's nascent Submarine Design Group (SDG) actually designed the ATV trained with Russia's Rubin design bureau. Funds for the ₹ 2,800 crore project were never a problem and were sanctioned from the Cabinet Secretariat, and the joint DRDO-Navy project was always a closed loop within the Prime Minister's office. After Indira Gandhi's assassination, the ATV baton passed on to Rajiv Gandhi, who was also the defence minister. "Rajiv understood both technology and strategy and was in favour of the project. He would keenly participate in our discussion on whether our N-submarine needed one reactor or two and the availability of enriched uranium for the 'reactors'," says a former project official.

Rajiv donned work overalls and boarded the INS Chakra as she steamed into Visakhapatnam to join the navy in January 1988. He became the only Indian Prime Minister to board a nuclear-powered submarine. The return of the Chakra at the expiry of its lease in 1991 coincided with the implosion of the former Soviet Union, the tectonic event that nearly killed the project. Officials say there was a perceptible lack of political interest in the project on both sides—on the one hand Boris Yeltsin in Russia and on the other Prime Minister Narasimha Rao. The SDG meanwhile began converting the Charlie-1 designs for industrial manufacture. Therefore, the Indian private sector was chosen to build the 104-metre long prototype, dubbed S2. Larsen & Tourbo (L&T) built the hull, Tata Power made the control systems and Walchandnagar Industries made the complex high pressure pumps and valves which carried saturated steam. The BARC had still not succeeded in perfecting the reactor, so the government decided to continue reactor development parallel to the construction of the first submarine.

In a quiet ceremony at the L&T's Hazira facility, the then DRDO chief, APJ Abdul Kalam symbolically cut the first steel plate of the ATV. The project picked up speed under the NDA and during the tenure of Atal Bihari Vajpayee, the Prime Minister who stunned the world by bringing India out of the nuclear closet. Vajpayee, who also headed newly established NCA, chaired the apex committee of the ATV.

The political and the executive councils were also the two other authorities the project has. The project remained under the direct control of Vajpayee through his National Security Advisor, Brajesh Mishra. Talks for the lease of another nuclear submarine with Russia were revived. In January 2004, India and Russia signed a secret $650-million inter-governmental agreement (IGA) for the completion and lease of one unfinished Akula class nuclear-powered attack submarine and training crew to man them. (The submarine, also called the Chakra, is undergoing trials in Russia and is expected to join the navy.) The crucial part of the IGA was the assistance to build the reactor, which had delayed the project by years.

During the Prime Minister Manmohan Singh's first tenure in 2004, the project entered its last mile. He attended several meetings and would often ask project officials, "Everything all right?" The query was a mere formality because the project received unstinting support. In 2005, the UPA government gave an in-principle clearance for building a follow-on series of larger ballistic missile submarines, costing nearly ₹ 8,000 crore a piece, or nearly twice that of the current series of ATVs and another line of nuclear-powered fast attack submarines to escort them. "If you need money, you will get it," the then Finance Minister P. Chidambaram had assured the project team. The last and most important milestone was reached in 2006. An indigenously-built version of the Russian VM-4 PWR successfully land-tested was sealed into the hull of the ATV the following year because it had propelled the Charlie-1.

8

WiFi: A NEW TOOL OF INTERNET TECHNOLOGY

WiFi stands for wireless fidelity. It is a new technology that helps the mobile Internet users take the advantage of Wireless Technology in a building, office or home. The user can connect his laptop PC to the Net through this technology. He has to insert a special card in this PC. This card can receive signals from a transmission tower that is installed in the building in which he arrives. This building could be an office, airport, residential complex, shopping mall, etc. The transmission tower would send Internet signals to the PC through this special card. The user can connect the PC through to the Net and exchange E-mails, V-mails and data. He can also surf through various websites of the Net. Finally, he can also download data from such websites. Hence, WiFi is a wireless connection that makes a PC Internet enabled. It is different from bluetooth, which is another wireless technology.

WiFi has arrived in West with full force. It has also arrived in India though only a few installations of this device cannot be deemed the harbinger of its arrival in the entire country. The airport terminal of Bangalore has WiFi facility. The primary advantage of WiFi is that Internet users can keep themselves in touch with the information superhighway of the world. As on date, it is a costly technique. However, its prices would fall soon, aver IT connoisseurs.

The user has to procure the special WiFi card to gain access to the Net when he is mobile. Frequent travellers would find it very useful. The Indians going abroad would also be benefited by WiFi. However, it may remain out of the reach of students and ordinary Net surfers at least for the time being. In a large building, several Net users can access the Net through a single transmission tower. Hence the need for complex circuits and long wires would be eliminated, if we adopt WiFi in our present computer networks. Net cafes and large buildings, where Net surfing is a routine task, can have WiFi with immediate effect.

There are many disadvantages of this new technology. Firstly, its tools and gadgets are costly. It may not become popular among the youth due to the high price tag attached to it. Secondly, the owner of the building also has to spend a lot on the WiFi infrastructure. If the number of Internet users in his building is not very large, the owner of the building may find this installation exercise to be wastage of time. Thirdly, unauthorized users can enter into any WiFi-enabled building and access the Net. In such cases, the real owner of the WiFi apparatus would lose revenues. Fourthly, the user of WiFi services must carry on Internet-enabled PC along with him at all times to avail this service. He can use the Net by spending time in any Net café. However, if he wants to be on his own, he needs a PC, preferably a laptop. Carrying a laptop could prove to be a nuisance for those travellers who prefer to travel light.

Every time a new technology that arrives at the global scenario, is viewed with awe. Later, it is accepted. What is more, its new uses are also discovered by intelligent users around the world. In the case of WiFi, we expect similar development to take place.

Now-a-days, laptops are not very costly vis-á-vis their desktop cousins. A person of average salary can afford to have it. A natural corollary of this fact is that they would be able to use WiFi. With the passage of time, the cost of the gadgets of WiFi is likely to come down. Hence, like laptops, WiFi too would be affordable. WiFi can be used in desktop systems as well. Hence, persons working in a large building can use a single Internet connection to access the information superhighway. Thus the ideal use of WiFi in desktop is not a distant reality in India.

To sum up, people should welcome this new technology which has yet to make deep inroads into the industries, Net cafes and business houses of our country. Its future is bright because it holds tremendous potential to explore the information superhighway due to its being easy to use.

9

NANOTECHNOLOGY

Whereas the 20th century was the era of macro-science, characterised by gigantic Boeings, soaring shuttles, huge dams, monstrous refineries and power plants, the 21st century is dominated by nano-science, featured by microscopic weapons, molecular surgical devices, ultra-thin packaging, minute light emitting diodes and molecular switches and circuits. As science processed in the last few decades, the importance of the emerging area of nanotechnology is becoming quite apparent to the Indian scientific community too. Nanotechnology is the design, characterization, production and application of structures, devices and system by controlling shape and size at the nanoscale. Eight to ten atoms span one nanometer. The human hair is approximately 10,000 to 80,000 mm thick. Nanoscience is the world of atoms, molecules, quantum and macromolecular. The vastness in ratio of surface to volume opens new possibilities in surface-science. Important aspect of the nanoscale is that the smaller it gets, the larger its relative surface area becomes its electronic structure dramatically too. Both effects lead greatly improved catalytic activity but can lead to aggressive chemical reactivity.

Nanotechnology has wider application in day to day life. Nanoparticles take advantage of their increased surface area to ratio. Their optical properties, e.g., Fluo becomes function of the particle diameter. When brought into a bulk material, nanoparticles can strongly influence the mechanical properties, such as the stiffness or elasticity. For example, traditional polymers can be reinforced by nanoparticles resulting in novel materials, e.g., as lightweight replacement for metals. In the coming days, one can clearly visualise the huge applications of nanoscience in different fields.

The biological and medical research scientists have exploited the unique properties of nanomaterials for various applications, i.e., contrast agents for cell imaging and therapeutics for treating cancer. Functionalities can be added to nanomaterials by interfacing them with biological molecules or structures. Thus, integration of nanomaterials with biology has led to the development of diagnostic devices, contrast agents, analytical tools, and therapy and drug delivery vehicles.

Diagnostics: Nanotechnology-on-a-chip is one dimension of lab-on-a-chip technology. Biological tests measuring the presence or activity of selected substances become quicker, more sensitive and more flexible when certain nanoscale particles are put to work as tags or labels. Magnetic nanoparticles bound to a suitable antibody, are used to level specific molecules, structures or micro-organisms. For example, gold nanoparticles tagged with short segments of DNA can be used for detection of genetic sequence in a sample multicolour optical coding for biological arrays have been achieved by embedding different-sized quantum dots into polymeric microbeads.

The overall drug consumption and side effects can be lowered significantly by depositing the active agent in the morbid region only and in no higher dose than needed. This highly selective approach reduces costs and human suffering. They could hold small drug molecules transporting them to the desired location. Some potentially important applications include cancer treatment with iron nanoparticles or gold shells.

Nanotechnology can help to reproduce or repair damaged tissue. This so–called "tissue engineering" makes use of artificially stimulated cell proliferation by using suitable nanomaterial based scaffolds and growth factors. Tissue engineering might replace today's conventional treatment, e.g., transplantation of organs or artificial implants.

Chemical catalysis and filtration techniques are two prominent examples where nanotechnology already plays a role. The synthesis provides novel materials with tailored features and chemical properties with tailored features, i.e., nanoparticles with a distinct chemical surrounding or specific optical properties.

Chemical catalysis benefits especially from nanoparticles due to the extremely large surface to volume ratio. The application potential of nanoparticles in catalysis ranges from fuel cell to catalytic converts and photocatalytic devices. Catalysis is also important for the production of chemicals.

A strong influence of nanochemistry on waste water treatment, air purification and energy storage devices is to be expected. Mechanical or chemical methods can be used for effective filtration techniques. Nanoporous membranes are suitable for a mechanical filtration with extremely small pores smaller than 10 mm. Nanofiltration is mainly used for the removal of ions or the separation of different fluids. On a larger scale, the membrane filtration technique is named ultrafiltration which works down to between 10 and 100 mm.

The most advanced nanotechnology projects related to energy are storage conversion, manufacturing improvement by reducing materials and process rates, energy saving, e.g., by better thermal insulation and enhanced renewable energy sources. Today's best solar cells have layers gathered to aboard light at different energies but they still only manage to use 30 per cent of the sun's energy. Commercially available solar cells have much lower efficiencies. Nanotechnology can help increase the efficiency of light conversion by specifically designed nanostructures. The degree of efficiency of combustion engine is not higher than 15-20% at the moment. Nanotechnology can improve combustion by designing specific catalysts with maximized surface area.

An example for an environmentally friendly form of energy is the use of fuel cells powered by hydrogen, which is ideally produced by renewable energies. The most prominent nanostructural material in fuel cells is the catalyst consisting of carbon supported noble metal particles with diameters of 1-5 mm. Suitable materials for hydrogen storage contain a large number of small nanoscale nanosized pores. Many nanostructured materials like nanotubes, Zeolites or alanates are under investigation. Nanotechnology can contribute to the further reduction of combustion pollutants by nanopours filters which can clean the exhaust mechanically, by catalytic convertors based on nanoscale noble metal particles or by catalytic coatings on cylinder walls and catalytic nanoparticles as additive for fuels.

Urgent high technology production processes are based on traditional top down strategies, where nanotechnology has already been introduced silently. The critical length scale of integrated circuits is already at the nanoscale regarding the gate length of transistors in CPWS or DRAM devices.

Novel semiconductor devices: An example of such novel devices is based on spintronics. The dependence of the resistance of a material on an external field is called magnetoresistance. This effect can be significantly amplified for nanosized objects, for example two ferromagnetic layers are separated by a non-magnetic layer which is several nanometers thick. The GMR effect has led to a strong increase in the data storage density of hard disks and made the gigabyte range possible. The so-called tunnelling magneto resistance is very similar to GMR and based on the spin dependent tunnelling of electrons through adjacent ferromagnetic layers. Both the GMR and TMR effect can be used to create a non-volatile main memory for computers, such as the so-called magnetic random access memory or MRAM.

In the modern communication technology, traditional analogy electrical devices are increasingly replaced by optical or optoelectronic devices due to their enormous wand width and capacity respectively. Two promising examples are photonic crystals and quantum dots.

These are nanoscaled objects which can be used, among other things, for the construction of lasers. The advantage of a quantum dot laser over the traditional semiconductor laser is that their emitted wavelength depends on the diameter of the dot. Quantum dot lasers are cheaper and offer a higher beam quality than conventional laser diodes.

Nanotechnology is already impacting the field of consumer goods, providing products with novel functions ranging from easy to clean to scratch resistant. Already in the use are different nanoparticle improved products.

Food: Nanotechnology can be applied in the production, processing, safety and packaging of food. A nanocomposite coating process could improve food packaging by placing anti-microbial agents directly on the surface of the coated film. Nanocomposites could increase or decrease gas permeability products. They can also improve the mechanical and heat resistance properties and lower the oxygen transmission rate.

The first sunglasses using protective and antireflective ultrathin polymers coatings are on the market. For optics, nanotechnology also offers scratch resistant coatings based on nanocomposites.

The use of nanofibres makes clothes water and stain repellent or wrinkle free. Textiles with a nanotechnological finish can be washed less frequently and at the lower temperatures. Nanotechnology has been used to integrate tiny carbon particles membrane and guarantee full surface protection from electrostatic charger for the wearer.

The traditional chemical UV protection approach suffers from its poor long-term stability. A sunscreen based on mineral nanoparticles such as titanium dioxide offer several advantages. Timanium dioxide nanoparticles have a comparable UV protection property as the bulk material, but lose the cosmetically undesirable whitening as the particle size is decreased.

10

INDIA'S MOON MISSION

India's first moon mission was finally launched with the take-off of spacecraft Chandrayaan-1 from the Satish Dhawan Space Centre at Sriharikota in Andhra Pradesh at 6.22 a.m. on October 22, 2008 by the PSLV CII with the Indian tricolour painted on its sides and a Sanskrit shloka written on one side. The probe marked India's presence on the moon and put India in the elite club of Russia, the US, Japan, China and the European Space Agency. With this India became the sixth country to launch the moon mission.

Chandrayaan-1 is the world's 88th moon mission shot over 49 years and it is the cheapest-ever at just over ₹ 380 crore. At 1,380 kg the spacecraft weighs a little more than two Maruti 800 cars. The estimated cost of Chandrayaan-1 project is ₹ 386 crore, much less than the amount spent by its Japanese and Chinese counterparts. The main goals of Chandrayaan-1 were to conduct high-resolution mineralogical and chemical imaging of the permanently shadowed north and south polar regions, to search for water, identify chemicals in highland rocks and map the height variation of lunar surface features. It also aimed to observe X-ray spectrum greater than 10 KV to create a 3-D moon globe and chemically map the entire surface of the moon.

After the great success of Chandrayaan-1, the Indian government has given the go-ahead to Chandrayaan-2. It is the second unmanned lunar exploration mission proposed by Indian Space Research Organisation (ISRO) and has a projected cost of ₹ 425 crore. The mission, proposed to be launched in 2013 by a GSLV launch vehicle, includes a lunar orbiter made in India as well as one lander and one rover built by Russia. The wheeled rover will move on the lunar surface to pick up spill or rock samples for on-site chemical analysis. The data will be sent to Earth through the Chandrayaan-2 orbits. The design of the craft was completed in August 2009, with scientists of both India and Russia together. It will be launched on India's Geosynchronous Satellite Launch Vehicle (GSLV) in 2013.

Russia will design and construct a soft lander and a rover. After the spacecraft reaches its orbit above the moon, the lander holding the rover will detach from the orbits and land on lunar soil, then the rover will roll out of the lander's platform. It will have six wheels and will be running on solar power. It will land near one of the poles and will operate for a year, roving up to 150 km at a maximum speed of 360 m/h. The NASA and ESA would actively participate in the mission by providing some scientific instruments for the orbiter. ISRO has said that Chandrayaan-2 will be fully indigenous one. Chandrayaan-II mission will aim to land a rover on the moon. The rover will move on wheels on the moon's surface and pick up rock and soil samples.

A spacecraft by NASA will send a heavy rocket crashing into moon's south polar region on a mission to find water that could support future crews bound for Mars. The water-seeking mission was conceived, developed and now is controlled by space scientists and engineers at NASA.

NASA has been looking not only to return astronauts to the moon but also to build a lunar outpost there by 2020. The NASA plan includes first sending next-generation robots and machines to the moon to create a landing area for spacecraft and a base where humans can live.

NASA also launched two lunar satellites as the opening act in the long-term mission to send humans back to the moon. The satellites—the Lunar Reconnaissance Orbiter and the Lunar Crater Observation and Sensing Satellite—were designed to provide them with new information about the moon.

In an October NASA mission, the Lunar Crater Observation and Sensing Satellite, known as LCROSS, slammed into the moon in an attempt to kick up what scientists believe is water ice hiding in the bottom of a permanently dark crater.

Scientists have been hoping that if a human outpost is created on the moon, people there could have access to water there instead of having to haul it up from Earth.

The NASA and ESA would actively participate in the mission by providing some scientific instruments for the orbiter and they have sent proposals to the ISRO in this regard.

According to Mr Armadurai, Project Director of Chandrayaan-1 and 2, "We are not duplicating efforts other countries have already made. Our instruments are state-of-the-art which did not exist a few years ago. It will be possible to build an international station on the moon to support a manned flight to Mars."

Chandrayaan epitomizes our space triumph; the rotten political scenario is a labyrinth. If only our political leaders and those in other walks of life were to think equally big and beyond themselves as our scientists do, the country will be on the seventh sky of progress—economic and scientific together.

11

THEORIES OF INTERNATIONAL RELATIONS

International relations theory attempts to provide a conceptual model upon which international relations can be analysed. Each theory is seductive and essentialist to different degrees, relying on different sets of assumptions respectively. As Ole Holsti describes them, international relations theories act as a pair of coloured sunglasses, allowing the wearer to see only the salient events relevant to the theory. An adherent of realism may completely disregard an event that a constructivist might pounce upon as crucial and vice versa.

The number and character of assumptions made by an international relations theory also determine its usefulness. Realism, a parsimonious and very essentialist theory is useful in accounting for historic actions but limited in both explaining systemic change (such as the end of cold war) and predicating future events. Liberalism, which examines a very wide number of conditions, can be very insightful in analysing past events. Traditional theories may have little to say about the behaviour of former colonies, but post-colonial theory may have greater insight into that specific area where it fails in other situations.

International relations theories can be divided into "positivist/rationalist" theories which focus on a principally state level analysis, and "post positivist/reflectivist" ones which incorporate expanded meanings of security ranging from class to gender, to post-colonial security, many often conflicting ways of thinking exist in IR theory, including Constructivism, Institutionalism, Marxism, Neo-Gramscianism, and others. However, two positivist schools of thought are most prevalent—Realism and Liberalism; though increasingly, Constructivism is becoming mainstream and post-positivist theories are increasingly popular, particularly outside the United States.

Realism

Realism makes several key assumptions. It assumes that nation states are unitary, geographically based actors in an anarchic international system with no authority above capable of regulating interactions between state as no true authoritative world government exists. Secondly, it assumes that sovereign states, rather than IGOs, NGOs or MNCs, are the primary actors in international affairs. Thus, states, as the highest order, are in competition with one another. As such, a state acts as a rational autonomous actor in pursuit of its own self-interest with a primary goal to maintain and ensure its own security, and thus its sovereignty and survival. Realism holds that in pursuit of their interests, states will attempt to amass resources and that relations between states are determined by their relative levels of power. That level of power is in turn determined by the state's military and economic capabilities.

Some realists (offensive realists) believe that states are inherently aggressive, that territorial expansion is constrained only by opposing powers, while others (defensive realists) believe that states are obsessed with the security and continuation of the state's existence. The offensive view can lead to a security dilemma where increasing one's own security can bring along greater instability as the opponent builds up its own arms, making security a zero-sum game only relative gains can be made.

Liberalism

The precursor to liberal IR theory was "idealism"; however, this term was applied in a critical manner by those who saw themselves as "realists", for instance E.H. Carr. Idealism in international relations usually refers to the school of thought personified in American diplomatic history by Woodrow Wilson, such that it is sometimes referred to as "Wilsonianism". Idealism holds that a state should make its internal political philosophy the goal of its foreign policy. For example, an idealist might believe that ending poverty at home should be coupled with tackling poverty abroad. Wilson's idealism was a precursor to liberal international relations theory, which would arise amongst the "institution-builders" after World War II.

Liberalism holds that state preference, rather than state capabilities, is the primary determinant of state behaviour. While realism where the estate is seen as a unitary actor, liberalism allows for plurality in state actions. Thus, preferences will vary from state to state, depending on factors such as culture, economic system or government type. Liberalism also holds that interaction between states is not limited to the political/security ("high politics"), but also economic/ cultural ("low politics") whether through commercial firms, organisations or individuals. Thus, instead of an anarchic international system, there are plenty of opportunities for cooperation and broader notions of power, such as cultural capital (for example, the influence of films leading to the popularity of the country's culture and creating a market for its exports worldwide). Another example is that absolute gains can be made through cooperation and interdependence—thus, peace can be achieved.

Democratic Peace Theory

The democratic peace theory argues that democracies have never—or almost never—made war on one another and have few lesser conflicts between each other. This is seen as contradictory especially one of the greatest disputes in political science. Numerous explanations have been proposed for the democratic peace. It has also been argued, as in the book *Never at War*, that democracies conduct diplomacy in general very differently from non-democracies. Realists disagree with liberals over the theory, often citing structural reasons for the peace, as opposed to the state's government.

Institutionalism

Institutionalism in international relations holds that the international system is not—in practice—anarchic, but that it has an implicit or explicit structure which determines how states will act within the system.

Institutions are rules that determine the decision-making process. In the international arena, institution has been used interchangeably with 'regime', which has been defined by Krasner as a set of implicit or explicit "principles, norms, rules and decision-making procedures around which actors' expectations converge in a given issue-area."

Institutional scholars hold a wide array of belief stemming from the central proposition that institutions "matter" in answering the question, what explains a particular outcome. There are four reasons for this:

They structure choices, they provide incentives, they distribute power and they define identities and roles.

English School

The 'English School' of international relations theory, also known as International Society, liberal realism, rationalism or the British institutionalism, maintains that there is a 'society of states' at the international level. Despite the condition of 'anarchy'—literally the lack of a ruler or world state.

A great deal of the work of the English School concerns the examination of traditions of past international theory, casting it, as Martin Wight did in his 1950s lectures at the London School of Economics, in which he made its three divisions:

1. Realist or Hobbesian (after Thomas Hobbes)
2. Rationalist or Grotian (after Hugo Grotius)
3. Revolutionist or Kantian (after Immanuel Kant)

In broad terms, the English School itself has supported the rationalist or Grotian tradition, seeking a middle way (or via media) between the 'power politics' of realism and the 'utopianism' of revolutionism.

Critical Theories

Many schools of thought in international relations have

criticized the *status quo*—both from other positivist positions as well as post-positivist positions. The former includes Marxist and Neo-Marxist approaches and Neo-Gramscianism. The latter include post-modernist, post-colonial and feminist approaches, which differ from both realism and liberalism in their epistemological and ontological premise.

Marxist Theory

Marxist and Neo-Marxist international relations are positivist paradigms which reject the realist/liberal view of state conflict or cooperation; instead of focusing on the economic and material aspects. It makes the assumption that the economic concerns transcend others; allowing for the elevation of class as the focus of study. Marxists view the international system as an integrated capitalist system in pursuit of capital accumulation.

Constructivism

Whereas realism deals mainly with security and material power, and liberalism looks primarily at economic interdependence and domestic-level factors, constructivism mostly concerns itself with the role of ideas in shaping the international system. (Indeed it is possible there is some overlap between constructivism and realism or liberalism, but they remain separate schools of thought.) By "ideas" constructivists refer to the goals, threats, fears, identities and other elements of perceived reality that influence states and non-state actors within the international system.

Constructivists believe that these factors can often have far-reaching effects, and that they can trump materialistic power concerns. For example, constructivists note that an increase in the size of the US military is likely to be viewed with much greater concern in Cuba, a traditional antagonist of the US, than in Canada, a close US ally. Therefore, there must be perceptions at work in shaping international outcomes. As such constructivists do not see anarchy as the invariable foundation of the international system, but rather argue, in the words of Alexander Wendt, that "anarchy is what states make of it." Constructivists also believe that social norms shape and change foreign policy over time rather than security which realists cite.

Functionalism

Functionalism is a theory of international relations that arose principally from the experience of European integration. Rather than the self-interest that realists see as a motivating factor, functionalists focus on common interests shared by states. Integration develops its own internal dynamic; as states integrate in limited functional or technical areas, they increasingly find momentum for further rounds of integration in related areas. The "invisible hand" of integration phenomenon is termed "spill over". Although integration can be resisted, it becomes harder to stop integration's reach as it progresses. This usage, and the usage in functionalist in international relations, is the less commonly used meaning of the term functionalism.

More commonly, however, functionalism is a term used to describe an argument which explains phenomena as functions of a system rather than an actor or actors. Immanuel Wallerstein employed a functionalist theory when he argued that the Westphalian international political system arose to secure and protect the developing international capitalist system. His theory is called "functionalist" because it says that an event was a function of the preferences of a system and not the preferences of an agent. Functionalism is different from structural or realist arguments in that while both look to broader, structural causes, realists (and structuralists more broadly) say that the structure gives incentives to agents, while functionalists attribute causal power to the system itself, bypassing agents entirely.

12

PARLIAMENTARY VS PRESIDENTIAL SYSTEM OF GOVERNMENT

The term parliamentary system does not mean that a country is ruled by different parties in coalition with each other. Such multi-party arrangements are usually the product of an electoral system known as proportional representation. India stands out as a shining symbol of democracy amongst the nations that emerged as independent states after the demise of colonial rule post-World War II. India's founding fathers opted for the Westminster model of parliamentary democracy as practised in Britain with some modifications. They did study the American and French presidential systems but opted for the parliamentary system of government. Parliamentary countries like India that use "first past the post" voting usually have governments composed of one party. However, parliamentary systems in continental Europe do use proportional representation, and tend to produce election results in which no single party has a majority of seats.

Some believe that it is easier to pass legislation within a parliamentary system. This is because the executive branch is dependent upon the direct or indirect support of the legislative branch and often includes members of the legislature. In a presidential system, the executive is often chosen independently from the legislature. If the executive and legislature in such a system include members entirely or predominantly from different political parties, then stalmate can occur.

In addition to quicker legislative action, parliamentarianism has attractive features for nations that are ethnically, racially or ideologically divided. In a unipersonal presidential system, all executive power is concentrated in the president. In a parliamentary system, with a collegial, executive power is more divided.

It can also be argued that power is more evenly spread out in the power structure of parliamentarianism. The premier seldom tends to have as high importance as a ruling president, and there tends to be a higher focus on voting for a party and its political ideas than voting for an actual person.

The Case Against

India is developing not because of the political system. India is developing in spite of the political system. With proper and accountable form of governance, India could have by now reached a super power status given the resources and the abilities of the people.

India experimented with parliamentary system of democracy, copied largely from UK. Unfortunately, it has not worked for India. India as a nation is deeply divided into several groups with conflicting interests. Indian democracy in practice has not been able to abolish caste system that divides the majority community into groups with conflicting interests despite many laws. Accountability is the major casuality in the Indian style of democracy.

The political parties often give importance to the winning chances based on the group and caste following a candidate has. Even in Cabinet formation, caste plays its role, many times in the formation of the Cabinet. Caste and communal divide made India into one of the most corrupt nations in the world. Some credible estimates put the annual corruption in India at 50 billion dollars.

To fight the twin causes of corruption and caste, may be India needs to debate on a presidential form of government on the US model. A strong executive president does not need the support of caste and communal vote banks. He can go ahead with reforms that make the administration more transparent, less corrupt and more accountable to the citizens and the nation. A powerful, committed and accountable administration is the need of the hour.

India's parliamentary democracy after more than half a century in existence today presents a sordid picture if the following features that have emerged are taken into account:

- Due to the compulsions of electoral arithmetic of parliamentary system, India has become politically more divisive and fragmented.
- India's political dynamics today are driven more by considerations of casteism, communalism and other sectarian factors.
- In India, today no political party can claim to be a national party of stature. Their influence may be predominant in some regions and negligible or even non-existent elsewhere.
- India's Congress Party claiming to be more than a century old has yet to nurture a leadership independent of the political dynasty that has held sway ever since Independence. In election after election to ensure their success, they look for their dynamic icon of the day to lead them.
- Election tickets for contesting elections are being given by all political parties to the progeny of existing political leaders, their wives, their kin or close aides down to personal assistants. Merit is not the consideration, nor a record of public service.
- The above has degenerated to the level of criminals, people chargsheeted in courts and those having considerable muscle-power to contest elections on tickets of political parties whose sole consideration is how many seats these notorious elements can bring along.
- In the absence of clear mandate, India has entered the era of coalition politics where political definitions are the order of the day and political loyalties are switched by the

number of briefcases full of millions of rupees that can change hands.

- Crucial portfolios in the Central Cabinet have been given not on the basis of the professional competence of the minister so appointed but by blackmail of withdrawing support to the coalition even though the minister may be a tainted one.
- In such a mileu, India's foreign policies are getting communised and communalised and national security priorities are given a go-by.

Why don't we debate the merits and demerits of presidential form of government and if it appears to be suitable, then why not go for it?

13

THE CHANGING FACE OF TERRORISM

Terrorism is not a new phenomenon. It has been with us for aeons. Even in the very first century there was the Sicarji, a terrorist group based on religion operating in Palestine. The 'Assassins', fed on hashish, terrorised the population in the eleventh century. But over the years, the face of terrorism has changed. It has become more lethal, more widespread and more difficult to control.

Terrorism is defined as the "threat or use of violence for political purposes when such action is intended to influence the attitude and behaviour of a target group other than the immediate victim and its ramifications transcend national boundaries." Contemporary terrorist groups are less organised than their forebearers and their depredations are unorganised acts with political motivation. At the same time, they are more implacable, less structured and more difficult to predict and penetrate. The unpredictability magnifies the effect of violence and makes it difficult to combat.

Terrorist groups have sprung up everywhere and there are too many targets. And if public places such as airports are watched over by security forces more vigilantly, the terrorists shift the focus to soft targets—schools, markets places, trains and buses.

Technological advances have helped the modern terrorists to arm themselves with small, portable easy-to-operate weapons. The entire range of weapons available for national defence is more or less there for the terrorists as well. Terrorists are also increasingly making use of bombs and explosions. Sophisticated timers are available to set off the explosives as and when the terrorists want. Detection of the perpetrators becomes almost impossible. Human bombs have been increasingly and successfully pressed into active service to eliminate a target. In Tamil Nadu, a live human bomb from LTTE, the dreaded terrorist outfit of Sri Lanka, killed the Indian Prime Minister, Rajiv Gandhi. 'Semtex' was the gruesome weapon of earlier terrorists. Now it is RDX and other advanced and much more lethal things.

Modern terrorists are constantly devising advanced and deadly ways to terrorise their targets. Deadly chemicals introduced in the water supply system, germs deliberately released into the air to cause disease epidemics, biological methods of adversely affecting the ecology—these are no longer in the realms of fiction alone; today, terrorists have the knowledge and capability to actualise them in this world. There were reports suggesting that modern anti-US terrorists were planning to paralyse the US by indulging in 'agro-terrorism', i.e., by deliberately introducing animal and plant diseases in the country.

The most worrisome trend in modern terrorism is their brutalization. These terrorist groups are without compassion or ethical considerations. Moral scruples do not weigh with them; they are mostly cold-blooded liquidators for whom there are no innocents. Most of the attacks are directed against people rather than property. It is because attacks on people get full media attention. In the horrible Beslan tragedy of Russia, Chechnya terrorists killed 155 innocent school children in cold blood and wounded many more to hog the limelight and to espouse their cause for a free Chechnya; these innocent children had nothing to do with these terrorists' so-called justified demands.

Today, terrorist groups have global networks or established contact with groups in different countries. The Al Qaeda, the terrorist outfit of Osama bin Laden, that was brought into existence in 1988, has 'branches' in practically every part of the world, notably in the Islamic nations. This organisation maintains a workable link between Muslim fundamentalists in various countries. This, in fact, becomes easy if states support various groups with finance, training and weapons. In India, too, contacts were detected between the ULFA and the LTTE of Sri Lanka, the NSCN and the Myanmar guerillas. In the not too distant past, Pakistan apparently helped the Khalistanis. At present, it is very active behind the militants of Kashmir. This networking, not only facilitates terrorists operations but also makes the task of combating it more difficult.

The focus has shifted from the ideological and anarchist brand of terrorism to so-called nationist, reparartist, religious and ethnic variety. Both religion and ethnicity have become dynamic forces. India has to contend with this kind of terrorism in different regions. For instance, in the north-eastern part of the country, the militants are battling with the Indian security forces on the ground of ethnicity. Another form is 'economic' terrorism which includes mass counterfeiting and mass fraud. Reports suggest that a number of Pakistanis are active in India minting fake coins and circulating fake currency to distabilise the growing Indian economy.

The economic disaster that constant terrorist attacks are capable of wreaking on a country today can be as appalling as that brought about by war. Even the U.S.A., which is a powerful and rich nation, found it tough to cope with the economic blow inflicted by the daring 9/11 attacks. Tourism is adversely affected. Women become victims of violence and are often forced into prostitution, as jobs become scarce and capital non-existent.

The nexus between terrorists and drug barons is another alarming trend. The Shining Path in Peru is an open example of terrorist-narcotics-smuggling link. The nexus is more covert, but certainly exists in India. That is the country is placed between two drug-producing regions—the golden triangle of Myanmar, Thailand and Laos, and the golden crescent of Pakistan, Afghanistan and Iran is a cause of concern to the authorities. It has been pertinently observed that the route for passage of drugs worldwide is full of violence. India being a passage country offering a narcotics exit in Mumbai, lays itself open to the terrorist-smuggler nexus. An ideology is grafted on to give the trade certain legitimacy. Narcotics dealers have enough funds to finance the terrorists who require ready cash to procure weapons. These weapons are also easily brought in with the help of the infrastructure set up by the drug smugglers. International banks are there to launder the drug money.

Terrorists are today adopting mafia tactics. They extort protection money from businessmen to fund their activities. Sometimes, ethno-political terrorist groups get succour from foreign governments which exploit the genuine or imaginary grievance of the terrorists. It is alleged that India capitalizes on the fact that LTTE is a Tamil terrorists' outfit and helps it covertly to keep its smaller neighbour Sri Lanka under control. However, hostile governments cannot create the necessary grievances or potential terrorists where they do not exist. It is unfortunate, perhaps, that the conditions—political and socio-economic—that encourage the growth of terrorism are now in existence in several regions. Religious revival grows out of dissatisfaction rising out of corruption and consumerism.

It soon grows into a rigid mould of what is termed "fundamental". Political infighting and instability again provides a suitable ground for the growth of terrorist groups. Socio-economic conditions of rising unemployment, lack of opportunity to earn a living , growing awareness of inequality in distribution of wealth and well-being, exploitation at the hands of powers that be—these factors create a situation which encourages youth to join terrorist groups and others to support them. In the north-eastern part of India, militancy is widespread on this very ground. A growing number of people of this region believe that successive Indian governments have deliberately neglected the economy of this region with a view to denying them the economic rights which by virtue of being Indians they rightly deserve. That the cadre strength of some of the local terrorist outfits such as ULFA is growing in this hostile region due to this very fact, cannot be denied. With the proliferation of such conditions, there is a spread and growth of terrorist groups in several regions of the world.

It needs to be emphasized that these groups lack the

ideological and moral fervour. That prompted the terrorists of an earlier era. The idealism is superficial now; beneath the veneer is the lust for power. This explains the mushrooming of many terrorist groups espousing the same cause—witness Afghanistan or our own Kashmir.

Democratic states find it difficult to deal with terrorist groups. Because of freedom of movement in a democracy, more targets are exposed to terrorist attacks. The terrorists take full advantage of the rights and freedoms granted in such a system and cynically exploit them. The media, too, publicizes terrorist attacks and gives the groups the publicity they desire. The terrorists of today find it smooth going with human rights groups speaking up for them and with modern means of communication and transport within their easy reach. There have been numerous instances when some of the human rights groups and activists in India are known to jealously safeguard the supposed violations of the human rights of the terrorists. But when it comes to speaking for the right of the common citizens or the security personnel, they are seldom known to rise to the occasion.

The terrorist groups are now decentralized and can spread their tentacles anywhere and everywhere.

The modern face of terrorism can be combated only by a superior intelligence network. Indeed, intelligence is the key to decide the tactics to be employed to deal with the actual threat. The law-enforcing machinery has to gear up—think faster and anticipate the moves of the terrorists—if it wants to meet the challenge. But ultimately, whatever short-term tactics are employed, the conditions that give rise to terrorism should be tackled and that can be done only on a political plane.

14

EUTHANASIA: CAN DEATH BE A THERAPY?

Death comes as the end. Anyone born in this world must perforce die, despite the advancement of medical knowledge and skill at present. And when that medical knowledge is quite certain that a person's sickness is not going to be cured, that he or she is not going to recover, in other words he or she is terminally ill, would it not be merciful to allow the person to die? Would not euthanasia—or mercy killing as it has come to be termed—be acceptable to the suffering patient as well as to those who are close to him or her?

Painless death, which is what euthanasia basically means, is something that each one of us desires even if we are not afraid of that final annihilation. Visions of being bed-ridden, suffering increasing and incurable pain, causing trouble and grief to those whom one holds dear, above all, being dependant on others with no hope of recovery—such visions do disturb the imagination of even the most robust in health and the most optimistic among us, at least fleetingly. At such moments the idea of an easy death is certainly attractive. To be able to end it all at a stroke, so to say, appears the better alternative to prolonging the misery.

The issue of euthanasia involves two aspects: passive and active. Passive euthanasia would be the right to refuse medical treatment which merely prolongs life technically but holds no possibility of a cure or a resumption of normal activity. It is something that many people have done. There can be little controversy about such a decision. Indeed, it is not callousness but a clear perception of reality to consider as a meaningless waste medication that is not going to do any good whatsoever. It would be far more dignified to die peacefully and naturally, free of the myriad tubes and pipes sticking out of one's body is an attempt to keep one artificially alive.

Refusing medical succor beyond a certain point is not a problem if a person's faculties are functioning normally. The decision is made by the individual. However, patients in a coma, or in an otherwise unfit condition, may not be in a position to make known their wish to forgo further treatment. Their families might hesitate to discontinue such treatment for fear of being accused of negligence. To meet such circumstances, there should be some legal provisions. If, for example, there is a written declaration by the patient made when he or she was fully conscious and mentally alert, that in case of terminal illness or irreversible coma, artificial means to sustain life, merely to prolong the process of death should not be used, the person's expressed wishes should be respected. Many of us, indeed, would favour making such a living will to spare our families the awful dilemma of deciding when the time comes, whether or not to continue with expensive but useless medical support systems.

It is when we come to the 'active' aspect of euthanasia that ethical dilemmas come to the fore. For it involves not merely a refusal to be medicated but a conscious and deliberate decision to end one's life in case of terminal illness, and beyond that the right of doctors to be protected from prosecution if they accede to a patient's request for mercy killing. Whether one takes the decision oneself or others have to take the decision, the issue is fraught with moral considerations.

'Active' euthanasia, in its essence, comes down to legalised suicide or legalised murder or abetment to suicide. There is a deep-rooted belief in most people that life is a a God-given gift and it is presumptuous on the part of a human being, howsoever merciful the motive, many would frown upon it as coming dangerously close to playing God. And if the patient is in coma, without having expressed any idea on the subject, who is to decide on actively terminating the person's life? The possibility of greedy and unscrupulous relatives colluding with an equally unscrupulous doctor to kill a patient, from whose death they stand to gain, is a real danger. Even if a doctor is sincere and honest, the dilemma will remain whether the decision to terminate life was right or wrong at a deep moral level. A doctor's duty is surely to prolong life and not assist in shortening it.

There is a wide difference between stopping irksome medical treatment to allow a dying person to attain a peaceful and natural end and, on the other hand, administering something in order to consciously induce death. What if after deciding to allow euthanasia and being administered the lethal drug, hovering between life and death, a patient wants to reverse his or her decision and does not want to die as yet?

It would be a horrendous situation for the patient as well as the doctor. Even those making a "living will" to die may yet feel like changing their mind toward the end, but drift into a coma before expressing their changed viewpoint. What then? Who can decide correctly for such a patient? The act of removing life supports and permitting death can be traumatic enough for some doctors and nurses, may be even abhorrent to their conscience. How then can they reconcile themselves to actively administering some lethal drug to shorten a patient's life?

There are times, of course, when the agony of a patient dear to us is difficult to see and bear, especially when everyone concerned knows that death is inevitable. And it is easy to understand and sympathise with the death of a patient suffering excruciating pain or the humiliating situation of losing control over vital bodily functions. It is not given to all of us to have the strength and courage to endure physical pain and mental anguish stoically, though many of us would, no doubt, yearn for such strength. At such times and for such persons, surely the choice of euthanasia should be made available.

In certain countries such as the Netherlands, the Northern Territory of Australia, Japan, Colombia and Belgium, law allows us the life of a person to be taken 'upon his/her explicit request'. In the United Kingdom, it has been considered legal to withdraw medical treatment and life support for a patient in persistent and vegetative state and allow him or her to die. In South Africa, even though euthanasia is not legally accepted, it finds widespread support. As a matter of fact, a survey by the Medical Association revealed that about sixty per cent of physicians in the country had performed passive euthanasia by withholding medication or procedure with the hope of speeding up death. In India, there are voluntary societies that are campaigning for the right of an individual to choose to live or die within the limits of law.

Any law on euthanasia should, of course, have clear safeguards to preclude any possibility of unscrupulous elements exploiting the situation. For instance, hiding behind euthanasia, the greedy relatives and doctors could kill the terminally-ill patient before time to make money and /or to settle the mounting hospital bills of the bed-ridden patients in question. The prime decision should come from the patient concerned, and that after long and deep thought. There can be no hasty decision in this matter. No one should try to influence a person to think in terms of terminating his or her life or in seeking active intervention from doctors in doing so. No effort should be made to terminate a patient's life unless he or she repeatedly requests such action, and there s no reason to doubt this desire to die. It is also important that euthanasia is considered only in case of severe mental and physical suffering with no prospect of relief, and all other options for the recovery of the patient have been exhausted. But some people disagree with this, claiming that allowing the so-called mercy killing, in all likelihood, would send wrong signals in the society, jeopardising the very sanctity of human life in the process. Besides, behind euthanasia lurks the grave danger of 'organ harvesting'. Incidentally, in 2005 the Andhra Pradesh High Court dismissed Venkatesh's requests for mercy killing on this very ground though he was terminally ill.

People, who staunchly oppose euthanasia, are blind to the

tragedy and sense of human waste when a person suffering from irretrievable brain damage is kept artificially alive, suspended between life and death. There are several persons in the world at present who lie in a 'persistent vegetative state'. Hence, it would be pertinent to recall that some time back a district court of USA, in perhaps the most heavily litigated right-to-die case in US history, passed a historic judgement allowing a terminally-ill patient, Terri Schiavo to die peacefully. In 1990, a heart attack had left Terri brain-damaged and she had fallen into coma; since then she had been leading a vegetative existence. Previously, death came when a person stopped breathing, now cardiopulmonary resuscitation and mechanical ventilators and respirators prolong life—or existence as some would have it—beyond what could have been imagined even some years earlier. In the circumstances, one has to consider the meaning of life itself, and not reject euthanasia out of hand as 'immoral'.

Euthanasia is a controversial subject, and there can be no unanimity about it. Myriad shades of opinion exist upon the rights and wrongs of it. Ultimately, it ought to be every individual's right to decide whether to ensure the suffering or to end it all, whether to continue with a treatment that merely prolongs a meaningless existence or to seek in death itself the final therapy. After all, the right to live would not be complete if the right to die with full dignity was not available to the people.

15

DISASTER MANAGEMENT IN INDIA

After Independence India began a process of rapid industrialisation. It inevitably lacked some framework conditions, such as an understanding of the risks of chemical hazards. Implementation of safety procedures, including regulatory approaches, soon followed and institutions such as the National Safety Council of India (NSCI) were created. There was much to do.

The Bhopal disaster (1984) did much to focus more attention on the need for a holistic approach to technology disaster management, and the role of ordinary people in emergencies. The government took several important measures, with major legislative and stronger institutional mechanisms. It set up Crisis Groups at Central, state, district and local levels. NSCI took the APELL process as a model, promoting awareness and training projects covering both hazardous materials transport and fixed installations.

India is also vulnerable to natural disasters. While well-established mechanisms for response, relief and rehabilitation were in place, major events such as the Orissa super-cyclone (1999) and the Bhuj earthquake (2001) emphasized the need for a comprehensive approach to mitigation and prevention for natural and man-made disasters.

Government Initiatives in Disaster Management

India is prone to multiple natural disasters such as floods, earthquakes, droughts, landslides, cyclones, etc. This is due to various factors like the geo-climate conditions, increase in population density, improper urbanisation, deforestation and desertification.

According to government data, about 60 per cent of the Indian landmass is prone to earthquakes of varying densities, over 40 million hectares is prone to floods, around eight per cent of the total area is prone to cyclone and 68 per cent of the area is susceptible to drought. In the last decade, the damage in terms of human suffering, loss of life, agriculture productivity and economic losses has been astronomical.

At the government level, there has been considerable concern over restricting socio-economic damage. Substantial scientific and material progress has been made in this field for more than five decades. However, the loss of human life and property due to natural or man-made disasters has not decreased. The basic responsibility of response mechanism, like undertaking rescue, relief and rehabilitation measures in the event of the disaster, rests with the state governments. And the Centre supplements the efforts by extending logistics and financial support.

The government has formed a National Disaster Framework covering institutional mechanisms, disaster prevention strategy, early warning system, disaster mitigation, preparedness and response and human resource development. The government has set up National Management Committee and Crisis Management Group. There is a National Committee on Disaster Management to suggest necessary institutional and legislative measures necessary for an efficient and long term strategy to manage natural disasters. Another committee—High Powered Committee on Disaster Management Plans—was constituted in 1999 to prepare comprehensive model plans for management of disasters at the national, state and district level.

The state governments have set up state crisis management groups headed by chief secretaries, institutes of relief commissioners and state/district contingency plans. There is a calamity relief fund (CRF) for each state. About 75 per cent of the CRF is contributed by the Central government and the rest is contributed by various state governments.

NSCI adopted several goals based on the APELL procedures; creating or raising public awareness of possible hazards within a community; stimulating development of cooperative plans to respond to any emergency that might occur; and encouraging accident prevention. Implementation in this vast country followed a two-track approach of development of awareness at the national level, and in-depth implementation in selected high-risk industrial areas (HRIA). We needed to gain first-hand experience through pilot projects in important areas. A National Advisory Committee and Technical Core Group was set up for periodical review guidance and technical education. In 2002, the first APELL Centre opened at NSCI headquarters in Mumbai. It was the first centre of this sort in the world.

The first project started in 1992 in six HRIAs also drawing on international collaboration from UNEP, USAID and WEC. In 2004, an APELL sub-centre opened in Haldia. A manual on cyclone emergency preparedness was prepared.

Transport issues were becoming urgent and a major new programme was based on UNEP's Trans APELL. A training module and seminars were developed for traffic police. A HAZMAT emergency van started work on a trial basis in Patalganga-Rasayani, and a broad based programme for transports was launched.

Several lessons may be learnt from this process. Widespread industrial development in a country like India requires comprehensive replication of the programme at local level. Sub-centres are essential with replication programmes involving local partners. Practical experience at local level has facilitated and has, in turn, been facilitated by national legislation such as the law setting up crisis groups and safety management in general. Crisis groups at district and local level require training and support tools—best practice studies, etc.—so there is an ongoing role for training organizations such as NSCI and its offshoots like NAC. Finally, the programme has pinpointed the need to treat transport as a priority issue, linking various locations in the hazardous material chain across the country. The experience has also aroused, much interest abroad, notably in China, South Africa, Jordan and Brazil, underlining the need to share experience internationally.

Emergency prevention and preparedness is a complex issue, and industrialised countries need to address the matter as an integral part of a larger sustainable development agenda. Experience in countries such as India can do much to streamline the process elsewhere, with growing pressures to better address disaster issues.

The disaster management policy of the government stresses on forecasting and warning using advanced technologies, contingency agriculture planning to ensure availability of food grains, and preparedness and mitigation through specific programmes. The Central sector scheme for disaster management focuses on setting up National Centre for Disaster Management, disaster management facilities in states and programmes for community participation and public awareness.

16

INDIA AND UNSC SEAT

New Delhi's unyielding intent to join the United Nation's Security Council as a permanent member was evident during recent visit of its upper layer politicians to various countries. Especially, while addressing the Indian Ocean island state's national assembly, Prime Minister Manmohan Singh appreciated the support extended by Port Louis for India's candidature to the coveted big boys' club. But what mattered was his conviction of India's determination and capacity to assume the onerous responsibilities of a permanent member of the expanded Council. The PM also asserted that India's membership would enhance the effectiveness, credibility and the legitimacy of the UNSC.

The event will turn out to be a momentous watershed in the 64-year history of the world body if it is able to push through the proposal of the candidature of India along with Brazil, Germany, Japan and possibly one of the major representative nations from the continent of Africa as new permanent members of the expanded UNSC with veto rights. Presently, the US, Russia, China, UK and France are the five permanent members.

New Delhi's Efforts and UNSC

New Delhi's patient perseverance seems to be paying dividends. The G4 countries—India, Brazil, Japan and Germany—have teamed up to support each other's bid for permanent seats. They plan to seek a vote in the Assembly on a resolution calling for UNSC's expansion. Many nations now fully subscribe to the fact that India, a country of 1.2 billion, not to be represented in the Security Council is something unfair. New Delhi, hence, has a solid reason to be optimistic in its decade-long endeavour as presently there appears to be increasing international support for its entry into the portals of the UN's exclusive decision-making club for maintaining world peace. However, India must reject the proposal being mooted in some quarters that if the country is at all permitted to enter the portals of the Council, it should be sans veto power.

The Security Council is given under chapter VII of the UN Charter, a virtual monopoly over the use of force to defeat aggression. States, alone or collectively with their allies, are entitled to use force only in self-defence as a temporary measure until Security Council starts to take effective measures. The UNSC's forces are supposed to be provided by individual member states by agreements made under article 43 of the Charter. Incidentally, India has all these crucial post-World War II years been a major source for the troops for peace keeping roles in the trouble spots all around the world.

A UN reforms panel has been at work for a couple of years to suggest ways and means of adding more permanent members to the Security Council in addition to the existing five nations. The present Council formed consequent to San Francisco deliberations of 1945 by the founder nations to establish the worthy successor to the defunct League of Nations has become totally irrelevant in the present day uni-polar world where the US power-play reigns supreme.

The UN General Assembly would require a two-thirds majority vote of the Assembly members to restructure the UNSC. The reform process would be considered a success only if an enlarged Council enhanced the representation of the developing countries from Asia, Africa and Latin America. Non-Aligned Movement (NAM) members would like expansion based on equitable geographical representation. As far as Asia is concerned, after China and Japan there is no other country but India which can justifiably represent the world's largest and most populous continent.

There is no denying that the present-day international peace and security calls for representative Security Council reflective of existing realities. In this context, the international community must take cognizance of the fact that a large geographical entity of over a billion people with 5,000 years of long history, civilization and cultural heritage needs to be given a justifiable place in the world body. The resurgent modern India, with its deep-rooted democratic system and growing economic potential, has the right credentials to champion causes of the developing nations.

India has struck the right chord when PM Manmohan Singh declared that the UN is the critical link in cooperative multilateral efforts to manage the challenge of global independence. The Security Council is an important UN organ whose primary responsibility is the maintenance of international peace, stability and security in the world. The UN Charter states that the Council may take military action against the offending nations by air, sea and land forces. India's size, its role in the world, its economy, its contribution to UN peacekeeping, all these make it a very serious and strong contender for permanent membership.

The Other Side: Why India Doesn't Deserve Seat in UNSC

India's UNSC bid creates noise every time there is a UN session in progress but really, it creates noise only in India. That is the irony of this bid which needs 2/3rd of 192 countries around the world to vote for India. Nobody is talking about it and nobody cares. It is important to discuss whether India really deserves that seat.

Agreed that one out of every six people in this world live in India, that India is the largest democracy, that India is a major contributor to UN peacekeeping missions, but is that enough to lay claim on permanent membership to UNSC? Just because you have been a loyal employee in a company and have worked honestly and diligently, it does not give you the right to lay claim to the Board of Directors. You should be in a strategic role to do that. You should have helped the company at a higher level to grow its business, to see through some crisis situations, or to enter new relationships. You should have done something that was impactful to the whole company.

Also, getting a UNSC membership is not just about national pride. Politicians, especially in the developing countries, have a habit of painting a utopian picture for the general public, taking them on fantasy rides, one after the other. And low literacy levels and low awareness levels in these countries do not help the situation.

India has to prove its case to become a permanent member with veto power of such an influential body. What is India's aproach towards other countries, what drives India's global relationships, what are India's ideologies, what principles does India stand for, these are important questions that need to be answered. Nobody knows what India's stand is on important issues such as the situation in Darfur, the Palestine-Israel conflict, the situation in Iraq and Afghanistan and many other such issues. Indian government did not consider them important enough to be commented upon. There are always more pressing domestic issues. And it hasn't been heard that India's stand is being discussed or covered by media for any major international conflict.

India fails to impress even in its neighbourhood. It has remained silent on the Myanmar issue. It didn't take a lead in helping to solve important crisis such as the Maoist rebellion in Nepal and LTTE issue in Sri Lanka. Even India's neighbours don't consider it their big brother, forget about other countries around the world. India is unpredictable. Change in ruling party changes the way India engages with other countries. Who would have predicted that the politics within the ruling party would derail the historic nuclear pact with US and in the process, deny energy-hungry India access to crucial nuclear technology, and send mixed signals to IAEA, France and Australia who were ready to help India build the nuclear plants.

India has inward looking policies that put national interest before anything else. Policies related to other nations are driven by domestic policy makers who don't have an international outlook. One of the reasons why India developed diplomatic relationships with some countries was to serve the interests of Indians in those countries and these relationships haven't evolved beyond fulfilling the requirements of the local Indians. India is just a big country that has existed in isolation for decades and has recently shown some economic growth and integration with global society. But largely, India is still not influencing any country's foreign policy.

All is not lost though. Consistency is the mantra India will have to adopt to become a permanent member of UNSC. India has to show consistent behaviour in all the things that it does that involves another nation. It has to show consistency in its stand towards foreign conflicts, in its economic policies that impact other countries and in internal policies that are related to human rights, child labour, etc. That is when nobody can oppose India's bid and India can proudly say that it deserves a permanent seat on UNSC with veto power.

17

SHOULD INDIA HAVE A NON-POLITICIAN PRESIDENT?

The President of India is the head of the State and is the head of the legislature, executive and judiciary branches of the Indian democracy. He holds a very important position. The president is not merely a chancellor sitting at the convocations, but an important constitutional functionary. The president is required to act independently and his actions require constitutional knowledge as well as political wisdom. The celebrity presidents may not have the wisdom and understanding of our political system and that of the mood of the people. By nominating celebrities, we are bringing down the dignity and importance of the position.

The president should be a person with a political background so as to understand the political situation and exercise the due diligence in performing his/her duties. The reasons behind this logic are: first he is the head of state of multi-dimensional politics and first citizen of India and the supreme commander of Indian armed forces, with real executive authority vested in the Council of Ministers, headed by the Prime Minister and is an authority mainly in forming new governments, as well as dissolving them in instances of crisis. He is supposed to be neutral with regard to consistency, and must have solid background of internal politics. The powers of the President of India are comparable to those of the monarch, king or queen of UK. The president also receives the credentials of Ambassadors and High Commissioners from other countries. Therefore, he is required to play external affairs politics too for the sake of international peace and harmony.

An example can be cited of one of the politicians and successful presidents of Singapore. His name was Ong Teng Cheong who was an architect, planner and politician. The key changes were to grant the President veto power over the issue of the country's reserves as well as over key government positions, but by Ong's own account, his job was not an easy one with the bureaucracy, but due to his solid background as politician and high technical knowledge, he faced all encounters and came out as the most successful president of the world in times of crisis. He uplifted the country to a very high level. Similarly, we need a president of high caliber and capacity with multi-dimensional politics to deal with Indian and international affairs.

Since Independence, we have had so many presidents and most of them carried dignity with that post. Dr. S. Radhakrishnan, Dr. Zakir Hussain, R. Venkataraman, Dr. Shankar Dayal Sharma, K. R. Narayanan and Dr. A. P. J. Abdul Kalam are a few names in the list who came from non-political background. It is better that the post is occupied by non-politicians who are knowledgeable, carry dignity, have contributed to the society, balanced, impartial and are popular but definitely not a politician. A politician will always be from a political party; he can seldom forget his earlier political affiliation. Of course, a non-politician president under political crisis can always be advised by the Cabinet, other political parties as well can rely on past precedents.

The above-mentioned Indian Presidents have carried out their duties admirably though most of them were either non-politicians or even if they belonged to some political party, they always maintained their dignity. A few names like Dr. Narayana Moorthy of INFOSYS – forget about the National Anthem Controversy, Dr. Moorthy is far too patriotic and has immensely contributed to nation building to be criticized by unscrupulous politicians whose contribution to society and nation building is worth mentioning – Dr. Karan Singh (though from Congress, still has the status to occupy the highest office), Dr Amartya Sen and Dr. M.S. Swaminathan, readily come to mind. Let us not go by their caste, religion, etc.

Current Scenario

With Pratibha Patil's victory, India had its first woman President. But this noticeable gender march would have been achieved after a fight in which each of the three main political groupings were seen to be more keen to play politics than be serious about electing a person for the country's highest constitutional post.

The CPI(M) has already angrily rejected a popular clamour for a non-politician as a president. For the BJP any candidate who looks less than friendly to it is a political lightweight. Sitting in the opposition, for the last three years, the BJP has shown distaste for debating issues in Parliament. Instead, it has set a new trend of rushing to the Rashtrapati Bhavan with all manner of grievances to the President. This looks like a dangerous attempt to politicize the office of the President of India.

The Constitution and convention have made it clear that the President of India will not be a political creature that can become a centre for friction with the government. At least once in the past India did have a president who acted like a politician, raising political temperatures in the country, particularly in a border state. It has been assumed that a non-political president cannot resonate with the conscience of the country while, say, returning a controversial bill.

The former president Dr. A.P.J. Abdul Kalam, was never in politics but he did apply his mind on occasions to controversial matters that were brought before him. It goes to his credit that he did not make it look like he was challenging the government. The country needs a president who acts with dignity and exercises his/her powers impartially — and certainly desists from putting his or her foot in the mouth. Those with an active and high profile political background do not necessarily foot the bill.

Our Constitution does not impose any disqualification upon an Indian citizen for holding this higher constitutional office. He can be a politician, a scientist, a literary figure or from any walk of life or discipline. In fact, at one time or the other, this highest office was decorated by individuals from one or the other of these disciplines. Take for instance, our present president is a politician and one of our former presidents is a celebrated scientist. Then we have had personalities like Dr. Rajendra Prasad, Dr. S. Radhakrishnan, Fakhruddin Ali Ahmed and the like. Dr. A.P.J. Abdul Kalam as well is a renowned scientist.

Preference should be not because of his being a politician or a non-politician. It is because he represents the collective genius and the vision of the country. Those asking for the non-political president have their own apprehensions. They fear that a political president will be no more than a puppet in the hands of the ruling party. This, they say, will adversely affect presidential neutrality. But those supporting the move of electing a political president are equally right when they argue that a non-political president may not be able to understand the intricacies of coalition politics. Instead of further complicating the argument and clamouring for a political or a non-political president, we must lay emphasis on sincere, educated president who commands respect and who is capable of winning our faith.

The truth is that we are yearning for a president that everyone likes, trusts and looks up to; a president who is free from prejudices; a president who unites everyone and divides no one; a president who transcends caste, creed, religion or region; a president who holds a clean image and truly desires the betterment of the country. Anyone who imbibes all these qualities in him truly deserves being the constitutional head of the country irrespective of whether he has a political background or not.

It is not the matter that the president should be political or apolitical. The post of the president has highest dignity in each country, though there is much difference in functions from country to country. In America, the president has all executive powers but in countries like UK or India, the Crown or the President does not directly have executive powers. In such countries, the prime minister and his cabinet work in the name of the president. As far as the question of Indian President, Dr. Abdul Kalam was a successful scientist president who gave a new vision to India. Besides doing his job with highest transparency, Dr. Abdul Kalam also maintained good relationship with legislature, executive and judiciary. Although the Indian President has been called a rubber stamp and works only according to the wishes of executive, it does not mean that he has no powers.

India needs a president with will power and a transparent character like Dr. Abdul Kalam who could morally inspire leaders and serve as example for our corrupt public representatives.

When a common man having will power can mould the society, then why is the president remaining only a rubber stamp? India needs a transparent president with will power for strengthening our democracy and curbing corrupt politicians. It is not important whether he belongs to any political party or not.

Definitely, we must have apolitical president like Dr. A.P.J. Abdul Kalam, who was non-controversial and apolitical. He has contributed a lot to science and technology, and was honoured with Bharat Ratna when he was a scientist. We must have an intellectual and learned president like him. India needs a man of his ability, vision and character to be the president. It would be appreciated if all political parties endorse candidature of an apolitical president at the time of the next election.

A political president will always be mired in controversy. All his actions will be viewed with suspicion as it will always be suspected that he is partisan towards the party he is associated with.

18

NAM IN POST-COLD WAR PERIOD AND ITS RELEVANCE

From the period of the formation of its vision at Bandung in 1955 and first summit at Belgrade in 1961, NAM has travelled a long and eventful path. Starting with a membership of 25 countries, its membership has grown to 118.There have also been shifts in its perspective and preoccupations necessitated by the change in international scenario. However, the changed perceptions that have come in the 1990s have placed NAM almost at crossroads.

With the disintegration of the erstwhile Soviet Union and break-up of socialist bloc, there have emerged new global situations and issues. The process of globalisation has also begun. Humanitarian aid to the developing world has greatly been reduced. Greater conditions are being imposed on the aid to the South, such as allowing access to transnational companies. Most of the developed and developing nations have adopted an open market policy. Again, these countries have formed an agenda of regional economic cooperation. The European Union has been established as a significant regional cooperation group. The Association of South-East Asian Nations (ASEAN) has also made remarkable achievement in forming a formidable economic bloc.

The North American Free Trade Agreement (NAFTA) has emerged as a strong economic bloc in North America and the Asian Pacific Economic Cooperation (APEC) has also been progressing well in creating a consensus for economic cooperation in Asia and Pacific region. Most countries, even NAM members, have started taking decisions pragmatically and individually. In the context of these far-reaching developments, there has started a debate about the relevance of NAM. It is being argued by some that in the changed situation, non-alignment and most of the policies associated with it have become irrelevant.

There is, however, a significant opinion in favour of continuous relevance and role of NAM in the post-cold war world. India, as one of the active founder members of NAM, is not only in the forefront of proclaiming non-alignment as the sheet anchor of its foreign policy but also advocating the continuous role of NAM with some changes in its perspectives and priorities. From the beginning of 1990s, the movement has realised the need to shift from an approach of confrontation to one of dialogue and cooperation with industrial countries. Also, circumstances over which many member countries of NAM had no control, compelled them to develop a variety of relations with super powers and their allies. But these states have not deviated from the basic criterion of non-alignment, namely, pursuit of policies that strengthened their existence as independent sovereign states, belief in coexistence of states with different political and social systems and support for national liberation movements and movements against racism.

The end of Cold War in many ways has vindicated the principles and policies of NAM. At the same time, it is a fact that though the Cold War is over, peace in the world is still threatened by forces of extremism, discord, aggressive nationalism, terrorism and piling up of large stocks of weapons of mass destruction.

The dynamics of globalisation has thrown a whole range of new problems for the non-aligned developing countries. While the developing world is largely supportive of mutually beneficial global integration, it has major concerns which are not being addressed in the global agenda. These are: equitable balance between rights and obligations of investors, particularly multinationals; extra-territorial application of domestic laws; intrusive and calculated invoking of human rights agenda; labour standards and intellectual property rights; and conditionalities of environmental protection and preservation and opting up of national economies tied to grant of aid and trade concessions. Developing countries are increasingly exposed to pressures to confirm to an agenda, which is being defined and driven by others.

The need for the articulation of the viewpoint of the disadvantaged is as strong as ever. NAM provides platform to these countries for consulting and developing common positions and coordinated approaches to safeguard their rights and promote their interests. The imperatives that propelled founding fathers of NAM to get together to speak with one voice and collectively declare their determination to assert their right to participate fully in the process of taking decisions on world issues in the light of their own national interests are still with us today.

Common to most, if not all, NAM countries are faced with problems of poverty, hunger, disease, ignorance, illiteracy, rising foreign debts, deteriorating terms of trade, inflation and unemployment. Therefore, the most important task that confronts the NAM today is to find ways and means to overcome these problems.

The scenario, once again, places India in a special situation. Though its problems are stupendous as a poor country, there is a measure of buoyancy in its economy. Its food position is satisfactory and its foreign exchange reserves are comfortable. Its advancement in the field of science, technology and industry permits it to render economic and technological assistance to many countries of Asia and Africa. Its economy is now much less vulnerable to external shocks or internal adverse factors. Thus, to a great extent India remains in a position to promote the ideal of collective self-reliance among non-aligned countries.

In 1977, at the 12th meeting of NAM, foreign minister, the former Prime Minister of India, I.K. Gujral, highlighted the points responsible for the re-emergence of new imperialism of the West. He said, "The G-7 are writing the global agenda, new labour laws and social clauses; selecting global investment regimes; preaching human rights environmental conditionalities, protectionism, etc. The five permanent members of UN Security Council are unwilling to give up the voto. Democratisation of the UN Security Council is blocked. Too many NAM countries are living on western dole. In several countries, treasured concepts of civilised behaviour have been abandoned. NAM, therefore, must deplore the fundamentalism of globalisation and the market."

The use of World Trade Organisation (WTO) for forcing developing countries to reduce tariff walls and observe labour standards is another case in point. This indicates another area of dominance by the developed countries in a period of recession in their economies. Unless the developing countries, which are also the members of NAM, put up united resistance against these onslaughts by the major allied powers, the prospects of world peace, security, equality of status for nation states and a voice for the underdeveloped world to procure foreign aid for development will remain a distant dream. At the Doha meeting of WTO in June 2002, India urged strongly on behalf of the developing countries.

Thus, even after the end of Cold War and demise of power blocs, non-alignment, both as an idea and a movement, continues to be relevant .The efforts of NAM have to be geared towards achieving security, peaceful coexistence , international cooperation in political, economic and cultural fields and in opposing all types of domination, neo-colonialism, hegemonism, fundamentalism, etc. India has a stake in these and is likely to play the leadership role that it has played so far.

Non-alignment was first developed as a conceptual factor in its foreign policy by India as a means to its enlightened national interest in the context of bipolarization of world politics and situation of Cold War. Later on, non-alignment became a movement of nations which had suffered the same fate of colonialism and imperialism. Prime Minister of India, Jawaharlal Nehru, with the cooperation of President Tito of Yugoslavia and President Nasser of Egypt, directed this movement towards peace in the world and also aimed at securing political and economic objectives of development. At the political level, the movement aimed to keep intact the independence of newly-decolonized countries and support the struggle for decolonization of rest of the colonies. It sought to forge unity among anti-colonial, anti-racial forces and liberation movements and help them in achieving their objectives worldwide.

The economic objective of the non-aligned movement is aimed at keeping the markets of developing countries free from domination of free market forces represented by Western capitalism and multinational corporations.

India remained in the forefront of the movement performing a leadership role as a founder member. In all the activities of NAM—struggle against colonialism, racism, and in favour of disarmament and cooperation for development, and dialogue with developed world, etc.—India not only provided policy inputs but has also played an active role. With the end of Cold War and bloc systems, NAM has in no way become irrelevant. If the essence of non-alignment is the assertion of independence, then non-alignment does not become irrelevant at any time. In fact, developing nations have no alternatives but to strive for a just world order through the forum of NAM.

While the relevance of NAM in the present day world is not in the doubt, it would serve its purpose if it focuses on the current problems that the developing countries are facing. In formulating its agenda for the future, NAM would have to incorporate in it both its traditional and emerging goals and objectives and take cognizance of emerging issues and priorities on the international agenda. The NAM agenda has to be typical and flexible thereby changing with the realities of time. To usher in peace, security and prosperity, NAM has to act in unison.

19

INDIA'S DEFENCE NEEDS IN A TECHNOLOGICAL SCENARIO

In the last century, science has transformed the world in almost all areas of activities. It follows that the corresponding economic, political, demographic and technological changes would also affect the military factor.

In fact, the demonstrated relationship between the advance of science and technology and defence is so strong that the future of warfare has been revolutionized. The world today, particularly the developed world, has progressed far ahead in the technological advancement of war-fighting. History has demonstrated that nations that fail to anticipate and adapt to changes are left behind.

India's defence industrialization and scientific know-how is widely acknowledged. It has, however, not attained the required degree of success as a self-reliant entity capable of meeting the needs of the country's armed forces and steering itself into the next millennium. Although the Defence Research and Development Organisation (DRDO) has achieved remarkable milestones in the area of nuclear and missile technology, it has failed to meet the basic needs of the infantry soldier, as was experienced in the recent war in Kargil. Priorities have gone wrong somewhere and unless defence planning and management strike the right balance, the potential of India's technological base may not be able to meet its defence needs.

In the current and future technological scenario, India has a wide spectrum of needs to cover. Some of these are: nuclear warfare, information warfare, satellite technology, missile technology, chemical and biological warfare, counter-insurgency, mobile warfare, air and naval warfare, high speed communications, underwater technology and cyber warfare.

After carrying out its nuclear tests in May 1998 and announcing that it has acquired a minimum nuclear deterrent, India committed itself to have the capabilities to sustain a first strike by a nuclear power and then to strike back, i.e., to have a 'second strike' capability. This would spell out the following needs:

a) Command and control systems with technological infrastructure to include C41, i.e., command, control, communication, computer and intelligence systems.
b) Widely dispersed command centres with duplicated command and control systems.
c) A multi-delivery system to include missile delivery, air delivery, and delivery by sea.
d) Widely dispersed and well-protected deployment sites, preferably underground hardened silos.
e) An integrated intelligence system.
f) Communication infrastructure.

India first needs to ensure that its nuclear weapons and delivery system are invulnerable to a first strike by nuclear weapons either by Pakistan or China or jointly by both of them. Secondly, it should have the capability of inflicting unacceptable damage on the enemy. In this respect, not only is the development of the medium range missile 'Agni' essential but what is also needed is a focus on its ability to strike targets even more accurately. In order to make its nuclear weapons invulnerable to first strike forces, India needs to create a strategic air command, protect its nuclear weapons sites, develop nuclear submarines and deploy anti-ballistic missiles.

Warfare today has changed radically due to the advent of information revolution. With the use of computers and modern communications, it has become increasingly important to ensure acquisition and security of information. The rapid growth of technologies to acquire and store information and the promise of improved command and control have generated the idea of 'dominance in the field of information'. The ability to see, hear and understand the enemy's command and control systems, intelligence sources and sensors have produced a new discipline known as 'information warfare'.

The information revolution and its related technologies are affecting all three pillars of national power, i.e., political, military and economic. India with its vast talented scientific population needs to overcome potential vulnerabilities, tame the microchip and use it to sustain tactical and strategic advantages that are available in information warfare. Broadly, these include dedicated military satellites for surveillance and communications, reconnaissance and target acquisition system, intelligence gathering and decision support system, airborne early warning platforms, digitalized mapping, etc.

Although India has forewarned the use of chemical and biological weapons, there are reports that chemical biological weapons, popularly known as the 'poor man's nuke', are increasingly being sought but certain government as an alternative to or in addition to nuclear weapons. Therefore, India needs to recognise the growing threat of chemical and biological weapons attack and take necessary steps for provision of counter-measures to protect its defence forces and civilians against such weapons of mass destruction.

Rapidly advancing technology and self-reliance go hand in hand. Keeping this in view, the DRDO needs to tackle a variety of new challenges in the field of basic battlefield needs. Higher levels of self-reliance in crucial sectors can only be sustained by close collaboration between the defence forces who have to combat disruptive forces in a variety of terrain and weather configuration and the research and development personnel who have to meet these critical needs. Good skills in design and manufacture lapsed after operational exigencies compelled direct buys from abroad and also resorting to licensed manufacture. Although the defence forces have been advocating their needs over the years in basic items like rifles, carbines, helmets, snow-boots and gloves, snow goggles, sound ranging equipments and other basic equipments for specialised operations, it is alleged that DRDO has failed to deliver.

This was dramatically demonstrated during the Kargil conflict when last-minute purchases from abroad had to be resorted to while the battles were being fought. The euphoria generated over success in the field of missile technology now needs to be transferred and transformed into active capabilities for design, development and production of more basic needs. Joint ventures could initially be undertaken with selected foreign manufacturers leading eventually to substantial self-reliance. China's success in this area needs to be emulated.

The evolution of new concepts of fighting is a direct outcome of the impact of technology on the conduct of land, sea and air warfare. The urgent needs of India's defence forces in present and future conflicts are: precision weapons, vastly improved means of real-time information, surveillance and target acquisition and improved clothing and equipment for high-altitude warfare. Advances in communications technology, computers, information systems, surveillance and target acquisition systems are critical for command and control. Equally important is the utilisation of the same means to destroy the enemy's means of command and control. Failure to meet these needs will have disastrous consequences.

As we have entered the new millennium, there should be no doubt that new technologies are transforming the way we conduct warfare.

To win, we need to adopt new war-fighting techniques, and for that our need for upgraded technology is absolutely essential. Existing gaps in these areas need to be eliminated without further delay.

20

THE RISE AND FALL OF THE MODERN STATE SYSTEM

Given practical form by the new nation states of Western Europe such as France in the late Middle Ages or Prussia in the nineteenth century, the old state system rested on the idea that by concentrating power in a single head or centre, the state itself could be sufficiently controlled and its environment sufficiently managed to achieve self-sufficiency or at least a maximum of self-sufficiency in a world which would inevitably be hostile or at best neutral towards each state's interests and in which alliances would reflect temporary coalitions of interests that should not be expected to last beyond that convergence. The old maxim: "No state has friends, only interest," typifies that situation.

The first powerful nation-states were monarchies, advocates of the divine right of kings to protect central authority and power. After a series of modern revolutions, first in thought, led by people like Hobbes, Spinozo, Locke and Rousseau, and then in practice as articulated in The Federalist, kings were stripped of their exclusive power and new power centres formed, presumably based upon popular citizenship and consent but in fact with the same centralised powers, only vested in representative assemblies and executive officers speaking in the name of the state.

Only in a few cases, where earlier dispersions of power has been constitutionalised, did they need to be taken into consideration. This led to the establishment of federations, forms of federalism that combined national supremacy with real constituent state powers, at least for purposes of foreign relations and usually defence.

The second defining element of the nation-state was its striving for homogeneity. Every state was to be convergent with its nation and every nation with its state. Where people did not fit easily into that procrustean bed, efforts were made to force them into it. This was done either through internal pressure as in France where the French government in the name of the state warred against Bretons, Occetanians, Provencals and Languadocians, among others, even denying them the right to choose names of their children that did not appear on the official Francophone list—or external (as in the Balkans where small national states with minorities outside of their state boundaries regularly warred with one another in an effort to conquer the territories where their fellow nationals lived and either exterminated or expelled those not of the same nationality). As a result, modern wars were basically of two kinds, either imperialistic wars designed to enable more powerful states to become even more self-sufficient by seizing control of populations, territories and resources that could be used in that direction or nationalist wars designed to reunite parts of the nation with the national state.

In the end, none of these three goals could be achieved. In many cases they were not achieved at all; in others they were achieved temporarily until those disadvantaged by them succeeded in revolting. In still others, they proved to be unachievable by any sustainable means, usually with a combination of all three factors that prevented their attainment. As a result, of the existing states in the world, 90 per cent contain minorities of 15 per cent of their population or more within their boundaries – like Crotia – and of the remaining 10 per cent, almost all have large national minorities living outside their state boundaries like Somalia. Since then, matters have gotten more complex, as we see by the great resurgence of ethnic conflict in one form or another throughout the world—a factor that has become one catalyst for the new paradigm in its reach for ways to overcome those conflicts.

As we approach the end of the era of the politically sovereign state, we also are beginning to recognise that state self-sufficiency, in reality, was never achievable. It is well to recall that modern economic liberalism, which was essentially based on the principle of free trade, emerged shortly after the emergence of modern statism with its economic basis in mercantilism which sought self-sufficiency, because of the problematics of mercantilism brought to the fore, inter alia, by the American revolution against Great Britain. When that policy failed, imperialism replaced it – for the powerful states —as the means to the end of self–sufficiency. Imperialism failed by the middle of the twentieth century, not only because the subjugated peoples rejected it, but because a democratic moral sensibility came to affect the subjugators. So, the world has had to find a new paradigm – and it seems that we have.

21

UNITY IN DIVERSITY IN INDIA

India has been known as the largest democracy in the world with a civilization more than five thousand years old boasting of multiple cultural origins. The cultural origins of the Indian subcontinent can be traced back to the Indus Valley Civilizations, the remains of which are cherished even today. Since the late 16th century, India was under the influence of the British Empire until 15th August 1947, the day when India gained Independence. India is a land of diverse cultures, religions and communities.

Cultural and Artistic Heritage

India bestows a rich cultural and artistic heritage. The fact that India was invaded and ruled by various kings down the ages is already reflected by its impact on Indian culture. The Gupta dynasty, the Mughal dynasty and many other dynasties influenced and contributed to the Indian culture. Music, inspired perhaps by the whistles of the wind or the splash of the waves, chirping of the birds or may be falling of the rain, exists on this land since the existence of humanity. They designed many musical instruments and innumerable ragas. Then they developed different notes for different times, seasons and feelings.

Different regions developed their own style of singing, not following the ragas but their own tunes and taking the lyrics in their own language and themes from their day-to-day life. One of the powerful attractions in India is the colourful and diversified attire of its people. The silk saris, brightly mirrored cholis, colourful lehangas and the traditional salwar-kameez have fascinated many a traveller of the centuries.

Majority of the Indian women wear traditional costumes, the men in India can be found in more conventional western clothing. Men from all regions in India wear shirts and trousers. However, men in villages are still more comfortable in traditional attire like kurtas, lungis, dhotis and pyjamas. The traditional lungi originaed in the south and today men and women wear it alike. It is simply a short length of material worn around the thighs rather like a sarong. A dhoti is a longer lungi but an additional length of material pulled up between the legs. Pyjama, like trousers, worn by the villagers are known as the lenga.

Both religious and regional variations mark Indian dressing styles and one is likely to witness a plethora of colours, textures and styles in garments worn by the Indians. Indian dance is a blend of nritta – the rhythmic elements, nritya – the combination of rhythm with expression and natya – the dramatic element. Most Indian dances take their themes from India's rich mythology and folk legends. Hindu gods and goddesses like Vishnu and Lakshmi, Rama and Sita, Krishna and Radha are all depicted in classical Indian dances. Each dance form also draws inspiration from stories depicting the life, ethics and beliefs of the Indian people.

The genesis of the contemporary styles of classicial dances can be traced to the period between 1300–1400 A.D. India offers a number of classical dance forms, each of which can be traced to different parts of the country. Each form represents the culture and ethos of a particular region or a group of people, such as Bharatnatyam – Tamil Nadu; Kathak – Uttar Pradesh; Kathakali – Kerala; Kuchipudi – Andhra Pradesh; Manipuri – Manipur; Mohiniyattam – Kerala; Odissi – Orissa.

Multiplicity of festivals is visible in India. Most of the festivals owe their origin to legends, gods and goddesses and mythology. As many communities there are, there are as many festivals unique to them. Colour, gaiety, enthusiasm, feasts and a variety of prayers and rituals characterize festivals here. There are a number of festivals celebrated in India. In fact, they are too numerous to count. Some important festivals are: Deepawali, Krishna Janmashtami, Onam, Dussehra, Pongal, Ramzan, Id, Baisakhi, Easter, Ganesha Chaturthi, Holi, Raksha

Bandhan, Ram Navmi, Christmas, Good Friday, Makar Sankranti, Moharrum, Shivratri, Durga Puja and many others.

The Raised Concerns

There is no uniformity in the Indian society, if looked by its various angles. This is a natural corollary to the fact that diversity is a part of Indian way of life. From region to region, diversity in the social structure is prominently seen. The north Indian social traditions and customs are markedly different and so those of the eastern India from those of other parts of the country. And here lies the tantalizing element of mystery associated with India.

To live peacefully has been our motto and this motto has helped us to achieve independence. As history tells us, there has been active participation from people of different castes and religions. In our struggle for freedom, people from different communities participated keeping one thing in mind that they all are Indians first. But unfortunately this peace and understanding among different communities has been endangered lately. India at present is facing many problems. The biggest of these is the problem of communalism. In their personal fight they are destroying their life only. In fact, it is the biggest threat to humanity and to the unity and integrity of India.

Notwithstanding the diversity factor, there is a common thread running through the Indians. Unity in diversity is best seen in India in a maze of seemingly disparate people. One social unifier is the Indian system of casteism adhered to by all racial groups belonging to the Hindu religious fold.

Lambasted by many as a retrogressive social tradition, this system has also given the Indians a sense of belongingness to a shared way of life. Though caste rigidity was prevalent in the olden times, now it has become flexible to a large extent. It is not uncommon to come across families of so-called incompatible castes entering into matrimonial alliance.

A major phenomenon causing concern in the Indian society is the gender inequality. The Indian society is highly prejudiced against the female gender. Basically, in a male dominated society, decision-making at family and political level is almost single handedly handled by the men. Customs such as dowry are worsening the process of subjugating women in the society. Of late, with the social awareness about women's vital role in the development of a community or the country, there has been a change in the perception of gender equations in favour of women. Education of women, giving the women a greater say in decision-making in the family and governance are emphasized. With the liberalization of economy, women are in top managerial position at par with the best men.

Though significant leaps have been made in the economic front, poverty is still a dominant reality. The majority of the population of India lives in utter poverty without access to health care, housing, drinking water and education. Major policy change has to be enforced to better the lives of these millions of souls if India is to become a truly desirable place to live in. Education is still a privilege in this country of over one billion people. Providing primary education has been the motto of the government. So far the government has not lived up to its promise with the result that one-fourth of its population is still illiterate. Lack of education is the primary obstacle to the nation's development. India should educate the masses if its aspiration of becoming the global knowledge superpower is to become a reality.

In conclusion, a varied diversity in every aspect is visible here. There is a great diversity in our traditions, manners, habits, tastes and customs. Each and every region of the country portrays different customs and traditions. But, though we speak different languages, yet we are all Indians. 'Unity in diversity' has been the distinctive feature of our culture.

22

HUMAN RIGHTS AND THE INDIAN ARMED FORCES

Historically, armed violence against civil societies was the regrettable fallout of wars between nations. Today, the unfortunate reality is that the targeting of civil population has become the scary strategy of the new breed of terrorism unleashed by fundamentalist forces. Innocent men, women and children become hapless victims of such violence and are caught in the cross-fire between the terrorists on the one hand, and the security forces on the other. While the freewheeling terrorists have no restrictions on descending into the worst methods of medieval mayhem to achieve their aims, the soldiers of the Indian Army face the daunting task of performing their duty in accordance with a high code of conduct and strict norms of behaviour with all odds stacked against them.

It was the appalling crimes against humanity by Nazi Germany in the extermination of millions of people that horrified the civilized world and aroused the collective conscience of the international community to do something to protect humanity against the violence perpetrated by man against man. This resulted in the Universal Declaration of Human Rights which was adopted by the General Assembly of the United Nations on December 10, 1948. The Declaration generally states that their lives, liberty, security and dignity need to be protected. This is the document of large body of human rights jurisprudence that has since come into being. In India, the Protection of Human Rights Act, 1933 defines human rights as the rights relating to life, liberty, equality and dignity of the individual as guaranteed by the Constitution or embodied in international covenants and enforceable by courts in India.

International humanitarian law deals with protecting victims of armed conflicts from violence and other violations of human rights. Standards have been codified in the Geneva Conventions (1949) for the protection of war victims and two additional protocols (1977). The combined goal of these instruments is to restrict the use of violence against those who are not engaged in armed fighting and to prohibit methods of warfare that cause unnecessary suffering. The conventions that cover the armed forces relate to the treatment to be given to sick and wounded military persons in the field, to sick and shipwrecked members of the armed forces in the sea, treatment of prisoners of war and protection of civilians in times of war.

Since Independence, the Indian armed forces have been engaged in four wars and in prolonged and continuous engagement in counter insurgency operations against terrorists and insurgents in Jammu and Kashmir and the north-eastern states. While combating insurgency, the army is very alive to the fact that it is a battle for the hearts and minds of the insurgents and that harmony between the interests of the individual and the state is essential. The problem arises when the dangers from across the border and from terrorism cross reasonable limits.

A nation and a society cannot tolerate terrorism when it endangers the security of the state and the welfare of its people. The state is bound to take stringent measures. The dilemma is how to execute such measures without disregarding the human rights aspect. It is here that the insurgent holds the trump card. The insurgent and terrorist use terrorism as a weapon which obtains for them disproportionate benefits in the political and military arenas. The terrorists are aware that the politicians are concerned mainly with the vote banks of their constituencies. Anything that disturbs chances of coming back to power disturbs them.

The terrorists, therefore, depend upon premeditated false statements to alarm the politicians. False evidence and outright lies are the weapons they use to degrade the capacity of the armed forces employed against them. It becomes incredibly difficult for the soldiers to be restrained when they see their comrades being killed, even as human rights organisations are swayed by the propaganda of the terrorists. Regrettably, the Press often publishes version of the terrorists, perhaps because it is more easily available. The terrorists, therefore, use the politicians, the Press and the public to get the human rights organisations to back them. Terrorists in Jammu and Kashmir have often fired at soldiers from within crowds of women and children, secure due to being in crowd they find themselves because soldiers will hesitate to fire back; or that if they do, then it is the armed forces who will get the flak.

It would be untruthful to say that there have never been excesses by the armed forces. There have been a number of cases where uniformed men have been found involved in serious violations of human rights of the civilians. For instance, some time back some jawans threw out some civilians from the standing Farakka Express at the Shikohabad station in Uttar Pradesh. The unfortunate civilians who fell on the adjacent rail track were run over by the incoming Sampoorna Kranti Express. And, as a result, several persons were killed. Further, in the guise of searching homes for the supposedly hiding terrorists, rapes and molestations of women by the men in uniform are also not unheard of.

However, before examining the record, one must also consider that when one uses the term 'armed forces', it includes not only the army but also the BSF, CRPF, ITBP, Assam Rifles and other paramilitary forces operating in the area. The fact that in the Indian system the Army is only called out when the police and paramilitary forces cannot handle the situation. Air Commodore R.V. Kumar and Group Captain B.P. Sharma, in their book *Human Rights and the Armed Forces*, have stated that less than one per cent of the complaints made against the army personnel are found to be valid.

The Army deals with human rights violations with a very heavy hand and where army personnel are found guilty, they are awarded severe punishment quite swiftly through court martial. In one case death penalty was awarded. Nonetheless, some people say that court martials, even while punishing the culprit swiftly, often do not do full justice vis-à-vis the gravity of the crime perpetrated by the guilty men in uniform. What makes matters worse is that the defence administration jealously maintains a complete secrecy and often shields the personnel concerned from the bounds of the media and the society for the sake of the so-called dignity and honour of the forces.

The Army is very conscious of the effect of the infringement of human rights by its personnel on the overall morale, discipline and motivation of the armed forces as a whole. It has, therefore, initiated a series of measures to educate its personnel in human rights awareness and correct procedures to be followed. There is a comprehensive list of do's and don'ts during, before and after military operations. In addition, human rights awareness is promoted by running various training courses at the level of pre-commission training, young officers courses and the defence service staff college course at Wellington. Most importantly, situational courses are run in counter-insurgency areas that take into consideration the on-the-spot factors that could vary from one situation to another. Although this training focuses on situations of counter-insurgency, provision is also made for the conduct of armed forces personnel during war.

The Indian Army personnel assigned for UN peace-keeping operations are given training not only in human rights but also on how to react to various situations they are likely to encounter. In order to sensitise the entire Army on human rights, the records of personnel are monitored and taken into account while considering promotions and postings to sensitive appointments.

Organisationally, the Army has instituted human rights cells. The charter of these cells is to monitor, receive complaints, investigate and submit reports for further action and also to be in touch with the National Human Rights Commission and NGOs working in this field with a view to minimise human rights violations.

The Chief of Army Staff in 1993 issued his Ten Commandments for strict compliance for forces engaged in counter-insurgency operations which included no rape, no molestation, no torture, death preferable to military grace, no meddling in civil administration, maintenance of correct relations with the media, respect for human rights, and fear only of God, to uphold the path of righteousness.

As a corollary to these Commandments, the concerned corps further issued Ten Directives for strict compliance which included display compassion and humanity towards the local populace; not to look down upon local customs and traditions; there are no insurgents here – only misguided countrymen; never molest women – they are our sisters and mothers; do not harm children – they are our heritage; no reprisals under any circumstance; treat apprehendees with respect; honour democratic norms and adhere to human rights.

The role of the armed forces in civic and welfare work in insurgency and disaster-hit areas – both natural and man-made – must not be forgotten. According to an assessment, the termination of the insurgency in Punjab was facilitated by the humanitarian work done by the Army when it was called out to assist the police in counter-insurgency operations. Army personnel attended the sick and the wounded villagers, shared their rations with the villagers and conducted classes in village schools. It is estimated that in Punjab and Jammu and Kashmir alone, the Army treated over 11 lakhs of sick and wounded civilians, gave free education to thousands of children, distributed free of cost rations worth million of rupees and helped in the construction of hundreds of kilometres of roads and tracks.

Towards the end of 2004, when the deadly tsunami struck the coastal areas of the south-eastern India, the defence forces were the first to rise to the occasion. They did for the victims what the local, state and Central governments failed to do. Apart from saving countless precious lives, the men in uniform provided food, medicine and shelter to thousands of victims and helped them in numerous other ways to take up a normal life once again. Similarly, in Jammu and Kashmir, when due to heavy snowfall, normal life is disrupted and when tourists are trapped, the Army and the Air Force are known to evacuate the trapped people and ferry them to safe areas. Defence personnel posted in the region even stop counter-terrorist operations during such times to provide relief to the beleaguered civilians. Further, on many occasions, the Army even provides more than half of its war reserves of oil and other resources for meeting the fuel shortage and other needs of the people in Kashmir. It may also be recalled that in the 1971 Indo-Pak war, India took 93,000 persons as prisoners. The Indian Army is reputed to have meticulously followed the Geneva conventions in the treatment of these prisoners. It is on record that Indian Army troops moved out of their barracks so that the prisoners of war could be housed. The behaviour of the Indian Army was exemplary, to say the least. The invisible results of this conduct probably won for the country the goodwill of these POWs and their families—a consequence as impressive as the victory achieved by the use of force.

Mr. K.P.S. Gill, who as Director-General Punjab Police, contributed substantially to the curbing of insurgency in Punjab, has highlighted a growing aberration which has received little public attention and is stridently denied by the human rights lobby. This is the systematic adoption of human rights litigation as a weapon against the agencies of the state by terrorists, insurgents and criminals who themselves reject democracy and seek the overthrow of lawful and elected governments. An overwhelming proportion of 'public interest' human rights litigation is today being initiated by front organisations of virulent underground terrorist movements in a systematic strategy to harry and paralyse security forces and the police.

The eventual judicial outcome of such litigations is irrelevant to the objectives of these groups. The very admission of the petition is sufficient to launch a media campaign based on fabricated information and charges that are reported without even a semblance of investigation or corroboration as 'facts'. Hundreds of such cases and complaints have been found to be utterly false. But there are no effective penalties attached to this abuse of the process of law – though statutes exist for malicious persecution, they have never been applied in a single case of this nature. This perversion of judicial process has to be countered to effectively resist the forces of destabilisation in the country.

It also must be borne in mind that personnel of the armed forces operating in areas of insurgency are also Indian citizens and, as such, are entitled to protection of their human rights. As a matter of fact, they face the grossest violation of several of their fundamental rights. They are constantly exposed to danger and torture of the worst kind. Instances of murder in cold blood, mutilation and torture have occurred in the 1962, 1965 and 1971 and in the Kargil war and in Jammu and Kashmir and in the north-east. However, human rights organisations have never ever protested against such acts. This has an adverse effect on the morale of troops who are kept on a tight leash when operating against insurgents with their own lives in danger, but have no support when their rights are violated. This needs rectification if the human rights issue is to have a balanced perspective.

The armed forces understand that they can function more effectively and smoothly if the civilian population is with them in their endeavours. This makes them more sensitive to civilian needs and human rights. This awareness will help in curbing the temptation to use more than minimum force and encouraging them to exercise restraint. It is desirable that the armed forces continue to emphasise the importance of human rights in the execution of their duties.

There is no place for the kind of events that have recently taken place in Jammu and Kashmir and Manipur; for instance, at the former, several innocent young men were killed as 'terrorists', in the latter, a women was allegedly abducted, raped and killed for 'being in touch with insurgents'. Equally, the armed forces too need our sympathy for the violation of human rights they constantly face with none to bring public attention to their plight.

The media can play an effective and important role in this. Instead of giving coverage of the human rights violations—both genuine and fake—of only those who pay scant attention to their victims' rights in the first place, they must also give coverage to the violation of human rights of the armed forces personnel, so that the morale of the uniformed men is kept high.

23

COALITION POLITICS AND NATIONAL UNITY

The breakdown of the national consensus on a parliamentary majority in India, a phenomenon which is an important characteristic of the parliamentary governments in the developing countries, has led to a dangerous trend, to identify the federal division of powers with sub-national pluralism. In an attempt to seek legitimacy for the coalition governments, which largely depends upon the support of several regional parties, a phenomenon specified to the Indian political system, many of the political parties which claimed to have demolished one-party dominance of the Congress, have called for the identification of the federal division of powers with sub-national identities representing the pluralist content of the Indian society.

Indeed, the proposals were aimed to evolve a centre of power in which the coalition constituents shared authority to sustain their power. The decentralization of central authority on horizontal basis, it was contended, would end the quest for identity of the regionalized sub-national cultures in India, otherwise compartmentalized in artificial administrative divisions of the Indian federal organisation.

The pluralisation of power at the federal centre in India and in the states, if came to be actively advocated, would dissolve the configuration of political power based on the traditional one-party parliamentary majority which reflects the diversity of the Indian society.

Besides the theoretical proposition that all forms of federal organisation are based upon territorial division of political authority on administrative basis, not even remotely related to any social pluralities, the practical implications of seeking any identification of the federal division of powers with sub-national identities, would be disastrous for such a large country as India and would, sooner than anticipated, lead to the disintegration of the Indian federal structure.

Federalisation and Indian Unity

Federalisation is a political process which underlines a division of powers on territorial basis. Whenever the territorial division of powers was sought to be identified with sub-nationalism, the federal structures disintegrated.

The Indian federal polity grew out of two diametrically divergent processes, which underlined the devolution of authority to erstwhile provinces of what was known as the British India before independence and the integration of the Indian princely states, which acceded to India in accordance with the Instruments of Accession. The Instruments of Accession laid down the procedure by which the Indian states acceded to India. The federal organisation of India was, therefore, constituted of the erstwhile Indian provinces and the Indian princely states, which were liberated from the British tutelage after the British colonial empire in India came to its end in 1947.

The federating process in India underlined a combination of the devolution of authority to the provincial governments on the one hand and the integration of the acceding states on the other. The Constituent Assembly favoured a conditional devolution of the power to the provinces. The rulers of the states, on their part too, approved of a conditional transfer of their authority to the federation. The Constituent Assembly of India, however, proved to be a great leveler and forged the provinces and the states into an irreversible union in which the Central government assumed paramount authority over the provinces as well as the states.

The political boundaries of the Indian provinces and princely states, as they evolved with the consolidation of the British power in India, overspread ethnic, cultural, religious and linguistic diversities. The Indian social pluralism did not represent any political boundaries. The ethnic divisions, religious commitments, caste gradation and cultural diversities cut across the political boundaries. The British described creating many interlocking segments. None of the interlocking segments presented any political uniformity and territorial contiguity.

The Indian federal organisation envisaged by the Constitution of India does not represent the division of political authority on the basis of the division of powers between the federation and the sub-national identities. The founding fathers of the Indian Constitution envisioned integration as well as autonomy in a concrete political system. The Indian federal organisation was embedded in an environment which was plural and diverse, but its boundaries were clearly defined.

The federal division of powers laid down by the Constituent Assembly transcended the cultural, religious and linguistic pluralism of the Indian society. The autonomy, now claimed for sub-national identities as the basis of what is called "cooperative federalism", is a prescription for the dissolution of the federal relationship evolved by the Constituent Assembly of India as the basis of the Indian federal organisation. Any attempt, made consciously or unconsciously, to change the territorial division of powers in the Indian federation will lead to its disintegration.

There is an inherent conflict between sub-national pluralism and political autonomy. Political autonomy is a residue of political authority and, therefore, complementary to national integration. Sub-national pluralism is basically a function of ethnic, cultural, religious and linguistic separation and consequently irreconcilable to national integration and nation building.

Coalition politics is not an attribute of parliamentary government. It is a dysfunctional feature of the cabinet system of government, which is essentially founded on an ideological and political consensus on national level. Regional aspirations, autonomy and social integration are an antithesis of a parliamentary consensus. Federalisation of power in India is reconcilable to the national consensus in a parliamentary government to the extent that it underlines on a political division of powers within the broad framework of a parliamentary order.

Coalitions are destructive of the parliamentary majority. If the trend to replace parliamentary majority continues, the parliamentary systems will not survive for long. Nor will the federal division of powers endure for many years because its basis in India is underlined by a consensus on a parliamentary majority.

24

SUSTAINABLE DEVELOPMENT AND ENVIRONMENT

Controversy has surrounded many major developmental and infrastructural projects in India, such as the Sardar Sarovar Dam on the river Narmada, the Chilka Lake in Orissa, the Konkan Railways, the East Coast Road, etc. Objections to these projects pertain to the extent of environmental destruction and uprooting of human settlements such projects may cause. But these environmental and social costs have been justified by the government and other protagonists as essential for any kind of development. This dichotomy reflects the essence of the debate around sustainable development. The process of resolving the perceived conflict between environment and development in all these issues, and the actual solutions that are worked out, will indicate whether the concept of sustainable development is implementable in a country like India.

Not only in India but almost everywhere in the world, "sustainable development" has become the new buzzword. Every international agency – from the World Bank to the UNICEF – and almost every country, is talking of it. But what does this sustainable development mean?

"Sustainable development is development that meets the needs of the present without compromising the ability of the future generations to meet their own needs." This definition has been offered by the World Commission on Environment and Development (WCED) in its report 'Our Common Future' (1987) and is widely accepted. Economists define it as an economic progress in which the quantity and quality of our stocks of natural resources (like forests) and the integrity of bio-geo-chemical cycles (like climate) are sustained and passed on unimpaired to future generations.

The eminent Indian economist, Sukhamoy Chakravarty

has pointed out that the success of sustainable development lies in the fact that it says nothing precise and, therefore, means anything to anybody! For a logging company it can mean sustained projects; for an environmental economist it can mean sustained stocks of natural forests; for a social ecologist it can mean sustained use of the forest; and for an environmentalist it can mean a clean heritage for our children. A western joke goes now, sustainable development for multinational companies, many of which have also embraced the concept, means simply 'sustained growth or sustained profits'.

Leaving aside its many uses and misuses, 'sustainable' here simply means keeping something going for and 'indefinite' period of time. However, when governments and industrial interests talk of 'sustainable' extraction of coal from coal fields, or oil from oil fields or coral from coral reefs, or of 'sustainable' farming by modern methods – which depends on the input of finite fossil fuels – it is often out of ignorance, greed or with an intent to mislead. The notion of sustainable development or sustainable 'exploitation' is not new; it has been with us for well over 100 years. Until the very recent past, however, it had not crept into conservation strategy. Today, the word 'sustainable' is tacked on to every major facet of human activity.

In its modern form, 'sustainable development' was born and developed in the World Conservation Strategy produced jointly in 1980 by the IUCN, WWF and UNEP. It aimed "to help advance the achievement of sustainable development through the conservation of living resources." It declared that "conservation, like development, is for the people," and thus implicitly assigned to all other species – plant or animal – a status of existence that is primarily for human use. That is the way all future development was to take place and be judged.

The concept assumed immense importance against the backdrop of the growth of human population and modern man's indiscriminate and unbridled exploitation of environment to gratify his ever-growing hunger for prosperity.

The two factors may soon exhaust the environmental resources and the planet will then not help in the survival of even human beings. People and planners must accept that there is a finite amount of habitable land and water on this earth. A specific concern is that those who enjoy the fruits of economic development today, may be making future generations worse off by over-exploitation of the natural resources and polluting the earth's environment.

Adding to the problems caused by population growth is the economic explosion. During the twentieth century, world economy expanded twenty times and industrialisation increased by a factor of five since 1950. This boom has depleted stocks of ecological capital (fuel, forests, soils, species, fisheries, water, atmosphere, etc.) faster than such stocks can be replenished. Our own success thus threatens to become our undoing.

Environmental degradation has already been massive. Yet not many seem to be aware of it. The natural resources are being exploited without much consideration for the future generations. Because of the holes in the ozone shield and the accumulation of green house gases, the world as a whole may slip to a critical stage. Indications of ecological degradation only reveal that economic growth of the present kind which depends on consuming the earth's natural and environmental resources is not sustainable. Thus, human survival and development today, more than ever, depend on two critical factors – a check on the population and a successful 'management' rather than 'exploitation' of the world's natural resources.

The process of economic transformation in recent years is seen to have involved a rapid increase in the scale of human pressure on the environment and also radical structural transformation, particularly in terms of urbanisation and industrialisation. Threats to environment can be linked directly with these rapid changes in several different ways. For example, as population expands, people move into previously 'empty' areas, generally involving destruction of various species of flora as well as fauna. Quite a different form of environmental degradation results from effluents, smoke and other wastes produced by industrial operations. The crowding of people into urban areas requires sanitary, transport and housing arrangements which are more complex and often more costly than those in the countryside, and all are accompanied by varying degrees of pollution.

Sustainability can never be absolute. It is not plausible that all natural resources can or even need to be preserved. Successful development will inevitably involve some amount of land clearing, oil-drilling, river-damming and swamp draining. But economic development and sound environmental management are complementary aspects of the same agenda. Without adequate environmental protection, development will be undermined; and without development, environmental protection will fail.

Each society experiments and learns from its own mistakes. Sustainable development cannot be thrust upon anyone by an external agent – whether it is the World Bank, the UNO, or the forestry department of a government – simply because it believes, at any point of time, that it has learnt all the lessons there are to learn. That will be a process towards unsustainable development.

Strong public institutions and environmental protection policies seem to be essential. Policy reforms must focus on changing agricultural and industrial practices so as to reduce drastically the amount of pollution, wastes and other environmental damage per unit of output. Environmental impacts need to be recognised; polices aimed at changing behaviour should rely heavily on economic incentives. Early action to prevent degradation will usually be much cheaper than attempting to reverse it later.

May be there should be a retrospective study of past practices, especially in agriculture, to see if they could not be applied without modifications to suit present needs. Several farmers are, indeed, discarding chemical fertilizers and pesticides and going back to traditional manures and biological pest control. Such steps certainly help towards making development sustainable.

Responsive and effective institutions must be developed. Dissemination of information and analysis must be improved to assist in setting up priorities and formulating policies. In the formulation of policies and decision-making, effective participation of the people on the spot should be ensured. Finding and implementing solutions to environment problems requires a partnership of efforts among nations. Industrial countries should assist in the transfer of less polluting technology to the developing countries.

These combined with other technical assistance would help developing countries to avoid or at least reduce environmental degradation. Further, the industrialised countries must take the lead in formulating and funding solutions to problems of worldwide concern as they have been the primary culprits on environment spoilage. But, above all, unless and until the world community strives in concert, to check population growth, no measure can work effectively.

People have always used the earth's resources and it is unreasonable now, with exploding populations, to expect them to stop. The solution to the human thrust on nature is not to cordon nature off, but to encourage wisdom in the exploitation of it, with the motto: "You must give back to the earth what you take from it." Man will have to shake off his predatory habit of viewing all natural products as his belongings and indulging his eternal greed at the cost of other species and ecosystems.

The agenda for reform is large and comprehensive. Accepting the challenge to accelerate development in an environmentally responsible manner will involve substantial shifts in policies and priorities and will be costly. Failing to accept the challenge will be costlier still. But the value of this challenge becomes clear only when we realise that humanity is not distinct from nature but a part of it.

25

HUMANS ARE THE WORST CULPRITS IN ENVIRONMENTAL DEGRADATION

Blest the infant Babe…
Nursed in his Mother's arms, who sinks to sleep
Rocked on his Mother's breast, who with his soul
Drinks in the feelings of his Mother's eye!
For him, in one dear Presence, there exists
A virtue which irradiates and exalts
Objects through widest intercourse of sense ….

— Wordsworth

We may not be as rapturous as Wordsworth about nature as mother of human beings; we know nature can be "red in tooth and claw" as well. But we cannot deny that humans owe much to the bounties of nature. However, humans have tended to take more and more from nature, robbing and looting nature's offerings, with callous lack of concern about the losses they inflict. In the process they do not just harm the environment; they harm humankind. Humans are, indeed, the worst culprits in the degradation of the environment.

Down the ages, humans have been in incessant pursuit of greater physical comforts and material prosperity. In this pursuit, they have steadily improved the technologies and other means necessary for higher production of wealth and for the availability of devices that could give more physical and mental pleasures. In this process, many social, political and cultural convulsions have happened. A great many wars have taken place, many human lives lost, and there have been instances of civilizations being wiped out. Nevertheless, human beings' relation with the environment remained almost unchanged for a long time; their interaction with nature remained harmonious based on the principle of mutual give-and-take.

The situation began to change rapidly with the advent of industrial revolution in the west in the eighteenth century, when human appetite for pelf and prosperity began to grow rapidly. Humans began to loot nature and pollute the environment without a thought for the consequences.

The industrial revolution led to a drastic escalation in air pollution. Coal was used in the emerging modern industries and factories on a very large scale. Later, it also came to be used in generating electricity. As a result, in the nineteenth and early twentieth centuries, many cities of Europe and US were covered with black shrouds of smoke. Industrial centres like Pittsburg and Pennsylvania developed an atmosphere so inky that automobile drivers were sometimes forced to use their headlights at mid-day. With the passage of time, the pace of industrialisation increased, with a corresponding increase in air pollution. Later, toxic wastes of the factories began to be dumped on land and in the waters of rivers and sea. Thus, land and water began to lose their quality.

When the western countries started fighting against the pollution caused by the industries after the 1930s, people in other parts of the world had already joined the race of industrialisation and blindly embraced all the concomitant ills. Consequently, today human activities have made the entire world's environment grossly polluted. Despite certain successes in controlling smoke, the pollution of air, water and land by other products of coal combustion – above all sulphur dioxide – and by nitrous oxides, hydrocarbons, and carbon monoxide—continues to worsen in most countries.

Industrialisation is not baneful *per se*. It is the method, technologies, impatience, intolerance and greed humans applied in this process that have caused havoc.

A corollary to the Industrial Revolution was the craving of human beings for urbanization. People began to throng to the industrial centres, towns and cities in large numbers without any regard to the capacity and limitations of a place in providing adequately the basic civic amenities to the inhabitants. As a consequence, large slum areas, filth and squalor grew. It became hard to maintain the sewage system as well as healthy sanitation. The crisis continues with greater intensity in the Third World countries.

Industrialisation and urbanisation also put pressure on the agricultural lands, the shortage of which began to be more acutely felt with faster and uncontrolled population growth. Remarkable progress made in the medical sciences has brought about a decline in the death rate. But no similar decline was attempted by the people in terms of birth rate. Two thousand years ago, humans scarcely numbered 250 million; it was only in the early 1800s that the figure reached one billion. A second billion was added in another 100 years, a third in 30 years, a fourth in 15 years and fifth in just 13 years.

What a pace of population growth! To feed the ever-increasing numbers, agricultural production was increased. Technological inputs certainly produced quick results. But the chemical fertilizers and pesticides have taken a big toll of the soil. They have also brought in their wake new pesticides – resistant pests which devour farm crops. The harmful chemicals get into the ecological cycle and lead to the large-scale damage to plants, animals and ultimately even to humans. Recently, a study found that the milk and cereals consumed by Indians contain high degree of toxic materials – all due to indiscriminate use of pesticides. Large scale agricultural production also encouraged huge irrigation projects with concomitant loss of forest land. Canal irrigation has laid waste large tracts of land due to unchecked seepage leading to salinity and alkanity of soil.

The scarcity of agricultural lands became an excuse for humans to clear the dense forests which, in fact, served to mitigate the harm and injuries caused by industrialisation and urbanisation. Trees are mercilessly felled to meet the industrial needs of various kinds as well as the needs of the vast urban population. With deforestation comes the growing menace of soil erosion, drought and other natural calamities. This act of deforesting the land is also ominous to the existence of many species of flora and fauna, even as the extinction of many marine species is feared due to the poisoning of rivers and seas by man-made wastes. The adverse impact on biodiversity may destabilise the ecological balance whose ill effects are quite intelligible.

The growing lust for luxurious and industrial products has recently further aggravated the crisis. The chloroflurocarbons (CFCs) released into the atmosphere because of the ever-growing use of refrigeration and cooling devices are depleting the ozone layer which protects the species on earth from being exposed to the harmful ultraviolet rays.

If we analyse the nature of environment degradation, we can only come to the conclusion that human culpability is, indeed, immense. To feed, clothe and shelter themselves, humans brazenly rob nature. The growing population almost renders it impossible to compensate the losses suffered by the environment or allow it the time required to recover. The urge to gain greater and greater material prosperity has not only degraded natural sources but also has certain other dangerous portents. The damage caused during the Gulf War to the seas and marine life shows the extent to which humans can go, without compunction, to achieve self-aggrandisement. The search for energy and defence superiority has led humans to further exploit the power of the atom. But they have shown a callous disregard for the accompanying dangers of radiation and tackling nuclear wastes. Unless human beings mend their ways, and fast, they will create another Venus or Mars on the Earth.

26

STATUS OF HUMAN RIGHTS IN INDEPENDENT INDIA

Like all other values, freedom is essentially an individual value. A society or a nation has no consciousness of its own. It is the individual who has consciousness and who either suffers from bondage or exults in freedom. A society or a nation can be said to be free to the extent to which the individuals composing it are free.

The expression 'human rights' as a term of art is of recent origin. However, the idea of the law or the law-giver, defining and protecting the legal rights of men, mainly the mutual rights of the members of the community, is very old. We find elements of the protection of human rights in the code of the Babylonian King. Hammurabi (about 2130 to 2088 BC). The Petition of Rights of 1620 and the Bill of Rights of 1689, the passages of the American Declaration of Independence, the Virginia Bill of Rights of 1776, the French Declaration of the Rights of Man and of the Citizen are the foundations of all human rights and democratic freedoms in the modern world.

Indians became familiar with the watchwords of American and French revolutions and modern Western values with the introduction of English education and British system of administration and jurisprudence, based on the rule of law, which in itself is a basic human right. The Indians got themselves acquainted with sciences and modern knowledge and the ideas about human freedoms and began to question not only colonial rule but also the harmful customs and institutions of foreign rule.

We got freedom. We framed our own Constitution and formulated system of administration. Most of the human rights listed in the Universal Declaration of Human Rights are incorporated in Part III of the Constitution of India. This part on fundamental rights declares that all laws in consistent with term are void and these fundamental rights are enforceable in courts of law. Some important rights of Indian citizens are — right to equality (Articles 14-18), right to freedom (Articles 19-22), right against exploitation (Articles 23-24), right to freedom of religion (Articles 25-28), and cultural and educational rights, protecting the interest of minorities (Articles 29-30).

Our Constitution incorporates a vast range of political, social, economic, cultural and religious rights of citizens. For ensuring the rights of all citizens, our Constitution allows for some special provisions for scheduled castes, scheduled tribes and other weaker and backward classes of society through the policy of reservation and other means. Untouchability is banned and is an offence. Primary education is free and secondary and higher education is subsidized and is being made progressively free. Physical and mental health is recognized as one of the social rights. India has recognized that human rights and democracy are inseparable and we cannot secure one without the other.

Over sixty-five years have passed since we attained independence. What is the real status of human rights in post-independent India?

In the region of civil liberties, some tangible improvements have been brought about. The judiciary, free press and voluntary non-governmental organisations have succeeded to a considerable extent in protecting and promoting the fundamental rights — civil liberties — of the people. The broader interpretation, given by the Supreme Court, of Article 14 – equality before law — and Article 21 — liberty of the person and of the life of individuals — and the system of public interest litigation have succeeded to a noticeable extent in establishing the rule of law and checking the arbitrary behaviour of politicians and public authorities. The role of the judiciary in the protection and promotion of civil liberties and human rights is impressive. Notable achievements have been made in science and technology, economic development, attainment of self-sufficiency in food, and improvements in health parameters — all leading to better human conditions. Efforts have also been made through the land reform movement and various developmental programmes to enable the weaker sections of society get possession of land. Labour legislations have been passed to ensure fair wages and healthy conditions of work to the working class.

However, the contradictions of the socio-economic order in our society have remained almost the same even after more than six decades of independence. Half a century is a considerable period of time in the history of a society to correct its mistakes and imbalances, but, unfortunately in India, neither the society nor the state has been able to resolve the contradictions. The socio-political scenario is marked by a sharp escalation in human rights violations by dominant groups. Despite the constitutional commitment of the state towards achieving the goal of equality, liberty and justice, the age-old structure of inequality has not been dismantled. The ideas of grassroot social democracy and distributive justice remain elusive. A considerable proportion of the Indian population is subjected to multiple deprivations.

The fruits of development have not been shared equitably. Poverty still remains a formidable challenge. Along with this, the basic amenities of life like health, education and drinking water are not available to one and all. Child labour and bonded labour exist in many areas, despite laws having been passed to prevent them. Women do not enjoy equal rights with men. There are many instances of violation of human rights of Dalits, tribals and ethnic and religious minorities. The right to information is right only on paper. Legislation is also necessary for protecting the the right to privacy.

Moreover, there are instances of violation of human rights by the state machinery itself. This was conspicuous during the emergency period. There are many instances of police torture during investigation into offences, sometimes resulting into custodial deaths. The Terrorism and Disruptive Activities (Prevention) Act (TADA) was misused. In many cases TADA was used against the members of the weaker sections of the society.

At present, the movement for human rights has been overshadowed by a dismal political scenario characterized by an all-pervading corruption in the political and administrative spheres of the country, criminalization of politics and the inability of political parties to form a stable government. Due to criminalization of politics, several sections are unable to use their right to vote or to vote freely.

A positive feature is that the citizens of the country are becoming conscious of their rights and are demanding an end to all kinds of exploitation. The role of the Indian judiciary in the protection and promotion of civil liberties and human rights is impressive and inspiring. A large number of human rights organisations have come up. Young men and women inspired by the spirit of human freedom are working in these organisations at grassroot level among the deprived and exploited sections of the people, such as the tribals, Dalits, women and landless labourers, to make them fearlessly fight for their rights. There has been an increased concern for protection of environment, itself a valuable human right. The National Commission for Human Rights has been set up to document, assess and act on human rights violations in the country.

In the end, we can say that despite some cases of violation of human rights, India continues to be a democratic and open society. "Freedom from fear could be said to sum up the whole philosophy of human rights." These were the memorable words of the first Secretary-General of the United Nations on the Universal Declaration of Human Rights. The world today is one global village. It is for the people of India to join hands with the people of the world in the global task of freeing all people from any sense of fear and of defending and promoting human rights and democracy that go together.

27

WOMEN SHOULD HAVE RESERVED SEATS IN PARLIAMENT

A democratic republic based on equality and liberty should ideally have no reason to have reservation for any segment of society in Parliament or elsewhere. However, we do not live in an ideal situation. Reservation is usually defended on the basis of the need to offer compensatory justice to rectify indefensible discrimination against certain sections of society, and the need to ensure equality through state intervention in support of the deprived and the underprivileged.

If we go by this justification for reservation, we see that women are indeed a discriminated lot as far as their representation in Parliament is concerned. The highest percentage of women through the Lok Sabha so far hovers around 8 per cent of the seats. In Rajya Sabha it reached 11 per cent or so once. And, in population terms, women form almost 50 per cent of the total number of people in India. In number terms, at least, the inequity of representation is more than obvious. Such imbalances need to be corrected and women need to participate more actively in the political process. So, why have more women not entered our legislatures?

In the existing patriarchal male-dominated socio-political system that prevails in India, women are not likely to get the opportunity to enter the political mainstream and be empowered. One had high hopes that discrimination against women would end once India got independence and progressive laws were made. Women have certainly made great strides in the economic world with several holding lucrative and important jobs in various fields of activities. But nothing much has changed within Parliament: Gender bias in political circles is very strong, and most parties are reluctant to give tickets to women for contesting elections. As a result, most women are left out of the political process at the very stage of selection of candidates. It is the reluctance that makes one feel that reservation of seats for women alone will help, indeed, force parties to give seats to women and seriously campaign for their victory so that they come to power.

Those who favour reservations also argue that only the presence of a substantial number of women in decision-making bodies would help in eliminating the centuries-old gender-based discrimination in socio-economic and political fields. It is because of the 'invisibility' of women at the decision-making level for a long time that the concerns of women and their specific need have not been adequately articulated, leave alone addressed. In 1990, the UN Commission on the Status of Women recommended a critical 30 per cent participation threshold to be regarded as the minimum for decision-making positions at the national level. It is well recognized that women's voices are seldom heard, and they are often forced to make compromises.

India, despite having a growing number of women in well-paid jobs, still ranks low in the gender-related development index as calculated by the UNDP Human Development Reports. Nor does it do too well in gender-empowerment measures. Progressive laws have, no doubt, been made aimed at empowering women in terms of employment, health, education and so on, but their implementation has been tardy. This suggests the absence of some vital catalyst and this catalyst could well be a more equal political space for women in Parliament. Reservation for women could well create a new class of politically aware women who would demand their rights with the force of conviction.

Most women do feel that empowerment through natural evolution of society as a whole, through the effects of education and family welfare measures, is to be preferred, but for that to happen within a reasonable timeframe, the right kind of foundations were needed to be laid long ago. Most women also prefer getting better representation without reservation. Since, however, that has not transpired, and since everything cannot be left to time alone, reservation has become a necessity. And practically, every political party solemnly affirms that this is so. Not one is opposed to the policy openly. And this is what is somewhat disturbing that no political party is firmly acting on this 'consensus'. Some or the other excuse is brought forward to postpone the introduction of the Bill, or, if introduced, to delay its passage.

One wonders even more when the same kind of reservation was eagerly pushed through at the Panchayati Raj level. One has a sneaking feeling that the men appeared so benevolent precisely because they were convinced that they were no longer concerned with jockeying for power at that grassroot level. It could well have come as a shock to see women readily coming out to contest and hold on the power. In spite of negative reports about the Panchayats being packed with women related to the men in power, there is evidence at least of some instances where the women have come in their own rights and done good for their villages. Unfortunately, these positive developments are seldom given the exposure they deserve. Anyway, it seems as if the men have realised that women can and do win and make a mark of their own, and now they are loath to give up even a minuscule amount of power. And they know that in the present circumstances, women would have to put up the kind of fight most of them are incapable of in the political arena – which is near brutish — without reservation. So, the opposition to reservation.

Reservation needs to be introduced, but on the interim basis, not to be extended as all such 'positive discrimination' measures tend to be in this country due to vested interests. Alongside reservation there has to be a concerted effort to train women and equip them to fulfill their obligations to the people who elected them. One promise for reservation is that certain characteristics predominantly 'feminine', as they say, such as altruism, self-denial and caring — which have been suppressed by patriarchy — will find a wider expression in the political arena. If that is so, we must go all out for reserving seats for women in Parliament which has seen some forgettable scenes in the recent past.

28

PROBLEMS OF WORKING WOMEN

No eyebrows are raised today at the thought of women going out to work. Plenty of lip service is paid to the idea of equality of men and women. And yet no one would deny that working women have to face problems just because of their being women. It may be relevant to say here that when we are talking of working women, we are referring to those who are in paid employment.

Social attitude to the role of women lags much behind the law. This attitude which considers women fit for certain jobs and not others, colours those who recruit employees. Thus, women find employment easily as nurses, doctors, teachers — the caring and nurturing sectors; as clerks and secretaries or in assembling jobs — the routine submissive sectors. But even if well qualified women engineers or managers or geologists are available, preference will be given to a male of equal qualifications. A gender bias creates an obstacle at the recruitment stage itself.

Then comes remuneration. Once again, the law proclaims equality, but it is seldom put into practice. The inbuilt conviction that women are not capable of doing more work than men or are less efficient than men governs this injustice of unequal remuneration for the same job. In the Republic of Korea women's wages are only 47 per cent of what men get. In Japan, they get only 51 per cent of what their male counterparts receive. And in India, too, there is widespread discrimination in this respect.

The age-old belief of male superiority over women creates several hurdles for women at their place of work. Women on the way up the corporate ladder discover that they must be much better than their male colleagues to reach the top. Once at the top, male colleagues and subordinates often expect much greater expertise and efficiency from a woman boss than from a male boss. What is worse, conditioned by social and psychological tradition, women colleagues, too, do not lend support to their own sex. Working in such conditions inevitably puts a much greater strain on women than what men experience.

These problems tend to make women less eager to progress in their careers. Indeed, many of them choose less demanding jobs for which they may even be overqualified. But such compromises do not work well for many, who become frustrated at jobs which do not suit their talents or listless because of the routine drudgery.

A woman's work is not merely confined to paid employment. She has to, almost, always, shoulder the burden of household chores as well—thankless unpaid work which could easily be put under the maintenance of essential services act.

Perhaps, the problems would appear less burdensome if at least social recognition was given to the invisible input of women in employment. But who cares to notice the routine work which many a woman does as a matter of course — cooking, cleaning, washing, rearing children and looking after the ill and elderly? If it is noticed, it is dismissed carelessly as a part of her 'duty'. While the man can come home from a taxing day at office and relax with a cup of tea and the newspaper or television, a woman is compelled to merely switch over from one kind of work to another on reaching home.

It is a much more hectic schedule for a working mother. Besides the regular housework, she is unfairly saddled with the entire responsibility of bringing up the children. In the circumstances, she has to face a high state of nervous tension and worry besides the physical stress.

A woman could still bear up with these problems if she had control over the money she earns. But in most families even her salary is handed over in toto to the father, husband or in-laws. So, a basic motto in seeking employment — getting economic independence — is nullified in many a woman's case.

Problems because of gender bias beset women in the industrial sector too. Technological advancement invariably results in retrenchment of women employees. Usually woman do not think of upgrading their skills. Maternity leave is seldom given. It is much easier to terminate the woman's employment and hire someone else. And trade unions do little to improve the lot of women workers. Women's issues do not occur on the priority list of these labour organisations.

Women going to work are often subject to sexual harassment. Public transport systems are overcrowded and men take advantage of the circumstances to physically harass women. Places of work are little better. Colleagues offer unwanted attention which can still be shaken off, but a woman is placed in a predicament if the higher officer demands sexual favours. If refused, the boss can easily take it out on the woman in other ways to make life miserable for her. On the other hand, if a woman is praised for her work or promoted on merit, her colleagues do not hesitate to attribute it to sexual favours conferred by her on the boss! The psychological pressure of all this can easily lead to a woman's quitting her job.

In small or big cities, the working woman finds it difficult to get suitable accommodation. House-owners are suspicious and hesitant to rent rooms to young — or even old — women on their own. Hostels or guest houses are rare and not enough to meet the demands. So, the woman is forced to seek non-transferable jobs and is thus restricted in her choice.

Most of the problems that beset working women are, in reality, rooted in the social perspective of the position of women. Traditionally, men are seen as the bread-winners and the women as house-keepers, child-bearers and child-rearers. This typecast role model continues to put obstacles before the working women.

The law too has hitherto served the interests of one gender—male—at the immense cost and disadvantage of the other—female. The framers, enforcers and executors of the law are by and large men, and women have little clout to influence the legal process, which has done pretty little to address even the basic issues pertaining to employed women. Besides, the number of working women is still not significant enough to be able to change their working conditions.

A fundamental change is required in the attitudes of the employers, policy-makers, family members and other relatives and the public at large. Marriage, pregnancy and child-bearing/rearing should be regarded by employers as a woman's important but not her only functions. The policy-makers must consider a woman as a distinct personality, not as an appendage of the male relatives. The family members, male or female, must share the indoor work of a woman if she works outdoor like a male. The public must regard and respect working women as significant contributors to the well-being and prosperity of the society. We all must recognize that providing good child care is a national responsibility if the women who work are short of time.

Flexible working hours would go a long way in easing the burden on the employed women. The system of paternity leave, paid or unpaid, can be introduced so that the father can share the household tasks and parent the new-born babe.

There is an urgent need to evolve a comprehensive national maternity and child-care policy incorporating the needs of working women in both the organised or unorganised — industrial, agricultural or service — sectors. Problems of harassment at the work place need to be seriously addressed. The offenders should be brought to book at the earliest. All efforts should be directed towards making the work environment congenial for the female employees.

In the final analysis, a clear-cut state policy, even if it cannot change attitudes and social perceptions overnight, can play a vital role in influencing and moulding social opinions.

The important aspect about state policy is that since it has the authority of law and sanction of the state behind it, it can change practices even if it takes times to change attitudes.

Social attitudes sometimes lag behind social realities in a period of transition. The role of the primary care-giver in a family needs to be redefined to include male members. If the social superstructure does not reflect the current needs, then it has to be changed. Perhaps, it is time for a few determined pushes to take the first step of reconstructing social structures so that they address modern needs.

29

ECONOMIC THEORY OF *LAISSEZ FAIRE*

Laissez faire is a French phrase literally meaning "let happen", or "let do". From the French diction first used by the 18th century physiocrats as an injunction against government interference with trade, it came to be used as a synonym for strict free market economics during the early and mid-19th century. It is generally understood to be a doctrine that maintains that private initiative and production are best allowed to roam free, opposing economic interventionism and taxation by the state beyond that which is perceived to be necessary to maintain individual liberty, peace, security and property rights.

In the *laissez faire* view, the state has no responsibility to engage in intervention to maintain a desired wealth distribution or to create a welfare state to protect people from poverty, instead of relying on charity and the market system. *Laissez faire* also embodies the notion that a government should not be in the business of granting privileges. As such, advocates of *laissez faire* support the idea that the government should not create legal monopolies or use force to damage the facto monopolies. Supporters of *laissez faire* also support the notion of free trade on the grounds that the state should not use protectionist measures, such as tariffs and subsidies in order to curtail trade through national frontiers.

In the free-market economy advocated by economic libertarians, individuals coordinate their economic decisions through the institutions of private property, freedom of contract and the free price system. Libertarians argue that the free market produces greater prosperity and personal freedom than other economic systems. In the early stages of European and US economic theory, *laissez faire* economic policy was in conflict with mercantilism, which had been the dominant system of the United Kingdom, Spain, France and other European countries during their rise to power.

Economic Theory

The *laissez faire* means that the neoclassical school of economic thought holds a pure or economically liberal market view: that the free market is best left to its own devices, and that it will dispense with inefficiencies in a more deliberate and quick manner than any legislating body could. The basic idea is that less government interference in private economic decisions such as pricing, production, consumption and distribution of goods and services makes for a better, or more efficient, economy.

The Austrian School of Economics and the Chicago School of Economics are important foundations of the economic libertarianism. Economic libertarians, as well as general libertarians, advocate *laissez faire* capitalism, where all the means of production are privately owned, economic and financial decisions are made entirely privately, goods and services are exchanged in a free market, and there is little or no positive state intervention in the economy. As a consequence, now-ubiquitous worldwide money regulating agencies such as the U.S. Federal Reserve System and other government owned and operated central banking systems are seen as artificial at best and damaging at worst.

Like most mainstream economists, the Austrian and Chicago Schools support the subjective theory of value, which says that only a buyer and seller, while using information shared and available in the market place, can determine how valuable goods and services are to them and thereby set a mutually agreeable price. Libertarians contend that supply and demand, as ordered by the incidence of independent, subjective valuations in the free market, are the only sensible means of establishing prices. Moreover, they believe that only prices rendered in a free market can synthesize and communicate the preferences and relevant, time-sensitive data to millions of consumers and producers alike, and any attempt to objectify these transactions by a centralized authority will fail. According to them, any government intervention such as regulation, trade barriers, or taxes, interfere with this judgement being reflected accurately in the price (though economists often argue that market failures can interfere with pricing as well). Most economists agree that accurate pricing is an important part of efficient markets, and thus important for maximising economic utility.

Market failures are a tremendous source of controversy amongst libertarians. This is what usually divides the mainstream ones who advocate for continued public ownership of policing, military and so forth and anarcho-capitalists who want full privatization of goods. For many of the hardline groups, the principle of liberty must overcome the goal of wealth. The public good of police, for instance, could be seen as immoral coercion, no matter how efficient it may be over private security.

Libertarians do not see unequal wealth distribution as a moral problem and firmly support the private ownership of land and capital. They oppose mandatory egalitarian redistribution of wealth because they believe this would qualify as initiation of force against individuals and their legitimate property. In addition, libertarians claim that redistribution of wealth takes capital from the most productive sectors of the economy, and that forcing economic egalitarianism reduces the incentive to work. They may further argue that any temporary equality of outcome gained by redistribution would quickly collapse without coercion because people have different levels of motivation and native abilities, and would make different choices based on their different values. Those that were more productive or traded more effectively would quickly gain disproportionate wealth, others would waste their resources, and some of those would choose to save for retirement or earn little on their own. Some may choose not to generate wealth preferring to spend their time in other areas they find more fulfilling like noncommercial artistic expression or religious growth — avenue libertarians do not oppose. However, they do oppose forced subsidisation of any such venture. Material in equality, they argue, is a necessary outcome of the freedom to choose one's own actions without imposing on others. To the extent that they accept any kind of welfare, libertarians tend to prefer Milton Friedman's negative income tax as an alternative — but not a supplement — to the existing system, arguing that it is simpler and has fewer of the "perverse incentives" of "government handouts".

Libertarians tend to believe that minimising the amount of money citizens pay to government minimises the ability of the government to fund bad programmes and prevents citizens from needing government assistance because they have more of their own money.

Because they oppose taxes, libertarians also oppose most programmes funded by taxes. Many libertarians do so in respect of government-run or regulated schools, hospitals, industry, agriculture and social welfare programmes. Others justify public schools on grounds of efficiency, fairness, or both, though most would prefer a school voucher system to the status quo.

Libertarians, especially the Cato Institute, have long supported Social Security privatisation as a first step to dismantling Social Security.

Lastly, many libertarians support the gold standard as opposed to paper currency because they do not trust the government to restrain itself from over-expanding the money supply which would result in inflation. Inflation is commonly regarded by libertarians as a surreptitious method of taxation employed to usurp value from privately-held money without levying an apparent tax and demanding physical transfer of money.

Laissez faire Today

Modern industrialised nations today are not representative of *laissez faire* principles or policies, as they usually involve significant amounts of government intervention in the economy. This intervention includes minimum wages, corporate welfare, anti-trust regulation, nationalised industries and welfare programmes among other forms of government intervention. Subsidy programmes for businesses and agricultural products, government ownership of some industry (usually in natural resources), regulation of market competition, economic trade barriers in the form of protective tariffs, quotas on imports or internal regulation favouring domestic industry, are the other forms of government favouritism.

According to the 2007 Index of Economic Freedom issued by the Heritage Foundation, the seven countries with the most free economies are currently the following: Hong Kong, Singapore, Australia, United States, New Zealand, United Kingdom and Ireland (all of them former constituents of the British Empire). Hong Kong is ranked number one for 12 consecutive years in the Index which attempts to measure "the absence of government coercion or constraint on the production, distribution, or consumption of goods and services beyond the extent necessary for citizens to protect and maintain liberty itself." Milton Friedman praised the Hong Kong *laissez faire* approach to the economy and credits that policy for the rapid move from poverty to prosperity in 50 years. Much of this growth came under British colonial control prior to the 1977 takeover by Communist China.

However, at a press conference on 11 September 2006, Donald Tsang, the Chief Executive of Hong Kong, said that "Positive non-interventionism was a policy suggested by a previous Financial Secretary many years ago, but we have never said that we would still use it as our current policy… . We prefer the so-called 'big market, small government' policy." Responses in Hong Kong were widely divided, some see it as an announcement to abandon the positive non-interventionism, others see it as a more realistic response to the government policies in the past few years, such as the intervention of the stock market to prevent brokering.

30

FIRST GENERATION – CONSERVING GOVERNMENT'S MOST VALUABLE RESOURCE

As public sector workers retire, they take important knowledge and skills with them – a situation bound to affect every corporation and private citizen. Savvy governments around the world are responding with innovative ways to recruit and train the next generation of civil servants.

As the post-World War II generation nears retirement world-wide, meeting their public welfare and social security obligations may be the least of the challenges confronting governments in the United States, Europe and Asia. Evidence is mounting that the real challenge for the public sector will be the loss of critical knowledge and skills as a result of the retirement of its own employees, a situation bound to affect every corporate and private citizen it serves.

When the government workers retire, important, sometimes critical, information and expertise can remain with them – knowledge civilians often take for granted. For instance, according to a manager at the US National Aeronautics and Space Administration, some time in the 1990s, NASA lost the knowledge it had developed to send astronauts to the moon. Extending this type of knowledge loss to other public sector services and agencies, from civil aviation to regulatory bodies to defence, a bleak picture emerges.

Government is not alone in facing this challenge, of course. In the private sector, the retirement of skilled workers has contributed to chemical plant explosions and airline maintenance problems, to cite just a few examples, and companies across a number of industries have moved aggressively to capture and retain knowledge.

But governments face unique challenge that cannot be overcome simply through the application of private sector solutions. For example, the civil service workforce is, on an average, older than the private sector workforce (which means that governments will, by default, be on the leading edge of solving the problem). In addition, some civil service employers also have an image problem that can hamper recruiting.

Long and complex hiring processes, non-competitive salaries, uncertain government budgets and bureaucracy all put government agencies at a disadvantage when it comes to competing for talent. As a result, even when governments institute programmes to help pass knowledge from older to younger workers, there may not be enough younger workers to inherit it.

Reactions and Responses

Governments in several countries have acknowledged these problems and are taking steps to address them. For example, to attract new talent, South Korea has opened up 20 per cent of its top civil service posts to applicants from the private sector. Meanwhile, a number of European governments have introduced a variety of inducements to make public sector employment more attractive, including more flexible civil service career paths, performance-based pay and hiring of executives on contracts. And many US States now conduct exit interviews with retiring public employees to understand why they are leaving and to determine what governments need to do to better attract and retain workers.

To preserve valuable knowledge, ministers and administrators in Canada have identified succession of planning as a pressing issue, and in response have established a mentoring programme. At the Kennedy Space Centre in Florida, where nearly 60 per cent of employees are approaching retirement age, NASA and the state have jointly funded a Web-based educational programme to capture and retain knowledge.

What is limiting the effectiveness of such initiatives,

however, is that there have been uncoordinated responses to one or the other specific consequence of workforce aging. Because workforce aging tends to be pervasive across departments and ministries, governments should instead approach the problem holistically, which involves three steps.

Diagnose the Problem

Each government agency must first determine the magnitude of its exposure to the threat of an impending worker shortage by answering the following questions: what percentage of employees is eligible for retirement in the next two to five years, and what skills will they take away with them when they go? Do current training and development programmes ensure that critical skills will remain in the organisation? Does the organisation have systems in place that capture the knowledge of workers eligible for retirement? Are current recruitment practices effective enough to compete with other agencies and the private sector for scarce talent? Are reward, recognition and compensation programmes competitive with the private sector? Does the agency provide flexible work options, such as flexible time, job sharing, telecommuting and part-time work, to meet the needs of a wider population of current and potential employees? Does the workplace environment "show" employees that they are valued and respected, so older workers want to stay and younger candidates want to join?

A diagnostic tool can then be used to pinpoint the specific nature of an agency's overall exposure to the problem of aging. One such tool is the Accenture Human Capital Development Framework. It measures the effectiveness of human capital processes and capabilities such as reward systems and career development and leadership, and enables organisations to logically infer potential linkages to public sector metrics such as tax revenue, taxpayer burden and taxpayer responsiveness.

By providing benchmarks along a number of dimensions against which they can measure themselves, the framework assists organisations in discovering their weaknesses and there they are at risk. For instance, it shows best-in-class human capital processes for areas such as reward systems and career development; best-in-class capabilities, such as leadership and talent management; best-in-class organisational performance drivers, such as productivity; and best-in-class business results or organisational outputs, such as return on invested capital and future value.

The framework has already been used in the private sector to address the aging workforce issue. For example, a North American financial services company used it to determine that although its payroll and benefits administration were excellent, it needed to improve career development, leadership and succession planning. But governments are also starting to use the framework to identify similar weaknesses, recognising the equivalent benefits of the tool in the public sector.

Develop a Human Capital Management Strategy

With the diagnosis in hand, an agency will have a clear picture of its human capital strengths and weaknesses, and can develop a holistic strategy tailored to its particular needs. A human capital management strategy should embrace both present and future workforce requirements.

First, the organisation should identify the skills and competencies most at risk as workers retire. It will then need to figure out how to retain, capture and transfer the associated knowledge.

The organisation should consider changes in retirement policies to retain critical skills, perhaps implementing phased retirement and alumni programmes. In the United States, for example, workers in more than 30 states now retire, at least on a part-time basis, with valuable skills and knowledge.

California and Ohio have offered a pension incentive to retain older teachers. And at the national level, partly to reduce the benefits of leaving workforce, the US government eliminated rules that penalised Social Security recipients for gainful employment after the age of 65.

Second, the strategy must address the critical skills needed for the future and how the organisation will attract, recruit, hire, train and develop the right type of people. Finally, to make it possible to do more with less, the human capital management strategy should consider other ways of delivering services, such as a shared services model.

Implement a Broad-based Solution

The third step is to enact comprehensive solutions, based on realistic, cost-effective and actionable steps linked to the strategy. For example, the US Department of the Treasury recently implemented a far-reaching solution that addressed the threat aging poses to its Senior Executive Service, its top tier of employees. The solution has two parts. The first uses a succession planning tool-kit to identify future leadership requirements, assess the depth of the talent pool, and determine necessary training and development. The second part involves benchmarking other senior executive development programmes and identifying best practices to plan mentoring and training for high-potential employees.

In 2003, the Queensland government in Australia opted to address these challenges with a shared services programme, which established stand-alone units to perform routine administrative tasks and transactions for several agencies. For example, instead of each agency maintaining its own staff to perform finance, purchasing and human resources, several agencies can share the services of one central unit.

This approach reduces the duplication of efforts and allows agencies to redirect their scarce budgetary resources into more productive applications. Estimates are that the Queensland's shared services initiative will trim as much as US $ 80 million from routine operating costs and make it possible to invest the money in areas of critical need, such as health, education and justice.

The US Transporation Security Administration took a slightly different approach when post-9/11 Congressional mandates required it to quickly recruit, evaluate, hire, train and deploy additional personnel. Instead of attempting to build an in-house human resources department capable of meeting the daunting challenges, the TSA became the first federal government agency to deliver core human resources functions, such as hiring, induction, personnel and benefits administration, through a shared services structure. In the first six weeks of service, the agency's partner began providing human resources for the TSA's approximately 55,000 employees, hiring up to 1,200 new employees per month. It also established a call centre that today handles as many as 750 human resource questions a day for TSA employees.

Demographic trends leave no doubt that fewer workers are in line to replace retirees. Even as workers have been aging, birth rates have been declining. The worldwide fertility rate has fallen by nearly half in the past 30 years and is below replacement levels in many parts of the developed world. By 2050, for the first time in history, the old will outnumber the young.

Meanwhile, budgetary pressures are forcing cuts at many agencies. It would be a mistake, therefore, for agencies to think that they do not have to worry about the wave of retirees and instead see it as a convenient way to reduce headcount. They need to establish the right knowledge retention programmes to avoid losing critical skills and expertise when these workers retire.

Recruiting and training the new generation will be a challenge. Studies in the United States and Europe show that young job seekers are far from eager to work in government sector. To their credit, governments have begun to recognise the problem, but so far the efforts to address it have been piecemeal. A comprehensive approach is necessary. If an organisation's human resources are its most important asset, then dealing with the impending loss of those resources must be the organisations's highest priority.

31

NEOCOLONIALISM : BETRAYED INTERNATIONAL ECONOMIC ARRANGEMENT

Neocolonialism is the term describing international economic arrangement wherein former colonial powers maintained control of colonies and dependencies after World War II. Neocolonialism can obfuscate the understanding of current colonialism, given that some colonial governments continue administering foreign territories and their population in violation of United Nations resolutions and private, foreign business companies continue arguing that their continued exploitation of the natural resources is beneficial to subjugated, colonial peoples. The economic control inherent to neocolonialism is akin to the classical, European colonialism practised from the 16th to the 20th centuries.

Economic Control

The contention is that governments have aimed to control other nations through indirect means. In lieu of direct military-political control, neocolonialist powers employ economic, financial and trade policies to dominate less powerful countries. Those who subscribe to the concept maintain that this amounts to a de facto control over targeted nations.

Both previous colonizing states and other powerful economic states maintain a continuous presence in the economies of former colonies, especially where it concerns raw materials. After a hastened decolonization process of the Belgian Congo, Belgium continued to control through The Société Générale de Belgique, roughly 70% of the Congolese economy following the decolonization process. The most contested part was in the province of Katanga where the Union Miniére der Hant Katanga, part of the Société, had control over the mineral and resource rich province. After a failed attempt to nationalise the mining industry in the 1960s, it was reopened to foreign investment.

Critics of neocolonialism portray the choice to grant or to refuse granting loans – particularly those financing otherwise unpayable Third World debt, — especially by international financial institutions such as the International Monetary Fund (IMF) and the World Bank (WB), as a decisive form of control. They argue that in order to qualify for these loans and other forms of economic aid, weaker nations are forced to take certain steps favourable to the financial interests of the IMF and World Bank but detrimental to their own economies. These structural adjustments have the effect of increasing rather than alleviating poverty within the nation.

Some critics emphasize that neocolonialism allows certain cartels of states, such as the World Bank, to control and exploit usually lesser developed countries (LDCs) by fostering debt. In effect, Third World governments give concessions and monopolies to foreign corporations in return for consolidation of power and monetary bribes. In most cases, much of the money loaned to these LDCs is returned to the favoured foreign corporations. Thus, these foreign loans are in effect subsidies to corporations of the loaning states. This collusion is sometimes referred to as the corporatocracy. Organisations accused of participating in neo-imperialism include the World Bank, World Trade Organisation, Group of Eight and the World Economic Forum. Various "first world" states, notably the United States, are said to be involved, as described in *Confessions of an Economic Hitman* by John Perkins.

Critics of neocolonialism also attempt to demonstrate that investment by multinational corporations enriches few in underdeveloped countries, and causes humanitarian, environmental and ecological devastation to the population which inhabit the neocolonies. This, it is argued, results in unsustainable development and perpetual underdevelopment; a dependency which cultivates those countries as reservoirs of cheap labour and raw materials, while restricting their access to advanced production techniques to develop their own economies.

By contrast, proponents of neocolonialism argue that while the First World does profit from cheap labour and raw materials in underdeveloped nations, ultimately, it does serve as a positive modernising force for development in the Third World.

Origins in Decolonization

The term decolonialism first saw widespread use, particularly in reference to Africa, soon after the process of decolonization which followed a struggle by many national independence movements in the colonies following World War II. Upon gaining independence, some national leaders and opposition groups argued that their countries were being subjected to a new form of colonialism, waged by the former colonial powers and other developed nations. Kwame Nkrumah, who in 1957 became leader of newly independent Ghana, expounded this idea in his *Neo-Colonialism : The Last Stage of Imperialism,* in 1965. In Africa, the French played a prominent role in charges of conducting a neocolonialist policy, and that French troops in Africa were – and it is argued, still are — often involved in coup d'etats resulting in a regime acting in the interests of France but against its country's own interests.

Denunciations of neocolonialism also became popular with some national independence movements while they were still waging anti-colonial armed struggle. During the 1970s, in the Portuguese colonies of Mozambique and Angola, for example, the rhetoric espoused by the Marxist movements FRELIMO and MPLA, which were to eventually assume power upon those nations' independence, rejected both traditional colonialism and neocolonialism.

Anti-neocolonialists' Allegations Against the IMF

Those who argue that neocolonialism historically supplanted or supplemented colonialism, point to the fact that

Africa today pays more money every year in debt service payments to the IMF and the World Bank than it receives in loans from them, thereby often depriving the inhabitants of those countries from actual necessities. This dependency, they maintain, allows the IMF and World Bank to impose structural adjustment plans upon these nations. Adjustments largely consist of privatisation programmes which, they say, result in deteriorating health, education and inability to develop infrastructure, and in general lower living standards.

They also point to recent statements made by United Nations Secretary General's Special Economic Adviser, Dr. Jeffrey Sachs, who heatedly demanded that the entire African debt – approximately $ 200 billion – be forgiven outright and recommended that African nations simply stop paying if the World Bank and the IMF do not reciprocate:

"The time has come to end this charade. The debts are unaffordable. If they won't cancel the debts I would suggest obstructions; you do it yourselves. Africa should say: 'thank you very much but we need this money to meet the needs of children who are dying right now, so we still put the debt servicing payments into urgent social investment in health, education, drinking water, control of AIDs and other needs," said Professor Jeffrey Sachs, Director of the Earth Institute at Columbia University and Special Economic Adviser to UN Secretary General Kofi Annan.

Critics of the IMF have conducted studies as to the effects of its policy which demands currency devaluations. They pose the argument that the IMF requires these devaluations as a condition for refinancing loans, while simultaneously insisting that the loan be repaid in dollars or other First World currencies against which the underdeveloped country's currency had been devalued. This, they say, increases the respective debt by the same percentage of the currency being devalued, therefore, amounting to a scheme for keeping Third World nations in perpetual indebtedness, impoverishment and neocolonial dependence.

Paternalistic Neocolonialism

The term paternalistic neocolonialism involves the belief held by a neocolonial power that their colonial subjects benefit from their occupation. This viewpoint has been described as both supremacist and racist. Critics have stated that the US "liberation" of the Iraqi people is a form of paternalistic neocolonialism because the US claims that it has liberated the Iraqis from the Saddam Hussein. The oppression of the revolutionary Shiite elements in Iraq under Saddam Hussein has been replaced by the oppression of the Sunni by the current Shiite-led government. This has cost the lives of one million Iraqis and has devastated Iraq socially and economically. Similarly, the United Kingdom viewed itself as a "civilizing force" bringing "progress" and modernisation to its colonies, a mindset that was seen again following British intervention in Sierra Leone.

Other Approaches to the Concept of Neocolonialism

Although the concept of neocolonialism was developed by Marxists and is generally employed by the political left, rhetoric of neocolonialism is now also employed by some promoters of conspiracy theories, specifically one world government, regardless of political views. One variant of the neocolonialist view suggests the existence of cultural colonialism, the alleged desire of wealthy nations to control other nations' values and perceptions through cultural means, such as media, language, education and religion purportedly, ultimately for economic reasons.

32

PLIGHT OF MINORITIES IN INDIA

Episodes like the large-scale disturbance directed against the Christian communities in various parts of India at the hands of its ruling party supporters, gunning down of totally unarmed by an upper caste gang, etc. and such incidents against Christians, Muslims and Dalits (previously called untouchables) are not very uncommon in India. These days Christian missionaries in India are being accused – by the fanatics and their friends – of 'inducing' people to convert to Christianity with 'educational and other facilities' provided to the converts. When did humanitarian and noble inducements like the provision of "education, hospital for the sick, shelter for the homeless" become a bad and reprehensible thing?

Calling these as inducements towards a change of religion is a stab at the heart of free speech and democracy. If attracting people with humanitarian good deeds is not right, then the promise of a good government by a party has to be taken as an 'inducement', and hence undesirable. If someone provides 'inducement' to somebody to commit a crime, the inducements that the missionaries provide are for something that they consider as elevating and liberating. It is only if one considers Christianity to be bad that one can denounce inducements for the same to be bad. But those who question the missionaries' mission won't come out and denounce Christianity to be bad because they want to wear the badge of 'tolerance' at the same time, claiming that Hinduism preaches 'tolerance'.

The truth is that no religion encourages its followers to go on a rampage of killing and looting others. The followers of any particular religion go on rampage only when someone or some group has something to gain out of the rampage. So, one has to dig deeper if one really wants to know as to who is behind current Hindu rampages, and what they are gaining out of it, or what they are afraid of losing without such rampages, be it against Christians, Muslims or Dalits. The 'tolerant' Prime Minister wants a national debate on 'conversion'. On the surface, it may look only as bad as questioning freedom, free speech or democracy. But it is actually much more sinister than that if we take the religious element into account.

First of all, there is nothing wrong with conversion as long as it is not forced. Secondly, even if one does not try to persuade another person into converting, the former can be accused of trying to induce others into converting, just because he or she belongs to another religion. That is why the bogey of conversion is far more insidious and treacherous than it looks on the surface.

So, what is really the motivation behind these sinister mischiefs? The family of Hindu fundamentalist parties, collectively known as Sangh Parivar (family of Sangh parties) under the umbrella of RSS (Rashtriya Swayamsevak Sangh) have found that whenever there is communal disturbance—riots against one religious minority or the other— they have fared relatively well in elections. This is because even though a vast majority of Indians, in spite of being castigated lower caste Hindus, they call themselves Hindus. One would find it unthinkable to believe in a religion that bestows upon that same person a lower level status than upon some others. But in spite of the fact that about 70% of Indians are regarded as low caste Hindus, they do call themselves Hindus and worship some form of Hindu gods or the other. And in the name of religion, the Sangh Parivar has found it easier to get them excited and vote for them – for the Sangh Parivar – when religious tension is festering. It is important to delve a little deeper into what causes people to follow and vote for the religious instigators.

In southern part of India, the distance of the devotees from their gods is assigned by the priests and it is managed to be in proportion to the distance of their caste from the top of the Hindu hierarchy—the Brahmins. Accordingly, the untouchables should not even be able to enter the temples, yet most of them call themselves Hindus. It seems that once one accepts the mysticism of god, one becomes willing to accept any amount of illogical things contained within that package. Any amount of inhumanity, any amount of degradation, any amount of indignities heaped on themselves or others become acceptable to the believers of god as long as all these irrationalities are contained within the enigmatic package that contains that god. The package seems to create a distance between its 'believers' and logic, rationality and questioning spirit of a person. It seems that all those rituals and stories that come wrapped up within the package, which one gets submerged in, and drilled with, from the time people are born puts a damper on the reasoning capacity of a person.

Otherwise, why would a person 'believe' in the religion that makes that same person a lowly untouchable being; why would a person want to believe in a god while he is forbidden even from hearing the verses of scriptures about the same god. If they somehow hear those scriptures, the scriptures command that molten lead be poured into the ears of those low caste individuals. If these low caste individuals perform a certain 'yagya' – a certain ritualistic prayer offering – the scriptures demand such low caste individuals to be beheaded, yet even to this day many of the same low caste individuals, including very prominent ones, aspire to perform that 'yagya'. What kind of rationality is that? What is it that makes them so devoid of sensible thinking? Could it be the unquestioning attitude one is drilled with from the time of his birth?

Any time there is a conflict between Hindus and persons belonging to a religious minority, it assumes a religious overtone because majority of people in India are Hindus. The Hindu band beaters stand to gain as fundamentalist vanguard of the majority. This should give a clue as to who are the instigators of the trouble in most instances. One would think that it would be mostly the illiterate masses who would be duped by this kind of trick of the fanatic Sangh Parivar. But unfortunately even the literate segment has come to buy into this kind of trickery and treachery, as vast majority of literate segment happens to be upper caste which has sold its allegiance to the Sangh Parivar. Why are they more attached to the Sangh Parivar today than in yester years? The reason is that the Sangh Parivar is the staunchest opponent of caste-wise distribution of jobs and other means of power dubbed as Mandalisation in India.

What is the Solution to the Problem?

The big question is where lies the salvation of India and its minorities? True salvation lies in Proportional Representation (PR) System of election prevalent in Europe and in many other parts of the world. Under PR system, parties are allocated seats in proportion to the votes that they get. In that set-up, no party would hope to get absolute majority, much less so in India. Most castes may be likely to vote for the best on their own caste or caste category or segment or religion or linguistic minority, as exigencies present themselves, and as they see it fit. BJP would be reduced to being just one of the several Hindu chauvinist parties, totalling not much more than their share of population (of about 15%).

After coming to Parliament in proportion to their population, the post-election alliances of various parties is going to be much more stable and more rooted in the needs of their constituents. As can be seen from the results of most countries that hold elections under pluralistic system, a party getting 30-40% of votes very often gets an absolute majority, at the expense of smaller parties. In United Kingdom, the Liberal Party has consistently obtained more between 20-25% of votes in the last several elections, yet as a minority party, they have been able to win only between 5-10% of the seats. As a result of several disadvantages faced by the minority parties, the countries having plurality system hardly have any minority parties. On account of such disadvantage, parties that might have arisen to redress the voice of segments' distress get wiped off in spite of their continued woe. This does not happen under a PR system.

Look at Germany. They use a mixed system of election under which the results are essentially proportional. Their Green Party consistently polls 6-7% of votes and they are allocated seats nearly in proportion to their votes. For their share of seats, they don't have to run around making unethical and uncouth alliances. Yet, for getting into the government they need an alliance. But to get their fair share of seats in the legislative bodies, they don't need to make pre-election affiliation or association. Such will never be the case in India or United Kingdom or the USA under their archaic plurality system. Under the plurality system, proportionality is more of an exception than rule.

All over Europe, except for UK and France, they have one form or the other of PR system. A party with 6-7% of popular support has no chance of gaining any seat except in anomalous circumstances. For the sake of survival, the smaller parties always get forced into unequal alliances, most of the time tilted disproportionately in favour of stronger parties. These alliances being uneven and unjust, almost always break down. The kind of continuous jockeying for artificially concocted and unjust advantage is the hallmark of plurality system.

Politics becomes synonymous with shrewd and unethical jockeying for power. On the other hand, under a PR system, party strengths do not undergo drastic changes subject to pre-election alliances, and 30-40% of votes is never going to be artificially converted into absolute majority. Besides, when people have parties of their own communities, they generally would not be persuaded to vote for an alien party on the basis of hate-bating tactics, so such a tactic would not even be tried.

As the upper castes and their interest control all of the major Indian newspapers, they never delve deep into the benefits of PR system of elections. Only passing references to PR system are seen once in a while, most of the time discussing its most outdated form with obvious flaws. For example, they assume that under the PR system people would vote for parties only, and that it is the party bosses who would decide as to who is going to go into the legislative bodies. This obviously has the flaw of giving inordinate power into the hands of party bosses. Concentration of power into the hands of political bosses leads to extremely corrupting and demeaning process of sycophancy among the followers of all parties. For the sake of personal gains, a cut-throat competition in flattery deification of the political bosses ensues. One solution to this flaw would be voting by the people for parties as well as for individual candidates in one and the same general election, unhindered by any nomination process.

Parties would be represented in the legislative bodies in proportion to the votes that they get. An electoral college of all the candidates, each carrying as many votes as they got in the general election, could decide who from within various parties would go to the legislative bodies. There can be many mechanisms of electing the final winners of seats in the legislative bodies, including several run-offs. The electoral college could even come up with the names of final two candidates who would go back to the country for a final run-off, to become the president, if a presidential set-up is found to be more desirable. The parliamentary system wherein the legislative as well as the executive power lies within the same body of representatives, does suffer from concentration of too much power within the single legislative body.

One could come up with innumerable ways of carrying out the will of the people, unfettered by intervention of any nomination process at the hands of political bosses. A solution does not have to be a permanent solution. In fact, it would be best for different states to choose different solutions and keep on changing them towards a better system of following the will of the people.

Only this kind of evolving PR system would be best able to evolve consensus and fulfill aspirations of all groups or segments of the society. It is in this kind of society that baiting, instigation and atrocities against minorities are not going to pay much dividend.

33

MASTERING THE DEVIL OF MATERIALISM

The inevitable superficiality of materialism has given rise to its deceptions and delusions. Materialism traps us unawares in a world of possessions ridden by irrational fears of likely loss and lurking dangers. Finally, it degrades creativity to consumption. The spiritual option is not to renounce modernity and demonise development, but to transcend the spirit of materialism.

The present global village is not partial to any of the existing religion. The civilization conflict, contrary to Samuel Huntington's hypothesis, will not be between Christianity and Islam. It will be, if at all, between religious and materialism, which is the rising religion of our globalising world. The conflictual model of inter-faith relationships that kept religions fighting with one another has enabled materialism – their common enemy – to steal a march upon them unawares.

Materialism is much more than it is understood in the form of affluence and lavish lifestyles. No religion preaches against material success gained the right way. The Hindus worship Lakshmi, the goddess of wealth. The Sikh gurus encounaged hard work, paving the way for the prosperity of Punjab.

The semitic religions see prosperity as a gift from God. At the same time, all religions recognise that our attitude to wealth is crucial to our personality. When affluence is idolised, it enslaves the individual and lures him away from the meaning and purpose of life. Materialism, unlike material prosperity, is a quasi-religion, complete with its own rituals, its own creed and its counterpart of the supernatural. Wealth pursued for its own sake is the god of materialism. Consumerism is its ritual and technology, is its "supernatural". Worldly success is its dogma. Escalating and interminable pleasure is the highway to its secular *nirvana*.

However, materialism is a pseudo-religion. Insisting that "matter alone matters", it brings about the subservience of the human to the non-human. The industrial culture degraded human beings into cogs in the machine. In the globalizing world, profit has already superseded people. The generation of wealth is a goal higher than the promotion of human welfare. The pathos of the dwindling stature of man, his growing insignificance and bewilderment, is a recurrent lament in modern literature. The secular-materialism dream of a new heaven and a new earth, on all available evidence, threatens to turn into a nightmare.

Decades ago, the French philosopher Bergson warned that we would be crushed, not by our failures but by our successes; and our souls could be smothered under the weight of our achievements. Studies now prove that materialism breeds despair, anger and irrational outbursts of violence, of which the infamous "road-rage" is a startling instance. Already in India, nearly a hundred thousand people commit suicide annually. The advent of prosperity has not translated itself into happiness.

The Anatomy of Materialism

By definition 'Materialism' is a worldview, based on superficiality. The reason for this is not far to seek. Matter, in a philosophical sense, is all surface and no depth. We cannot get into the depth of a material object. A stone, for example, has no inside, strictly speaking. Break a stone and we get several stones; we do not reach the "inside" of a stone. Nor can we access the depth of a stone by drilling into it. Drilling creates, at best, only an illusion of depth. The deceptions and delusions of materialism stem from its inevitable superficiality.

The surface spoken is a sphere of vulnerability, insecurity and unfulfilment. That is so because the surface is governed by the inexorable law of change. Change, for the sake of change, breeds restlessness. It unsettles. Whatever is on the surface, it keeps poorly. It has no stable or settled value. It is for this reason that material possessions tend to lose their value soon after they are acquired. As long as it was being struggled for, it was an idea. Attainment turns this idea into an object; and an object exits no longer in the depth but on the surface, where the magic evaporates. This inevitable dissatisfaction with what is attained keeps the mill of acquisitiveness grinding. It also makes fulfillment elude our group.

While superficiality is inhospitable to human stature, personality is a depth-phenomenon, which also means that it has a spiritual core: a core of mystery. It is only from a superficial perspective that a person's worth can be equated with his possessions. Such an approach perforce brings about an imbalance between "being" and "having".

The more obsessed one gets with "having", the less capable or keen he gets of "being". This leads to a situation in which material riches are secured to the neglect of, even at the expense of, one's inner wealth. In other words, the wealthier a person gets materially, the poorer he gets humanly. It is a glaring fact of history that the culture of materialism and its coordinate of liberal individualism have failed to produce individuals of stature. When personality is reduced to a materialistic concept, we get stuffed shits where we expect great men and women.

This also explains us the reason that the degradation of human worth into "having" and the corresponding erosion of human dignity together constitute the perverse logic of corruption. The perpetrators of mega are not driven by the need to meet their basic needs. They are possessed and driven by the spirit of covetousness, having equated their worth with their material possessions. Their richness is a matter of being seen for what they have, of which the craving to hog the social limelight is an irresistible corollary. Sadly, they realise too late that they are poorer for their ill-gotten wealth. The more they have, the poorer they are. And that is so, even if they manage to evade detection and public infamy. Can a man's affluence avail him if it has already cost him his self-respect? The irony is that public respect is purchased at the cost of self-respect. That is too great a price to pay.

In a culture of superficiality relationships suffer. The logic of change operates with equal effectiveness on relationships as on fashions. Both remain vulnerable to change and are driven by convenience. Since this is an intuited reality all through, relationships bristle with anxiety and mistrust. Mutual trust can exist only in personal depth, the depth of total mutual acceptance in love. Mistrust activates control-orientation, which breeds cruelty. All the values we cherish – such as love, truth, compassion and justice – have their roots in human depth; and they evaporate in a culture of superficiality.

Besides, superficiality is a domain of compromised freedom. According to Swami Vivekananda, man is free only in the sphere of the spirit. He can have the illusion of freedom in the domains of matter and mind. Freedom is at the root of our humanity. The thirst for freedom cannot be assuaged by the glitter or comfort of the prison to which we are confined. This is why mansions of affluence often hold oceans of misery. Downy pillows and plush mattresses are, somehow, incomplete without sleeping pills. The world of materialism is strewn with irrational fears of likely loss and lurking dangers. It reduces human freedom to the logic of taking and receiving, and erodes the freedom to give. "The freedom only to receive is, at best, only an illusion of freedom. It degenerates sooner or later into the compulsion to extort, which makes thieves of those who can thrive at the expense of others. Significantly, in the Indian tradition as well as in all other spiritually informed schools of thought, the basic ingredients of human freedom are self-control, generosity and compassion.

Finally, materialism has degraded creativity to consumption. Creativity like personality, to which it is originally related, is a depth phenomenon, as is proved by the mystery that inheres in it. On the surface, there could be suspense, but not mystery. Creativity is an outward flow. Consumption is a pull in the opposite direction. Consumption is not merely a dental activity. It is a larger and comprehensive metaphor of a personality orientation. Consumption affords pleasure. But it is only creativity that engenders enduring joy. Pleasure, in comparison, is superficial and transitory. It breeds a craving to consume ever-increasing doses in the futile chase after elusive fulfillment.

It is an undoubted fact that consumerism has powerful psycho-social and pseudo-religious overtones in materialism. It is the ritual of materialism. In materialistic cultures a person's social worth is measured wholly by the consumables he can afford. This includes not only exotic cuisine, expensive wardrobe and other catalysts of "social envy", but also pointers like expensive medical treatment, exclusive education, elite residential locality and so on. One familiar pointer to the psychological implications of consumerism is what has come to be known as "retail therapy".

This refers to the false sense of well-being that people derive merely from shopping for the sake of shopping. When peace returns after a domestic quarrel, for example, the husband and wife celebrate the occasion by going on shopping spree that may include the ritual of 'eating out'.

The agony and poverty of materialism is that in its keenness to fatten the body, it leaves the spirit starved. It is reflected in the foolish assumption that the hypervitaminosis of the body would, somehow, spill over and become nourishment for the soul. The mounting agony of the world, however, roundly condemns the willful blindness of this secular dogma.

34

NEGATIVE THOUGHTS – THE UNWELCOME HOME GUESTS

Imagine enjoying a peaceful day at home when suddenly the door flies open and in comes a crowd of unruly people. They are loud, obnoxious and condescending. They push past you as if you were not there, heading to the kitchen for something to eat, piling on to your sofa in front of your television, barging upstairs to take a nap in your bed. They seem overbearing and headstrong and even though you may want to tell them to leave, you feel powerless to do so.

As the days wear on, they keep inviting more and more of their friends to stay also, until your home is cramped and uncomfortable. They are with you in the shower, in your bed, while you eat your meals, in your car as you drive to work. You feel that your life has been taken over by these barbarians, and you wonder when you lost control of your life and your home.

Who are these creeps, you ask? They are negative thoughts. And they will take over your life if you don't take control of them. We often don't realise how overrun with negative thoughts we are, until we become extremely uncomfortable, just like the example above. Negative thoughts can be sneaky, slipping in undetected, yet having a powerful impact on our moods and emotions. Over time, they will begin to take over our thoughts altogether.

Think of the following scenarios and see if you recognise yourself in any of them:

- Our spouse is 30 minutes late coming home from work and suddenly the telephone rings. Do you immediately imagine the worst? Does your heart start racing at the thought of an accident?

- You apply for a great job and feel excited by the possibilities. A few days go by and you don't receive a phone call requesting an interview. Do you begin worrying about errors you might have made in the application or whether your skills are up to par? Do you assume that you won't get the job and resign yourself to a low-paying, unfulfilling career for the rest of your life?
- You are driving in fast-moving traffic and you see a large truck approaching from the opposite direction. Do you automatically begin feeling anxious that the truck could veer to your lane and crush your compact car – even though the driver of the truck has given you no indication that this is a possibility?

These examples demonstrate how easily our thoughts can move into a negative place. It is actually quite common, so don't despair if you identify with these situations. There is something you can do about it. It is important to point out that these examples reflect situations that are completely out of our control. Even if they did happen, there isn't much we could do about it. We'd simply have to deal with it, just as we do with all of life's challenges. Obsessing over the horrible things that could happen to us only makes us feel powerless and frightened.

What if we choose to turn our thoughts around and focus on happy things instead? We can, you know! That does not mean negative thoughts will never pop into our heads. Of course, they probably will. But we don't have to allow them to stay. Just like our unruly house guests described above, we need to be firm and unyielding about the type of thoughts we want to welcome in. So, what can we do when frightening images pop into our heads? The best course of action would be to kick them right out again. Don't entertain them. Simply turn the thoughts around to something positive – or at least neutral – instead.

Rather than assuming your spouse is late because of an accident, assume he or she is late because of heavy traffic, a last minute request from the boss, or a quick stop at the supermarket. Rather than assuming you didn't get the job, assume that it will take time for the hiring manager to get through all the applications. Acknowledge that even if you didn't get this particular job, there are plenty more great jobs out there if you take time to look for them. And yes, rather than assuming that you'll be killed by a large truck, assume you won't be.

Turning these thoughts around will take time and consistent effort, especially if you are used to letting them take over your mind. Remember that unwelcome house guests don't usually respond to subtlety. You may need to display immense determination and kick some major butt before they will leave. But if you keep at it, they will eventually grow weary of the hostile atmosphere and leave you in peace.

Overcoming Negative Thinking

Would you consider yourself to be an optimist or pessimist? Are you always on edge, waiting for the next disaster to strike? Or do you look to the future with anticipation and joy? One of the biggest lessons has been understanding that "like attracts like". I used to believe that I would be happy if I could only meet the right man, find the right job, lose enough weight, etc. But I didn't work that way. I did, indeed, do some of those things, but I still wasn't happy. I had to learn to become happy first, and then everything else in my life began to transform to more closely match my attitude.

The majority of us tend to let our experiences influence our thoughts, rather than the other way around. One negative experience can ruin our mood for the day, which will cause us to act and think in ways that attract even more negatively, which puts us in an even worse mood, and on it goes! It creates a chain reaction of negativity that affects us and everyone around us.

Obsessive fear and worry are also facets of negative attitude. A certain amount of these emotions are normal, of course. Worrying about our performance in a job interview or feeling fearful in a dangerous situation are to be expected and can actually do us good by keeping us sharp mentally. But how many of us take these to the extreme? Worrying excessively about things that are out of our control can do more harm than good.

I come from a long line of worries and I married into a family that has just as many. It's like a genetic tendency or something. I always tease my husband that his family's legacy is, "Be careful"! It is uttered at least once or twice every time we get together with them usually as a farewell. Instead of "goodbye", they say, "be careful"! Just once I am tempted to reply, "No, actually I'm thinking of trying recklessness for a while, see how that goes." Somehow, I don't think they'd get the joke.

There is a difference, of course, between worry and common sense. I'm not saying we should throw caution to the wind and ignore safety. By all means, we should do what we can do to minimise the potential for disaster. But constantly focusing on the bad things that could happen to us and even expecting them to happen, can only keep us stuck in negative thought patterns. Does that mean if we think only positive thoughts, only good things will happen to us? No, unfortunately, I don't think that is true either. I think there are certain experiences we need to go through in life for the purpose of strengthening us and helping us grow. Even though they are not fun at the time, they serve our highest good in the long run. Those situations aside, we do have control over much more of our lives than we realise. We need to remember that our thoughts have tremendous power. What if we decided to use that power in a conscious, focused way? What would we be capable of creating?

One of my favourite quotations is : "If you want to know what your thoughts were like yesterday, look at your body today. If you want to see what your body will be like tomorrow, look at your thoughts today." How powerful is that? And, of course, the concept can be carried further than the state of our bodies, to include the state of our lives too. Look around you. What have your thoughts created? Can you see a connection between your attitude in the past and your circumstances today?

You can still change. It is never too late for an attitude shift. It will require practice and patience, of course. Remember that many of us have been thinking negatively for years, and old habits die hard. But if you set your mind to it and keep focusing on the positive, positive circumstances will begin to bloom in your life. Make a conscious decision to expect the best at all times. Even if you don't end with "the best", you might still end up with something really good.

35

COMPASSION IS THE BASIS OF ALL MORALITY

There is no need to define morality; let man be simply compassionate. This sentence expresses the basic essence of morality: the extent to which it relies on compassion for its definition. For, when we think about it, is not that truly human feeling of compassion the basis of all morality?

Morality rests for its very meaning on the concepts of 'good' and 'bad', where good refers to all thoughts and deeds that do not aim at or cause any harm or injury or do not involve an attempt to inflict suffering on others. Thus, morality — or what is not morality — is based on man's ability to understand, being able to sympathise, feel kindness and sorrow for and identify himself with the sufferings of his fellowmen. So, only compassion can give rise to moral thoughts and feelings.

If we consider all those thoughts and deeds that are truly moral in character, we will see how compassion drives morality. Depriving people of what is theirs or what must belong to them — what is called stealing — for selfish ends, taunting or insulting others through words or actions for the purpose of self-gratification, violence—expressed verbally or as acts of torture, killing, etc. — for the sake of violence contradict morality as well as an inner feeling of kindness and compassion.

Truth is indeed a controversial aspect of morality. But almost always it can be justified as a moral principle on the basis of compassion. When we talk about speaking the truth in order not to hid what, if hidden, will only prove damaging to others, we are emphasizing the ability to 'feel' for others. Again, often we purposely keep ourselves from communicating the truth as, once revealed, it may hurt someone's feelings and sentiments. But keeping a person in the dark or denying him or her knowledge which he or she ought to have amounts to cheating another soul of its rights to know that with which it has a concern. An anxious feeling to see that a person is not cheated of what is due to him or her may make us reveal the truth ultimately. It is the same feeling of being truthful in order not to betray another person that constitutes sexual morality in any relationship. A deep-felt concern for the companion's feelings of hurt and rejection is necessary for the moral aspect to prevail.

When we talk about social morality of any kind, what comes into play is our ability to feel for the well-being of our society. A certain moral code of conduct is ultimately necessary to ensure that the society does not fall prey to degeneration of values, which would lead to rampant sufferings and ultimately chaos. It is a concern to help the society by safeguarding it from unwanted ills and malaises and ensuring its well-being that is at the root of social morality. Society's concerns are our concerns: anything capable of causing a detrimental impact on it in the short-term or in course of time is ultimately bound to affect us and our children.

There is the need to realise that human beings must continue to feel compassion for the sake of themselves as individuals as well as the society. But like any other human trait, compassion ought to be continually exercised if it is to remain a dominant force. Unfortunately, in modern society what we witness is a complete lack of kindness and sympathy among fellow beings. One can only shake one's head and say that just like other cherished values, even compassion is getting eroded in the hustle and bustle of the mechanical existence of these times. What remains is material values that look only towards immediate personal gains and in the process rid humans of whatever 'humanness' is left in them. Morality is fast disappearing, it seems. But it need not be so if only we would tell ourselves that genuine feelings of the human heart, mainly compassion, need to survive for the betterment of the human society and mankind as a whole.

After all, can humans rid themselves totally of all feelings of compassion trying as hard as they may?

It is only by feeling for others' sorrows and sufferings that one can sympathise with them and help those in need. This is the underlying principle of all morality which has to survive and that too abundantly if human society is to prosper in the real sense.

36

THERE IS NO LIMIT TO WHAT YOU CAN DO

Have you ever thought about what you could do if you really decided to? I am not merely talking about what your skills, education and talents are capable of. I am talking about what is really possible for you. There is a very real possibility that you can do virtually anything. Not alone, not without new information, but certainly within your ultimate grasp.

Now many people would say to me, "Be realistic. Some things are just not possible." To them I say, a "realist" is simply a pessimist who does not want to admit it. I've never heard a "realist" take an optimistic posture on any topic. They always say, "Let's be realist," and then go on to explain why your idea can't be done. Imagine a realist saying, "Realistically, we don't yet know what the possibilities are. This could be easier than be think." Better, eh? One thing I have learned over the years is that luck really does come to those who commit to a goal. Scientists and philosophers call it "synchronicity". It is when things come together in an unexplainable way to help you reach your destination. Sometimes you just happen to meet someone who has the answer you need or shares your interests. At other times, it is written off as "timing" or blind luck.

I don't see it that way. I believe that there are some universal principles at work which most people miss. There have been references to this phenomenon in philosophical and religious literature throughout history. When any person makes a decision to bring about a certain outcome, the entire universe starts the process of making it happen. As long as the person persists in the belief that they are creating the desired result, the process continues. When doubt, hatred or fear dominate the person, the process stops and other forces direct the world's energies in other positive directions. This is why there is "power" in positive thinking.

Sometimes, we express a strong desire and the result occurs immediately. We call this a miracle. At other times we strive long and hard without visible progress. The operative word there is "visible". There are too many elements in the world for us to be conscious of how they all interact. But the moment we decide to do what it takes to create a result, the universe bends towards us to assist. This continues unless we do something to stop the process.

That is why I say there is nothing you can't do. There are things that might not be worth doing but almost anything can be done somehow. To do such things requires a certain state of mind. It requires optimism, determination, clarity, love for all mankind and humility. Optimism is the only productive way to think. Not Pollyanna blind faith in spite of the facts, just the continuing belief that there is a way and that you will ultimately find it. Determination is to do what is necessary even if it is not convenient if you are not in the mood, if it takes more than you expected, and if it is not fair, meaning that you have to contribute more than others.

Clarity of focus is essential in order to activate things in your favour. So, goal setting in writing is essential to get things going. The clearer your focus, the more compelling your influence becomes. When you believe unflinchingly in your cause, others will be drawn to you. Love of all humanity means respect for the dignity of and sensitivity to the needs of others. Contrary to Gordon Gekko's live in the movie "Wall Street", greed does not work, because it separates you from others. Only love and respect will connect you to all who might ultimately help.

And finally, humility. The biblical way of expressing this thought is, "Not my will, but thine, be done." If we realise how little we know, we will be a lot more humble. Emerson said, "Desire is possibility seeking expression." If you truly want something, the possibility of it surely exists. This does not mean that it is a good idea for you. It just means that it could happen. But if you are dedicated to achieving something deeply and sincerely, then it is incumbent upon you to pursue it.

Where the problems arise is when we decide that we already know what it will take to do the job. Far too many variables exist for us to really "know" what it takes in any instance. So, we must move forward based on what we know, while listening to the messages the world is sending us. We sometimes find that an even better outcome is available to us through a simple change in the direction. At other times, we simply need to learn the lesson life has to teach us at a given point and then move on in a new direction. We never know how valuable that life lesson will be later on as we pursue a greater goal.

So, I encourage you to be realistic. There is no limit to what you can do by yourself and by influencing other people. Now the questions arise as to why do people say 'yes'? How can we get them to comply with our requests?

37

BIODIVERSITY

Biodiversity or biological diversity implies infinite variations in the species, both plant and animals, of nature and their living environment. Species diversity is represented by morphological, physiological and genetic features, whereas ecosystem diversity shows the difference in habitats and biological communities.

The process of species diversification started soon after the origin of life on the planet. It is a gradual process, influenced by various geophysical and climatic factors, and resulting in the emergence of new strains of the species. Species which are not able to adjust themselves with the changing conditions gradually become extinct as evidenced in the case of the giant dinosaurs and other large mammals and birds of the past. However, on the whole, diversification has prevailed over extinction. As a result, estimates of the number of plant and animal species living on the earth range from three million to more than ten million, though to date only about 1.5 million species have been recorded in scientific literature. About most of these, little more is known than their appearance and location. It is possible that several million insects and plants – along with fewer members of other animal classes – await discovery, mainly in the tropics.

Biological diversity plays a significant role in nature. It provides major clues to the scientists about the origin and the evolution and the specification process of various flora and fauna. It also acts as a major tool for assessing the impact of various factors in influencing the process of species diversification. Rich biodiversity is an indicator of the health of a particular habitat and its potential to sustain life.

In ecology, biodiversity plays a significant role. It enriches soil, maintains water and climate cycles, humidity and precipitation and helps in recycling and converting waste material into nutrients. All the living creatures, from unicellular organisms and planktons to higher species, help maintain equilibrium within various components. Ecological diversity is of great significance to human society. Food, medicine and raw materials for industry and household purposes are obtained from various living resources.

During the past few centuries, with the increase in human population, biodiversity has come under tremendous pressure. Biological extinction which led to the disappearance of one species in several hundred years has now been replaced by an accelerated rate of extinction – one species every year. This is the result of the extensive habitat changes wrought by mankind. If the same pace continues, an estimated one-fourth to one-third of species is likely to become extinct within the next few decades. Overall, roughly 1000 birds and mammals are now thought to be in jeopardy. Although endangered animals, e.g., tigers in Asia, Cheetahs in Africa, Whales in the Antarctic, whooping cranes in North America, etc. receive great public attention, plant extinction is often more significant ecologically. According to Peter H. Raven, Director of the Missouri Botanical Garden, a disappearing plant can take with it ten to thirty dependent species such as insects, higher animals and even other plants. The International Union for Conservation of Nature and Natural Resources (IUCN) finds about ten per cent of the world's flowering plants to be dangerously rare or under threat.

These estimates of species at risk understate the true problem, for they deal only with known and higher life forms. It seems probable that many unnamed species are disappearing in scientifically unchartered tropical area. In his book *The Sinking Ark,* Norman Myers surmises on the basis of extrapolation that right now, at least one species might be disappearing each day in tropical forests alone. Even outside the tropics, many small, obscure organisms such as worms, mites, beetle and herbs may be disappearing without our knowledge. Besides, an examination of the survival prospects of all forms of plant and animal life – including obscure ferns, shrubs, insects, mollusks, elephants and wolves – indicates that the huge numbers of them have little future. Loss of such a multitude of species would constitute an irreversible alteration in the nature of the biosphere even before we understand its working – an evolutionary Rubicon whose crossing *Homo Sapiens* would do well to avoid.

The loss of biodiversity has immediate and long-term effects on human survival itself. The majority of the world's population still depends on wild plants and animals for their daily food, medicine, housing and household material, fodder, fuel wood, spiritual sustenance and intellectual stimulation. For these billions of human beings the loss of biodiversity is a direct and irreversible attack on their livelihood and social security. The loss is even more direct in the case of domesticated biodiversity. Traditional farmers of the world have developed an incredible variety of crops and livestock. This too has been eroded over the last few decades, with literally lakhs of traditional crop strains and hundreds of domesticated live stock breeds being replaced by a harmful of laboratory-generated hybrids or by dominant cash crops.

The traditional diversity was bred to meet diverse human needs of nutrition, taste, colour, ritual, smell and to resist drought, flood and pests. It provided several kinds of insurance to the farmer against crop failure.

Modern hybrids, on the other hand, while substantially increasing the grain yield and monetary profits, have forced the farmers to look elsewhere for their daily needs – especially fodder – and left them dependent on the vagaries of markets, governments and private corporations.

The ways in which humans destroy other species are legion. The excessive hunting or collecting of animals for food, profit or recreation is a time-honoured means of extermination. From the Stone Age to this date, hunters and collectors remain significant threats to many mammals, birds, reptiles and fishes.

Animals have become endangered in the pursuit of their

hides, heads or tusks; there are, besides poachers, some unscrupulous zoo suppliers who imperil rare species. The lure of spectacular profits offers the impetus for trade in endangered species and derivative products; for example a Bengal tiger coat sells for $ 95,000 in Tokyo!

An important cause of extinctions over the next few decades will be the destruction of habitats. As both populations and economies grow and human settlements sprawl, undisturbed natural areas are bound to shrink. Wildlife breeding zones, migration routes and browsing and hunting domains are paved, inundated with water, grazed or ploughed.

Forest lands are denuded by farmers or timber companies and then given over to cattle, crops or non-native tree species. Plant species unique to a small locality along with the animals that feed on them can be erased from the earth by a single bulldozer; predators dependent on a complex food web may disappear once the wild area around them is compressed below a critical minimum level.

The problem of habitat destruction exists in every continent, but it is particularly serious in the humid tropics which is where major species losses are predicted. Viewed in terms of biodiversity, the moist tropical forests of Africa, Asia and Latin America hold an importance far beyond land area they occupy. Suffused with exceptional amounts of light, warmth and moisture, the tropical rain forests house a remarkable variety of ecosystems and species. The rain forests, home to half of the world's life forms, continue to be destroyed at the rate of over 100,000 sq km every year.

The roots of biodiversity destruction lie in the relations between the communities within each nation and between the nations themselves, point out certain observers. This is responsible for cornering the vast biological resources for the benefit of a small minority within the poor nations and for the wasteful consumption patterns of the North. Eighteen million hectares of Amazonian forest have been cleared in Brazil to meet the European and American demand for coffee. Germany causes the degradation of 200,000 hectares of rain forest a year for timber. Adverse terms of trade, protectionist policies of the North, dumping of environmentally destructive technologies and materials in the South and a host of other factors continue to cause severe and widespread biodiversity destruction.

The exploitative policies followed by the elites within the southern countries are no better. Vast natural habitats have been plundered to meet the ever-growing needs of this minority, aided by laws which legitimise urban-industrial control over resources. The poor are forced to overstrain the meager resources that are left in their control, and are then portrayed as ecological culprits. In countries like India, the development policies and projects have rarely been sensitive to the need for biodiversity conservation and that of the local communities. The government's failure to remove poverty and curb consumerism has led to conditions in which sensible natural resource management assumes a low priority.

In the last few years the world has started realising the significance of biodiversity. Several conventions and agreements on conservation and protection of various organisms have been drawn up since 1970, when UNESCO held the first Man and Biosphere Convention.

At the Earth Summit at Rio in June 1992, the majority of the world's nations signed a convention on biological diversity. Though the expectations from the Rio Summit were very high, the polarization between the North and the South on various issues such as funds and use of biodiversity has raised certain doubts about the applicability and implementation of various programmes. Funds are certainly going to have a major impact on conservation programmes, especially in developing countries.

India's biodiversity is immense mainly because of its unique biogeographical composition, comprising living components of three different realms, namely, Palearctic, Indomalayan and Ethiopian. With just two per cent of the world's land mass, the country has about five per cent of living resources and, therefore, stands as one of the 12 mega-diversity states in the world. The country faces problems such as overpopulation, large number of cattle, growing demand for land, energy and water supply. Unplanned developmental works and overexploitation of resources have made its living resources most vulnerable. Overexploitation has not only resulted in shortage of various materials but also left our biodiversity exposed to various ecological threats.

Showing the loss of species entails much more than the ratification of international treaties, the passage of national conservation laws and the policing of national park boundaries, essential as all these steps are. The future shape of the biosphere will depend in good measure on the shape of political and economic policies affecting employment, land tenure, income distribution and population growth. The extermination of a species seldom poses such an obvious threat to humans as other kinds of environmental deterioration such as air pollution and the spread of deserts. Yet for many reasons, a decline in the diversity of life forms should worry everyone. The impending large-scale loss of species is without precedent and will result from the disruption of complex ecological systems. Not surprisingly, no means exist for qualifying the costs. But the biological impoverishment of the earth will certainly mean economic as well as aesthetic impoverishment of humans.

We made progress so far as our relationship with nature was on a sustainable level. We will be doomed if, in our greed, we kill the goose laying the golden egg.

Unprofitably travelling towards the grave

Like a false, steward who hath much received

And renders nothing back.

38

HISTORY NEEDS TO BE REWRITTEN

History has been taught and is still being taught as a continuous narrative of pre-selected events. To this is added the fact that recent and contemporary research is almost never incorporated in textbooks and other works on history. Thus, the history of a particular ruler or a ruling class or dynasty qualifies as a history of that time and society. Similarly, the personal religion of the ruler or the ruling class often emerge as a determining factor when it comes to interpreting history.

Most literary material which has survived the ravages of time and which serves as the basis on which to construct the history of that period, relates to elite or dominant groups. This is based on the fact that only the elite groups have a right and access to education. They, therefore, recorded their lifestyles and portrayed the elite sections of the society in these written records. In other cases, people who have recorded history, if not belonging to the elite group themselves, have invariably been people associated with the court. Mostly, it is this literature which has survived and made its way to us as historical records. But to suppose on the basis of these records that conditions in the whole society at that time were such as have been portrayed, would be wrong. To suppose that every section of the society indulged in luxuries and maintained a rich life style because the 'palace' was splendid, would result in a historically inaccurate picture. These portrayals tend to be one-sided pictures of particular and specific sections of the society at that time.

The writing of history is not free of all prejudice. In fact, every historian writes with specific interest, even at times with a bias in mind. Histories might have been written to please rulers and gain a position at the court.

That prejudices and self-interest are involved in writing history is illustrated well by the Indian example. The British, as part of their colonisation process of India, thought it necessary to rewrite Indian history to portray Indians as unable to govern themselves, and thus justified their imperial cause. The freedom struggle was, therefore, portrayed as a mutiny. After India won Independence, Indian historians have constantly been trying to portray the real situations during that time.

Some of them though have been misappropriating this need to satisfy vested political interests by portraying a history which can be interpreted to satisfy nationalist sentiments. History invariably is prejudiced to serve certain ends.

Similarly, one can see in our present day the inclusion of a glorification of the past in the political agenda of various parties. Even large and responsible political parties in India are resorting to a glorified portrayal of India's past. The subjective element thus plays a very important role in writing and interpreting history. Often historical portrayals do not depict the reality, but what a particular historian, due to one or the other reason, wishes to portray as having occurred.

There is an imminent need to change our whole approach to history. The need calls for moving from a study of individual rulers or dynasties or events relating to the elite to a more complete study of society as a whole. Dynastic history constitutes only a part of history and shows the distribution of power. What needs to be studied along with this part of history includes the development of the whole society from one point of time to another and changes in social systems and social organisations. Political history should necessarily also include analyses and developments of various regional, religious and social groups.

This is particularly necessary in the Indian context to promote a genuinely secular approach. It would help us to understand why and how communal disharmony and intolerance surface and how best to avoid them. In contrast, the nationalists and communalists have tended to highlight only particular aspects of history, while suppressing others.

The communal view and interpretation of history can virtually be done away with if history is written and studied in a wider sense with a broader mind. To illustrate this point, economic history, for example, would reveal class interests and antagonisms which would cut across religious frontiers. Similarly, social history would reveal that Hindu or Muslim rulers were not partial in their treatment of Hindu or Muslim masses. The common people, whether Hindu or Muslim, were equally poor and oppressed. Political history, when viewed carefully, would reveal that the politics of Indian states was based on economic and political interests and not on religious considerations. Similarly, socio-cultural history would reveal harmonious Hindu-Muslim relations at the base level.

One of the most important tools for reviewing and revising history is archaeology. While literary records pertain to the lives of certain people belonging to elite groups, archaeological evidence is more complete and incorporates evidence of the lives of common people. Site excavations of ancient cities, for example, reveal life styles of all sections of the society at that time. Archaeological proof fills in gaps while at the same time providing clues to trade and commerce, and migration of people.

It is thus essential to review and rewrite history and prevent its abuse for political purposes.

39

HISTORY REPEATS ITSELF

History is a record of the past, especially in connection with the human race. It offers as a glimpse into acts, events, ideas, characters of the past, thus helping us to know more about those centuries gone by. When we trace history right from its beginning to the recent times, we cannot fail to notice that some events and characters have shown a repetitive quality. It is almost as if such acts and ideas were meant to occur over and over again in different centuries though in a slightly different manner each time. What is the significance of such repetition?

The ancient Greeks, for instance, regarded history as a cycle of events that repeated itself endlessly. Viewing history from where we stand today, we may find that there is no dearth of historical material to justify this view. Wars and destruction have lingered through history as factors responsible for creating many events. It is as if they have kept the wheel of time in motion. Causes for the origin of wars have also been more or less the same – almost always a lust for power and greatness, or else to prove the superiority of a set of values, be it social or political in nature, or for economic gain. Thus, if the Persian monarch, Darius 1, invaded territories far and wide to establish his power over kingdoms and wide to establish the power over kingdoms, large and small, thus extending the dominions of the empire, so did Alexander of Macedonia, the Roman monarchs, Chenghiz Khan and the Mughal Babar. The consequences of war and destruction have also been similar: the emergence of new powers, new rulers not very different from their predecessors as far as their goal of conquest is concerned.

Almost every century has seen the rise of a great leader – though as to what constitutes 'greatness', is a debatable matter. Messiahs, truly concerned about the welfare of mankind in general, have come and gone, almost always emphasizing a similar set of values and virtues for the good of man. Reformers and leaders genuinely concerned about the condition of the society in their times have always stressed the importance of similar essential values for man. Thus, the fundamental message delivered to humanity by the Buddha, Mahavira, Guru Nanak and Mahatma Gandhi is very similar.

History is thus nothing but man's one long struggle for survival to preserve his existence, identity and values. The struggle has often borne more than a slight resemblance in the methods used and the manner adopted in each period. Such repetition of historical facts – events, ideas and acts – sometimes makes us think that there is nothing coincidental about it; that it is a planned sequence leading towards a pre-destined goal.

However, in spite of history repeating itself time and again to reveal the mistakes and pains that have, it seems, worked against man's struggle for a better life. Man has never actually learnt from his past experience. Wars continue to this day, rather on a global scale. Man's lust for ambition and power continues to destroy peoples and nations. All this points to only one thing – man's inherent nature and his basic approach or manner of responding to the historical experience which has been the same ever since civilization began.

40

RIGHT TO INFORMATION

The right to information is an effective tool to control corruption, make governments accountable and curb arbitrary use of power. A movement of securing for the people the right to information is necessary to make democracy more meaningful. The Right to Information (RTI) is derived from our fundamental right of expression under Article 19. If we do not have information on how our government and public institutions function, we cannot express any informed opinion on it. This has been accepted by various Supreme Court judgments since 1977.

Democracy revolves round the basic idea of citizens being at the centre of governance – rule of the people. We need to define the importance of the concept of freedom of the Press from this fundamental premise. It is obvious that the main reason for a free Press is to ensure that citizens are informed. If this is one of the main reasons for the primacy given to the freedom of the Press, it clearly flows from this that the citizens' rights to know is paramount. Also, since the government is run on behalf of the people, they are the owners who have a right to be informed directly.

In a government of responsibility like ours, where all the agents of the public must be responsible for their conduct, there can be but few secrets. The people of this country have a right to know everything that is done in a public way by their public functionaries. They are entitled to know the particulars of every public transaction in all its bearing. Their right to know, which is derived from the concept of freedom of speech, though not absolute, is a factor which should make one wary when secrecy is claimed for transactions, which can at any rate have no repercussion on public security.

Right to Information Act promises to be a single piece of legislation that can result in the victory of participatory democracy. The Right to Information Act is a codification of important right of citizens. The right has existed since the time India became a republic, but was difficult to enforce without going to court. The Act and its rules define a format for requisitioning information, a time period within which information must be provided (30 days), method of giving the information, some charges for applying, and some exemptions. The principle is that charges should be minimum – more as a token: They are not at all representative of the costs that may be incurred. Citizens can ask for information by getting Xerox copies of documents, permissions, policies and decisions. Inspection of files can also be done and samples can be asked for.

All administrative offices of public authorities have to appoint Public Information Officers (PIO). Citizens can apply for information to the PIO of the office concerned. If it is not provided or is refused, the citizen can go to the Appellate Authority who would be an official in the same department, senior to the PIO. If this too does not produce a satisfactory result, one can appeal to the State or Central Information Commissioner, an independent constitutional authority being established under the Act. Thus, when exercised in rightful manner, Right to Information can become a tool for realising democracy.

The Right to Information Act provides for a time-bound and defined process for citizens to access information about all sections taken by public authorities. The penal provisions are the real teeth of the Act, which ensure that the PIO does not treat citizens demands for information in a cavalier manner. The primary power of RTI is the fact that it empowers individual citizens to requisition information. Hence, without necessarily forming pressure groups or associations, it puts power directly into the hands of the foundation of democracy—the citizens. There will certainly be an attempt to subvert this revolutionary right by the ruling coterie, since it strikes at the basics of their power. This can easily be countered if enough citizens use the Act. Citizens can use the right from their own houses – and it usually does not take more than about two hours to make an RTI application.

A few million applications across the country by the concerned citizens on issues that interest them will bring a major change in India and be a determined move towards the Swaraj we desire. There is a great need to spread the usage of this countrywide, so that transparency and good governance triumph. We now have the power; we only need to use it. It is simple to use and the benefits are immense.

Recent Controversy

The public outrage over the recent attempts of the government to tamper with the national Right to Information Act (on the issue of file notings, etc.) may have subsided for the moment but the storm has left some indelible marks on the history of Indian democracy. In a never-before alignment that rose above caste, class, gender, economic, political, professional and whatever have been your considerations, the government's move paved the way for a neat two-way split centered around one guiding principle: do we want to progress towards a clean and true democracy or not?

The proposed amendments have evoked mass indignation not only because the government was attempting to water down the RTI Act, but it was doing so while maintaining that it was making it more progressive, in addition to acting without any public consultation whatsoever. In fact, well into the Parliament session, no one, not even the members of Parliament, had even seen the official text of the Amendment Bill.

The language of the amendments leaves little room for doubt that the December 2005 attempt to exempt the file notings (with some minor exceptions) has worked its way back into the proposed amendments to the Act. Furthermore, the new sub-section 8 (m) reads almost identical to section 8(e) of the old Freedom of Information Act, which the government had pledged to improve upon. Worse, it now lengthens the list of exemptions by excluding "information pertaining to any process of any examination conducted by any public authority or assessment or evaluation made by it for judging the suitability of any person to appointment or promotions." In every sense, these amendments violate the fundamental principle of minimum exclusion that would make for a progressive Act.

Areas of Concern

There have been lot of concern areas regarding the Right to Information Bill as originally passed. The Bill contains a few provisions that have diluted its effectiveness. The provision in the original draft that criminal liability, with punishment by imprisonment, would extend to those who furnished false information or those who destroyed it, has been deleted. Another important change relates to the selection of the Information Commissioner and his or her deputies. The draft Bill envisaged their selection by a team comprising the Prime Minister, the Leader of the Opposition in the Lok Sabha and the Chief Justice of India (CJI). However, the Bill as passed by the two houses has amended the draft to replace the CJI with "a Union Cabinet Minister to be nominated by the PM", thus making the selection process somewhat more partisan. These and some other flaws in the Bill should not detract from the fact that it is a substantial improvement over the Freedom of Information Act and other freedom of information laws, passed by various states from 1997 onwards. While the right to know is not explicitly spelt out in the Constitution, the Supreme Court has held in several cases that this right is inherent in the right to freedom of speech and expression (Article 19) as well as the right to life and liberty (Article 21). The effectiveness of the Right to Information Act will depend substantially on how prepared the Central and state governments are in implementing it – in both letter and spirit.

Experiences of common citizens using the RTI Act since it was passed point to extensive ground level problems in the implementation of the Act. But neither the government nor the media seem inclined to pay attention to these seemingly mundane problems which could prove debilitating in the long run. Nearly a year since the Act came into effect, the status of *suo motu* disclosures by public authorities across the country is woefully unclear. The procedure for accepting application forms and fees is yet to be streamlined, even in large public offices such as collectorates. Although in theory the Act provides for redress through a two-step appeal procedure, the working of State Information Commissions – the second and final public authority at the State Government level—in many states puts the entire Act's credibility under a cloud.

While public pressure is easier to mobilise against blatant attempts to hold democracy hostage, such as the latest amendments, it is in the apparently insignificant details that the government could succeed in breaking down the patience of common citizens who are putting their new-found tool to test. This is a danger that RTI activists, the media and the public should anticipate and guard against.

Positive Side of the Picture

The Freedom of Information Bill aims to empower every citizen with the right to obtain information from the government. The change from the repressive regime of the Official Secrets Act to the notion of freedom of information as a citizen's right has taken 77 years, but it marks a significant paradigm shift for Indian democracy. The right to information has both intrinsic and instrumental value. Its intrinsic value comes from the fact that citizens have a right to know. More tangibly, in a country like India it can promote action for development and, therefore, has considerable instrumental value.

Information enables people to make enlightened choices and keeps tabs on elected representatives and officials who claim to act on their collective behalf. Thus, accountability and transparency are both enhanced radically. In the last few decades, freedom of information has been recognized as an internationally protected human right, and societies across the world have been moving away from opaque and secretive administrative systems to open and transparent systems.

However, there is a doubt about the revelation of complete information on the point by the government as the Bill reinforces the controlling role of the government official, who retains a wide discretion to withhold information. For example, requests for information that involve "disproportionate diversion of the resources of a public authority" can be shot down by the public information officer. From the gatekeepers of the Officials Secrets Act, they now become gatekeepers of the freedom of Information Bill.

However, despite the shortcomings, the new law could be the tentative beginning of a more inclusive development process – what Amartya Sen describes as "a momentous engagement with the possibilities of freedom."

41

ADVERTISING AND SOCIAL RESPONSIBILITY

There is much to celebrate about advertising. Wherever there is a market economy there is competition, and the more competition there is, the more important becomes the role of advertising. It is the most visible sign of the lively competition which results in satisfied customers to whom it promises more choice, better value, more new and improved products that are widely available and easily accessible.

The reach and influence of advertising is truly mindboggling as its tentacles reach into every segment of society today. Competition to sell goods and services through a relatively new medium, the Internet and the web, is developing at a tremendous speed and is sure to extend the boundaries of advertising manifold. It has also become an attractive hunting ground for the unprincipled operator as there are far too many obstacles to the enforcement of codes and self-regulation becomes doubtful.

Advertising is essentially about informing customers about product availability and prices. Every product can be distinguished from its rivals, with the help of advertising, thereby helping the customer to exercise choice. Advertising is thus important in establishing brands that customers can recognise and rely upon. The economy too stands to benefit as advertising builds up volume by creating demand, especially for new products, which, in turn, can lead to lower prices.

While this proves that advertising – and its corollary competition – is highly beneficial to the economy and is accepted as a fact of modern life, it is also clear that advertising works within the social milieu. It must reach out to individuals in the community in order to inform, convince or cajole. These individuals are a part of the greater social fabric. So, it becomes the responsibility of advertising to make sure that in its efforts to attract maximum customers it does not tear or slash this tenuous fabric. Advertising is all about reaching out to society just as much as society can stand being reached out to. Society survives on an unwritten code that delineates roles, functions, actions and behaviour of its members. It is the duty of advertising to respect this code and use the influence it has over the customer's mind to strengthen this code and not put it in a cocktail shaker just to make a particular product sell. Essentially, advertising is justified provided it strikes a balance between hard-sell and regulatory ethics.

Unfortunately, imperfections which still cling to human nature often tilt the balance in favour of stronger motives of self-interest, rather than higher or loftier ones. E.F. Sehumachu has described the market as "the institutionalisation of individualism and non-responsibility." This instinctive rivalary and strife to capture the market, even though it may result in benefits to the customers, can prove detrimental to society as a whole. This happens especially when the myriad morals, traditions, values and principles upon which the societal edifice is based, are sacrificed without compunction.

The idea of advertising having to be legal, honest, decent and truthful, has been around for a long time and regulatory bodies such as the Advertising Standards Authority have taken it upon themselves to draw up regulatory codes to guide all advertising. The problem is that there are many grey areas between what is banned by law and what exceeds the standards of honesty, decency and truthfulness as set out in the codes. In many cases, the approach becomes subjective and the conscience of the individual advertiser is the only check to overstepping certain unwritten limits.

The advertising legend David Ogilvy of Ogilvy and Mather always believed that "good products can be sold by honest advertising because if you tell a lie you will be found out." Strictly speaking, this is not ethics but business prudence. But honesty in its pitch should be one of the main principles of all advertising. Advertisers should not exploit the credulity, lack of knowledge or experience of customers. This is especially pertinent in the case of advertisements relating to financial services where there is a great deal of small print that the public fails to read and understand. Exaggerated claims such as "best", "smoothest", "whitest" are, of course, subjective and part of standard advertising practices. What is much more serious is the concealment of relevant information, for instance, withholding statutory safety warnings for specific products such as tobacco, paan masala and certain drugs, as also showing risky acts of daredevilry and bravado encouraging false notions of masculinity and heroism.

There is a phrase in advertising called "knocking copy", which in effect means unfairly attacking or discrediting other products. Of course, comparative advertising is widely practised and accepted but comparisons should be clean and fair because an attack on rival products induces negative thinking in the customer. Many products are advertised by attempting to denigrate, discredit or take unfair advantage of a competitor, as is found in the case of soaps, detergents, drinks – soft and hard. This affects public values as it encourages fault-finding attitudes.

Indecency in advertising tries to fulfil the ultimate objective – to use shock tactics to draw attention to the product. The most obvious example is the often irrelevant exploitation of sexual images, especially those of women. Attitudes to indecency are subjective and vary enormously. Nevertheless, such advertising is increasingly being viewed as unnecessary and avoidable even in the advertising world. Very often, only the titillating image remains with the customer who later has no recollection of the product which is in fact counter-productive for the advertiser. Besides, even for the consumer who does not wish to be labelled a prude or a feminist, such advertisements reflect bad taste and promote moral laxity and licentiousness simply by the association of ideas.

Shocking claims and images are also used to instill fear, especially by insurance companies. But raising such apprehensions should not be disproportionate to the risk as it could result in spreading panic. Instead, appeals to encourage prudent behaviour or discourage dangerous or ill-advised actions would be more acceptable ways to attract customers.

The advertising of alcohol is a very controversial and widely-discussed aspect of responsible advertising. No matter how subjective the approach of different individuals, society as a whole agrees that it is ethically vital for the advertiser to keep alcohol abuse and damage to health—in all age groups—in mind while advertising the product. This also holds good for the tobacco industry where manufacturers and advertisers insist on the right of freedom of commercial speech, but have come to acknowledge that the right also carries with it certain responsibilities and constraints must be exercised for the sake of health as well as ethics.

In the modern world, advertising has an awesome impact in its ability to influence lifestyles, attitudes and priorities of millions. It has the power to create demand and make people believe they must have something which they would have never dreamed of before. This is significant in developing countries where newer artificial needs are being created, often at the expense of necessary public services. Making non-essential products fashionable amounts to wasteful expenditure in poor countries, while the seemingly inexorable march of consumption fuelled by advertising in developed countries raises a more fundamental environmentalist question of the damage it is doing to the planet – and to a lesser extent perhaps the moral question of excessive devotion to the acquisition of worldly goods.

Advertising has, no doubt, become an essential part of modern life. But it must be made to act responsibly and abide by certain values and ethical codes. It must stick to standards and stay within bounds. Though it would be ridiculous to expect advertisers to act as the moral guardians of society, any advertising that shrugs of responsibility and rides roughshod over the customer is, ultimately, self-destructive. Socially responsible advertising has the power to influence, educate and motivate the community towards positive and desirable behaviour and this would be the guiding principle behind all advertisements.

The magical power of words and images should not be misused so that *caveat emptor* or "buyer beware' becomes a warning against exploitation and manipulation of society by unscrupulous near-sighted advertising.

42

ARE SCIENCE AND ART ANTITHETICAL TO EACH OTHER?

Science from the word *Scientia* which means 'knowledge', is supposed to concentrate on verifiable facts, reasoned arguments and firm conclusions. Art, on the other hand, is considered to be too closely linked with imagination, feelings and emotions to stand the test of reality. Facts certainly form the basis of any work of art. Poetry is a writer's response to reality, outer or inner; novels weave social details and human characters into a story; paintings depict a scene or a human being. But the reality underlying art cannot be called the reality of fact. It is reality transformed by the colours of the imagination, the permutations and combinations in the artist's mind, and given shape by the magic of words, paint or sound. Reason is not excluded by the artist but it is a regulatory factor, not the chief motivation as in a scientific inquiry.

In yet another aspect science and art seem to diverge: the matter of accuracy. It aims at making its knowledge more and more approximate to truth, and in this effort constantly revises its repertoire of principles, formulae and theories.

Art does not aim at that kind of accuracy. A work of art does not reveal all that can be expressed about a subject. Essence is more important to art enabling the reader, hearer or viewer to gather much more than what the mere words or paint depicts on the surface. Aesthetic joy is not confined to superficial accuracy.

A scientist's method is different from that of an artist's. Analysis—the breaking down of a phenomenon into its components—is basic to the scientist's way of trying to understand reality. Looking at a star, he cannot rest content wondering about what it is. He has to analyse its ingredients, and come to the triumphant conclusion –

By the spectroscopic Ken
I know that you are hydrogen.

The artist's method is different. He looks upon and collects bits and pieces of the outside world and experiences – a colour from here, a smile from there, a song from elsewhere – and integrates it all into a whole which cannot be dismembered into its constituents. Of course, poems are 'analysed', and paintings and musical compositions 'dissected' in order to be 'critically appreciated', but the enjoyment of a work of art lies in taking it as a whole.

Are science and art then truly antithetical to each other? The gulf in attitude and approach may suggest that it is so. And yet, there are so many ways in which the two interact, so many points at which they meet. Many a great discovery of science has its roots in the same intuition and imagination that find expression in works of art. Reality is ultimately the subject of both science and art, only perspectives may differ. Truth itself is no hard and fast single, dull entity. It is multi-faceted and is approached by divergent paths. If Keats found beauty and truth in a Grecian urn, Blake found eternity in a grain of sand, and Einstein found it all in a matter of relativity.

It is a matter of interest that scientific interests and discoveries have spurred art to look for new perspectives in beauty. Newton's *Optics* seems to have sparked off innumerable colour images in English poetry. Before the invention of photography the landscape painter depicted with meticulous care what he saw in nature as it was; after photography took over this kind of depiction, art developed impressionism. The landscape was seen in terms of light and vivid tones of colour. Psychological advances too have had an impact on art. If James Joyce used the 'stream of consciousness' technique, the surrealism of Salvador Dali opened up entirely new possibilities in painting. Picasso's portraits are, indeed, considered as an attempt at space-time coordination in painting. Shades of Einstein! Today, computer graphics show how the artist's imagination can be combined with scientific and technological skill and precision to produce something totally new.

Technology has helped art in its various forms to reach the masses. The printing press – and now the Desktop printer – have multiplied the accessibility of common man to written word. Radio has brought into every home the music of many lands. Television and cinema have created vivid forms of entertainment; indeed, the audio-visual media are justly art-forms in themselves. Science has created tools which the artist in human mind learns to use with effect. The information technology has revolutionised the reach of art forms as well. And since information is a two-way process, the access to what is happening in remote places also has a suitable influence on artist's work.

Science with its cold clinical approach has killed the joy and wonder of life, say some. Not quite true. With the spread of knowledge, one knows that the rainbow is merely light broken up into its spectrum, and that the moon is made of rocks, but that does not quite deaden our appreciation of the rainbow or the rain clouds or kill our ability to enjoy Wordsworth and Shelley. A poet could now rhapsodise over what a drop of blood looks like under a microscope or the distant star through a telescope and make a reader marvel afresh at the universe.

In any case, those who reduce science to bare reason are doing an injustice to it. The human mind which is responsible for creating a work of art is equally responsible for discovering laws of nature and universe. Neither can be done without the spirit of imagination. Science fiction exemplifies how the imagination creates words and events that science of the future renders into reality. Leonardo da Vinci not only painted the famous "Mona Lisa" but also drew models of flying machines. H.G. Wells looked forward to man's landing on the moon. Asimov's robots are threatening to come alive. And the very recent successes at experiments in cloning found an artistic outlet in the creation of dinosaur clones on the screen, though most people would rather not have a Jurassic Park for real. The effects for the movie, incidentally, were created by the most sophisticated computers in conjunction with the human brain. What better illustration of the harmony of art and science could be there than the fact that some of our most reputed 'scientists' have been great 'artists' as well? Einstein was a good musician. Who can, in the circumstances, draw five lines to demarcate the end of art and the beginning of science?

Life is a many-splendoured entity, and reality has more than one plane. Art and science, far from being antithetical to each other, are part of the same reality. It needs a comprehensive vision to see them as parts of a whole; to compartmentalise them within narrow boundaries would be detrimental to human welfare. The head and the heart are equally important for a meaningful life.

43

MORAL DILEMMAS INHERENT IN SCIENTIFIC PROGRESS

Humankind, over the centuries, has made tremendous progress in the field of science. Scientific advancement in the last century has been overwhelming: by making the most productive use of various scientific discoveries and technological breakthroughs, humans have excelled in various fields in an unprecedented manner. We can explore the depths of oceans, send teams of astronauts to space to know more about the planets and the moon. We have made many wonderful scientific inventions and discoveries. We have been able to increase longevity, arrest the gradual decay of human body and control the spread of lethal diseases by making extraordinary life–prolonging drugs and medicines. A number of killer diseases are now curable. Cancer, for instance, now is not feared as much as it was earlier.

Scientific progress made by human has made possible a number of miraculous developments in most fields. From telecommunications to medical science, from space explorations to mapping the unfathomable depths of oceans, man has been performing amazing feats. The technological breakthroughs achieved in telecommunications has now made it possible for us to stay in touch with the world easily and cheaply. As a matter of fact, now the world has become a small global village of sorts where everyone knows everyone. But the biggest and perhaps one of the most amazing scientific achievements by man has been in the field of cloning of animals. Scientists have cloned animals with great success and it is said that the day is not far when they would be able to clone human beings to produce perfect, healthy and disease-free specimens of human beings.

However, the scientific developments and advancements have been accompanied by dilemmas of morality and ethics.

The truth is that moral dilemmas and human ethics are inherent in scientific progress. Are all the progress and breakthroughs achieved in this field morally justified and in sync with our moral values? Are they ethically right? For instance, by aspiring to clone human beings, are we not trying to become God in a world where even good human beings are hard to find and where despite all the progress made in various walks of life, thanks to scientific progress, the fact remains that we are still beasts by nature and by instinct? Humans have tamed nature to a great extent and assumed its powers to make their own laws that have disturbed the delicate balance in nature. By assuming roles we were never destined to play, we have become more selfish, greedy and insensitive to each other's sufferings. We destroy and kill helpless and mute animals and, at times, human lives are also sacrificed, for carrying out medical experiments, all in the name of scientific advancement.

The fact is that scientific experimentation in the laboratory cannot proceed largely without involving destruction. Even an atom is split – smashed – to release energy. Animals are regularly dissected – killed – and the environment is experimentally modified – interfered with – all in the name of creative and scientific thought. Many such scientific efforts leave behind in their wake highly toxic waste products and this toxic waste creates environmental hazards and pollution of the worst kind. But this aspect does not cross the mind of the scientific and progressive modern man in pursuit of scientific knowledge and the benefits he can derive from it.

Progress made in the field of sciences comes at a great premium. For all the progress achieved through scientific discoveries and creations, the world today is not a better – or safer and happier – place to live in. There is a great deal of violence that has made the world a dangerous place to live in. It appears that science has not been very successful in contributing to solve the world's real problems or in improving the overall life of man. In addition, since science lays more stress on physical aspects of a health/medical problem and often seeks to find solutions accordingly, most of the time it manages to solve such a problem on faulty basis. Take for instance, the case of drugs and medicines. Despite the hullabaloo made, the preventive field in medical science is almost entirely undeveloped compared to curative medicine. This is obvious in cancer research where the destruction of cancer cells has long been considered to perfect panacea. But most scientific attempts have focused on therapies that can actually prevent the disease, strengthen the patient's immune system and even effect permanent cures. Therefore, in spite of many billions of dollars spent on cancer, deaths by cancer continue to occur in great numbers.

Despite giant strides made by man in achieving remarkable breakthroughs in various fields, the fact remains that the average age of man is still more or less the same. The scientific progress in the areas of military and war has seen creation of deadly weapons and technologies that have the capability to destroy not only human beings but also the entire planet. Individual nations now have the power to destroy the world if they wish to.

Biological and chemical means of warfare have already taken a heavy toll worldwide. Often helpless prisoners of war are subjected to torture and forced to undergo the so-called scientific experiments to discover more about the destructive abilities of dangerous weapons, gases and drugs. Most importantly the fruits of scientific progress are largely enjoyed by a select and privileged few. The majority still remains unaffected and untouched by the blessings of modern science. Isn't it true that despite sending teams of scientists to space many times over, people still cover long distances on foot?

Suffice it to say, scientific progress has been a double-edged sword for humankind. Scientifically, we may have achieved much and we can boast of advances in telecommunications, communication, transport, nuclear science, space and health; however, where humanity and moral values are concerned, there is still a great deal of pain, suffering and insensitivity in the world. None of these has been mitigated by science; rather, the world is now a more unsafe, unhealthy and sad place. Excellence in science and technological breakthroughs have, by and large, been at the cost of our moral and human values.

44

IF HUMAN BEINGS CAN BE CLONED

Cloning is not something new. Mammals have usually been cloned by nuclear transfer technique which involves fusion of a donor cell and an egg cell. Until now, this fusion was possible only when the donor cell was taken directly from an embryo and not from an older cell. However, Dr Ian Wilmut and his colleagues at the Roslin Institute in Scotland achieved a breakthrough in cloning by using an adult cell. By using an adult cell, the team proved that even cells that have already differentiated and become specialised, do not forget the genetic instructions to create an entire organism. It is this development that has generated a lot of controversy. Dr. Wilmut has pointed out at the possibility of cloning human beings in a similar fashion, i.e., producing not two identical childern but a child identical to the parent. Although this possibility is remote at present, it does exist, raising a plethora of moral, social, cultural and economic, apart form scientific questions.

If human beings can be cloned, then the technique can be used to recover a loved one who is no more. In cases of infertility, a person can give his/her own cells to produce to a clone. There are many who see human cloning as an attempt to improve the human race. Scientists argue that cloning may be used to study genetic diseases. It could also be used in human beings to treat diseases by replacing diseased cells.

However, skeptics regard cloning to be a dangerous technology – a technology that would threaten the very foundation of human civilization. Since it involves genes from a single parent, concepts of parenthood, family and society would undergo tremendous change. Such an order of things would be beneficial neither for the parent nor for the child.

Cloning is a departure from the natural order of things: It is deliberate and artificial since it involves asexual reproduction and asexual lineages of species have not lasted long. There is also a fear that human cloning might result in ethnic cleansing as the technique could be used to propagate one species at the cost of another. In other words, if misused, the technique could lead to the unfolding of man's commercial potential in the face of a new technique.

The UNESCO has declared that practices which are contrary to human dignity such as reproductive cloning of human beings shall not be permitted. The National Bioethics Advisory Commission of the USA called for a ban on cloning experiments. The Pope declared that each human being has a right to a unique human genome. The European Union has also adopted a ban on human cloning.

Dolly, the sheep, cloned by Dr Wilmut and his colleagues was born after 277 attempts, of which only 29 of the fused udder cells actually became embryos, which were implanted in 13 ewes of which one became pregnant and gave birth. In the much more complex human system, the odds of success are much lower, making human cloning an event of the far future.

No view can be absolute. It would be highly impractical to completely ignore the benefits of the new technology and over-emphasise ethical issues. In fact, several techniques which had a moral tag attached to them, have in the long run proved beneficial to mankind. Most of the scientists are deeply concerned that laws prohibiting human cloning will stifle important research. James Watson, the Nobel laureate, called for a halt to the abuses of cloning human beings rather than stopping research associated with it. The question ultimately is that if human beings can be cloned, then how do we ensure that the power of the technology is not abused for selfish gains by a few. A reasonable legislation to prevent unscrupulous use of the technology would be the first step towards ensuring human benefit. It the ill-effects of human cloning that can be guarded in some way, the idea of further research on the issue might not be bad at all.

Weighing the advantages and disadvantages of human cloning, the odds of success are quite low. The new technology would make human reproduction into a customized, mass production of identical human beings, assuring better quality and a degree of design predictability, long associated with industrial production. Human cloning would certainly make life more mechanical as opposed to the organic.

45

THE IDEAL AND CONCEPT OF WELFARE STATE

The English term "welfare state" is believed by Asa Briggs to have been coined by Archbishop Willam Temple during the Second World War, contrasting wartime Britain with the "Warfarestate" of Nazi Germany. Friedrich Hayek contends that the term derived from the older German world Wohlfahrtsstaat, which itself was used by nineteenth century historians to describe a variant of the ideal of Polizeistaat ("police state"). It was fully developed by the German academic Sozialpolitiker – "socialists of the chair" – from 1870 and first implemented through Bismarck's "state socialism". Bismarck's polices have also been seen as the creation of a welfare state.

There are three main interpretations of the idea of a welfare state:

(a) The provision of welfare services by the state.

(b) An ideal model in which the state assumes primary responsibility for the welfare of its citizens. This responsibility is comprehensive because all aspects of welfare are considered; a 'safety net' is not enough, nor are minimum standards.

It is universal because it covers every person as a matter of right.

(c) The provision of welfare in society.

In many "welfare states", especially in continental Europe, welfare is not actually provided by the state, but by a combination of independent, voluntary, mutualist and government services. The functional provider of benefits and services may be central or state government, a state-sponsored company or agency, a private corporation, a charity or another form of non-profit organisation. However, this phenomenon has been more appropriately termed as "welfare society" and the term "welfare system" has been used to describe the range of welfare state and welfare society mixes that are found.

The Development of Welfare States

An early version of the welfare state appeared in China during the Song Dynasty in the 11th century. Prime Minister Wang Anshi believed that the state was responsible for providing its citizens the essentials for a decent living standard. Accordingly, under his direction the state initiated agricultural loans to relieve the farming peasants. He appointed boards to regulate wages and plan pensions for the aged and unemployed. These reforms were known as the "New Laws", "New Policies", or "xin fa".

Modern welfare states developed through a gradual process beginning in the late 19th century and continuing through the 20th. They differed from previous schemes of poverty relief due to their relatively universal coverage. The development of social insurance in Germany under Bismarck was particularly influential. Some schemes like those in Scandinavia, were based largely in the development of autonomous, mutualist provision of benefits. Others were founded on state provision. The term was not, however, applied to all states offering social protection. The sociologist T.H. Marshall identified the welfare state as a distinctive combination of democracy, welfare and capitalism.

Examples of early welfare states in the modern world are Germany, all of the Nordic countries, the Netherlands, Uruguay and New Zealand in the 1930s. Germany is generally held to be the first welfare state. Changed attitudes in reaction to the Great Depression were instrumental in the move to the welfare state in many countries, a harbinger of new times where "cradle-to-grave" services became a reality after the poverty of the Depression. During the Great Depression, it was seen as an alternative "middle way" between communism and capitalism. In the period following the Second World War, many countries in Europe moved from partial or selective provision of social services to relatively comprehensive coverage of the population.

The activities of present day welfare states extend to the provision of both cash welfare benefits (such as old-age pensions or unemployment benefits) and in-kind welfare services (such as health or childcare services). Through these provisions, welfare state can affect the distribution of well-being and personal autonomy among their citizens, as well as influencing how their citizens consume and how they spend their time.

After the discovery and inflow of the oil revenue, Saudi Arabia, Kuwait, Qatar, Bahrain. Oman and the United Arab Emirates all became welfare states. However, the services are strictly for citizens and these countries do not accept immigrants; those born in these countries do not qualify for citizenship unless they are of the parentage belonging to their respective countries.

In the United Kingdom, the beginning of the modern welfare state was in 1911 when David Lloyd George suggested that everyone in work should pay national insurance contribution for unemployment and health benefits from work.

In 1942, the "Social Insurance and Allied Services" were created by Sir William Beveridge in order to aid those who were in need of help, or in poverty. Beveridge worked as a volunteer for the poor and set up national insurance. He stated that "All people of working age should pay a weekly national insurance contribution. In return, benefits would be paid to people who were sick, unemployed, retired or widowed". The basic assumptions of the report were the National Health Service, which provided free health care to the UK. The Universal Child Benefit was a scheme to give benefits to parents, encouraging people to have children by enabling them to feed and support a family. This was particularly beneficial after the Second World War when the population of the United Kingdom declined. Universal Child Benefit provided encouragement for new babies which sparked the Baby boom. The impact of the report was huge and 600,000 copies were made. He recommended to the government that they should find ways of talking the five giants being: Want, Disease, Ignorance, Squalor and Idleness.

He argued that to cure these problems, the government should provide adequate employment. Before 1939, health care had to be paid for. This was done through a vast network of friendly societies, trade unions and other insurance companies which counted the vast majority of the UK working population as members. These friendly societies provided insurance for sickness, unemployment and invalidity, thereby providing people with an income when they were unable to work. But because of the 1942 Beveridge Report, on 5th July 1948, the National Insurance Act, National Assistance Act and National Health Service Act came into force. Thus, this is the day that the modern UK welfare state was founded.

Debating the Welfare State

The concept of the welfare state remains controversial and there is continuing debate over governments' responsibility for their citizens' welfare. Here it is crucial to clarify what exactly one means by welfare state. Firstly, the welfare state is not a state-run economy. The welfare state refers to the programmes paid by the government that provide basic temporary and conditional financial help to those legally unable to provide to themselves because of their current economic situation due to health problems, mental diseases, etc. or because of a major natural disaster or terrorist attack.

Arguments in Favour

Humanitarian – the right to the basic necessities of life is a fundamental human right, and people should not be allowed to suffer unnecessarily due to lack of provision.

Altruism – helping others is a moral obligation in most cultures; charity and support for people who cannot help themselves are also widely thought to be moral choices.

Utilitarian – the same amount of money will produce greater happiness in the hands of a less well-off person than if given to a well-off person; thus redistributing wealth from the rich to the poor will increase the total happiness in society.

Religious – major world religions emphasize the importance of social organisation rather than personal development alone. Religious obligations include the duty of charity and the obligation for solidarity. However, before the welfare state in the UK, charitable donations were normally 10% of a person's income and the number of charities in the UK were enormous as was the amount of support given by them to the paupers. Therefore, though this is fulfilled by a welfare state, it is actually a concept of welfare, not necessarily welfare provided by the state.

Economic – social programmes perform a range of economic functions, including regulation of demand and structuring the labour market.

Social – social programmes are used to promote objectives regarding education, family and work.

Market failure – in certain cases, the private sector fails to meet social objectives or to deliver efficient services due to such things as monopolies, oligopolies or asymmetric information.

Social justice – the money the state provides comes from the nation's labour and natural resources through universal taxation. The rich manage the wealth that is often inherited and do not necessarily contribute more than the average worker. Therefore, it is a matter of justice to provide for the private individual who cannot legally provide to himself. Further, there will also be members of societies who through disability, health problems, or other causes out of the individual's control, are unable to provide for themselves.

Economies of scale – some services can be more efficiently paid for when bought "in bulk" by the government for the public, rather than purchased by individual consumers. The highway system, water distribution, fire department, universal health and national defence are some examples.

Anti-crime – people with low incomes do not need to resort to crime to stay alive, thus reducing the crime rate. Empirical evidence indicates that welfare programmes reduce property crime.

Arguments Against

Moral (compulsion) – libertarians believe that the "nanny state" infringes upon individual freedom, forcing the individual to subsidise the consumption of others. They argue that social spending reduces the right of individuals to transfer some of their wealth to others, and is tantamount to a seizure of private property.

Reduced morality – the introduction of the welfare state and benefits that support people who do not contribute to the national good, reduces the compulsion to contribute.

Religious / paternalism – some Protestant Christians and an increasing number of Catholics also believe that only voluntary giving (through private charities) is virtuous. They hold personal responsibility to be a virtue, and they believe that a welfare state diminishes the capacity of individuals to develop this virtue.

Anti-regulatory – the welfare state is accused of imposing greater burdens on private businesses, of potentially slowing growth and creating unemployment.

Efficiency – the free market leads to more efficient and effective production and service delivery than state-run welfare programmes. They argue that high social spending is costly and must be funded out of higher levels of taxation. According to Friedrich Hayek, the market mechanism is much more efficient and able to respond to specific circumstances of a large number of individuals than when run by the state. An example of the inefficiency of the state is that in the UK, there is one non-teaching civil servant for every classroom in the country, whether they be administrators, managers or inspectors.

Motivation and incentives – the welfare state may have undesirable effects on behaviour, fostering dependency, destroying incentives and sapping motivation to work.

Charitable – by the state assuming a larger burden for the financial care of people. Individuals may feel it is no longer necessary for them to donate to charities or give to philanthropies.

Managerial statecraft – this paleo-conservative view posits that the welfare state is part of an ongoing regime that remains in power, regardless of what political party holds a majority. It acts in the name of abstract goals such as equality or positive rights, and uses its claim of moral superiority, power of taxation and wealth redistribution to keep itself in power.

Crime – state-provided welfare normally incurs high tax economy. This, in turn, leads to people feeling protective over their earnings and, therefore, looking for ways to cheat the tax system to pay less tax. This, in turn, reduces overall morality. People dependent on welfare state have been found by surveys to be more depressed and have a lower self-esteem than working people. This, in turn, often leads to them feeling rejected, hopeless and/or abandoned by the populace at large. Therefore, they have a lower self of national unity of community responsibility and may turn to crime to get back at society or just fill the time.

Abuse – state-provided welfare benefits often finish by being fraudulently claimed by those who are not in real need. To counter this effect, more and more requirements are introduced for welfare claimants to prove their eligibility to obtain benefits. This results in creating complex and costly bureaucratic procedures whose effect is often adverse to the desired – the poor and needy persons who are not able to do the required paperwork are left behind while others get specialised in overcoming the bureaucratic hurdles (often by fraud or bribery) and claiming the benefits.

Discussion of Some of the Criticisms

Some criticism of welfare states concerns the idea that a welfare state makes citizens dependent and less inclined to work. Certain studies indicate that there is no association between economic performance and welfare expenditure in developed countries and that there is no evidence for the contention that welfare states impede progressive social development. R.E. Goodin et at., in *The Real Worlds of Welfare Capitalism* (Cambridge University Press, 1999) shows that on some economic and social indicators the United States performs worse than the Netherlands, which has a high commitment to welfare provision. However, the United States leads most welfare states on certain economic indicators, such as GDP per capita (although in 2006 it had a lower GDP per capita than Norway). The United States also has a low unemployment rate (although not as low as Denmark, Norway) and a high GDP growth rate at least in comparison to other developed countries (its growth rate, however, is lower than Finland's and Sweden's, two nations with relatively small population but comparatively high commitments to welfare provision. The United States' growth rate is also lower than the world's overall). The United States also leads most welfare states in the ownership of consumer goods. For example, it has more TV's per capita, more personal computers per capita, and more radios per capita than what people would call welfare states.

Another criticism comes from Classical Liberalism, namely, that Welfare is the theft of Property or Labour. This criticism is based upon classical liberalist ideals, wherein a citizen owns his body, and owns the product of his body's labour (i.e., goods, services or money). Note that in this definition property that is inherited is not included. So, to remove money through legal mechanisms set by a democratically elected assembly from the working or non-working citizen and give it to a non-working or handicapped citizen or to a child is argued to be a theft of the worker's property and / or labour and a violation of the property rights.

The third criticism is that the welfare state allegedly provides its dependents with a similar level of income to the minimum wage. Critics argue that fraud and economic activity are apparently quite common now in the United Kingdom and France. Some conservatives in the UK claim that the welfare state has produced a generation of dependents who rely solely upon the state for income and support instead of working even though assistance is given only to those unable to work so that actually being able to work and instead relying on the state for income is a criminal offence. The welfare state in the UK was created to provide a carefully selected number of people with a subsistence level of benefits in order to alleviate poverty, but that as a matter of opinion have been overly expanded to provide a large number of people indiscriminately with more money than the country can afford.

Some feel that this argument is demonstrably false: the benefits system in the UK hands out considerably less money than the national minimum wage, although people on welfare often find that they qualify for a variety of benefits, including benefits in kind, such as subsidised accommodation which usually makes the overall benefits much higher than figures show. On the other hard, benefits handed out in the US often exceed $ 10 an hour (varying state to state). When one accounts for all the free services provided – free housing, free food, free welfare checks – such that it's wiser economically not to work, rather than to accept $ 6 at the local retail store. One must not forget that even working families may be eligible for benefits when even while working their income does not cover their or their children's basic needs.

The fourth criticism of the welfare state is that it results in high taxes. This is usually true, as evidenced by places like Denmark (tax level at 50.4% of GDP in 2002) and Sweden (tax level at 50.2% of GDP in 2002). Such high taxes do not necessarily mean less income for the nation overall, since the state taxes go directly to the people it is taxed from. The real issue is that they all result in a major redistribution of that income from the citizens on the productive side of the equation to the citizens on the welfare state side. Thus, the productive, self-reliant citizens subsidise the lifestyle of others.

The fifth criticism of the welfare state is the belief that welfare services provided by the state are more expensive and less efficient than the same services would be if provided by private businesses. In 2000, Professors Louis Kaplow and Steven Shafill published two papers, arguing that any social policy based on such concepts as justice or fairness would result in an economy which is Pareto inefficient. Anything which is supplied free at the point of consumption would be subject to artificially high demand, whereas resources would be more properly allocated if provision reflected the cost. However, it is not clear how this would apply to services such as health and education, where individuals are unlikely to demand more services that are actually required, where the benefits of providing the service flow through to all levels of society (by reducing disease, and increasing the wealth creation abilities of the population).

The most extreme criticisms of states and governments are from anarchists, who believe that all states and governments are undesirable and / or unnecessary. Most anarchists believe that while social welfare gives a certain level of independency from the market and individual capitalists, it creates dependence to the state, which is the situation that, according to this view, supports and protects capitalism in the first place. Nonetheless, according to Noam Chomsky, "social democrats and anarchists always agreed, fairly generally, on so-called 'welfare state measures' and anarchists propose other measures to deal with these problems, without recourse to state authority." Anarchists believe in stopping welfare programmes only if it means abolishing government and capitalism as well.

46

INDIAN CINEMA AND SOCIAL RESPONSIBILITY

Since its beginning in India with the film "Raja Harishchandra" (1913), the cinema has remained a very important medium of mass communication. In its ability to combine entertainment with communication of ideas, it leaves the other media – except, of late, the television – far behind in reach and appeal. Also, like literature, it has mirrored different times and has left an impact on successive generations. Any work of art reflects the conditions of the society in which it is born, and the hopes and aspirations, the frustrations and contradictions present in any given social order. Cinema is no exception.

There are different views regarding cinema. The producers and financers consider it a lucrative business. For the actors and actresses, it is a means to earn money as well as satisfy their cravings for glamour and fame. The director and other artists look at it as yet another form of art. To some it is an audio-visual translation of literature and its message, if any. For the government, cinema is a potential area of employment and revenue. But for a majority of film-goers, it is comparatively inexpensive and interesting form of entertainment. Whatever it may mean to different people, cinema is generally regarded as an art form meant to entertain the people by presenting before them motion pictures on the screen, incorporating a gamut of elements – story, dance, song, thrills, comedy and pathos.

Beyond what the cinema means to individuals, however, the wide mass appeal of the cinema has invested it with a great deal of social influence. The nature of its influence – good or bad – naturally depends upon the social awareness of the people involved in it—the film-makers, the artists, the audience and the government. Should cinema as an art form be required to have social responsibility? Social responsibility involves behaving in a manner that does not impair the values of society, does not lead to disintegration of society or cause it to become degraded in any way. Cinema may be socially responsible by depicting reality. At the same time, with its power of influence – and here we are accepting the view that the audio-visual medium has the power to influence the viewer – it could easily gather support for progressive changes even while castigating social evils.

Most of the early Indian films like "Achhoot Kanya", "Godan" and "Awara", pursued their themes with social responsibility. Business or profit motive was certainly there – one cannot deny that – nor can one object to it. But these films did not lose sight of the needs of society at large. They tried to promote nationalism, communal harmony, mutual cooperation and social solidarity. Films like "Paigaam" strove to mitigate class conflicts, while others attacked evil social practices like caste exclusiveness, untouchability and child marriage.

Over the years, Indian cinema has lost touch with social responsibility and has become a slave to the 'box office syndrome'. It is all a question of hits and flops at the box office. 'Right' ingredients are squeezed in, necessarily or unnecessarily, into the films to make a hit without thinking that these ingredients – sex, violence, etc. – cause great injury to the social fabric and the people. At least, this is the trend in commercial or feature films. To cap it all, some film personalities have repeatedly asserted that their object is not to reform society.

The low aesthetic quality of today's films is directly proportional to the large number of unscrupulous, fly-by-night producers who are interested merely in profit-making without any concern for the society. The financer who comes forward to back the production of a high budget commercial film pleads that if he cannot be sure of handsome returns on his investment, he would rather turn to something else; why risk his money on a dubious venture? Worse are the distributors who will not touch a film if it does not have the 'right' ingredients. The economics of production has also sounded the death-knell for the 'art' films. But the people concerned must remember that many films with costly sets, top stars, sex and violence have flopped while low-budget films with light comedy, melodious range and lacking the 'right' ingredients do good business.

Indian cinema, deeply influenced by the stage, began with scripts based on mythological and historical plots. Gradually, themes came to be taken from novels, plays and stories of leading Indian litterateurs with a broad social and moral vision. This tradition continued for a considerable time. Then the progressive messages of the books gradually made a silent exit. Cheap scripts are now generally the norm, often openly plagiaristic. Variety is lacking. Double meaning dialogues are another common features; at times, it is explicitly vulgar.

An audience's right to entertainment is quite just. It is also true that a majority of the audience today demands cheap entertainment afforded by the display of violence, sex and obscenity in films. The general public has little interest in realistic 'art' movies and is only attracted by big names: something the low-budget movies cannot indulge in. The government also does not seem to be truly concerned about the affairs of the cinema, notwithstanding the ritualistic award-giving ceremonies, film festivals and tax concessions for pious sentiments such as secularism and patriotism. The Censor Board's ambiguous standards do not help matters much. For the Censor Board, kissing is obscene but rapes, gruesome killing and vulgar dialogues do not invite the scissors.

The overall result is that a majority of films today are juvenile stuff devoid of any social purpose, relevance or significance. The hero of a typical Indian film generally does not have to do anything for a living. His sole occupation in life appears to be winning the heart of his dream-girl and fighting with the world for her sake. Or, if he does something for a living, his lifestyle is much at variance with what he would earn from such a living. Similarly, the heroines do little except singing, dancing and crying with the hero. An effect of this is that a majority of the youth outside the screen are turning into incurable romanticists. This attitude forces the youth to turn their eyes from the hard realities and essential duties in life. Such youth cause harm to themselves as well as to others.

Today, the portrayal of women in Indian films has touched the nadir. There are few films in which heroines have been required to play stellar roles. She is an atrociously made-up piece required to dance, sing, expose and vanish. Revenge being the *leit motif* of most films, she is frequently raped and the hero vows to take revenge. This reinforces the feelings of girls and women that they are weak, unimportant, and the world of males is after their body and vanity.

A rape scene has become almost mandatory in most films and this is picturised in such a manner that instead of generating pathos and horror, the scene produces sexual excitement in the viewer. This perverse depiction of women as glamorous props and objects of titillation and victims of violence, and of this violence as an exciting and adventurous act could well be partly responsible for the increasing atrocities against women.

We have always had genre-based movies abounding in nauseating stereotypes like the long-suffering wife and mother, the corrupt and lecherous politician, the avaricious landlord and trader, a weak-kneed judiciary and a thoroughly corrupt and inept police. This trend is now reinforcing prejudices towards certain sections of the society and encouraging cynical disbelief in the entire system.

The stunning luxuries of the filmi villains and their varied methods of collecting wealth help people to overlook the tendency to make fast money by hook or by crook. This is, consequently, eroding the social norms and values which are generally established in a society after great industry and pain. When films glamorise violence, the impressionable minds in the audience feel tempted to imitate it in real life. Some fall prey to criminal tendencies and get increasingly brutalised, while the social psyche in general gets desensitised to the violent acts as they see them repeatedly. It cannot be denied that violence holds a natural appeal for exuberant but immature minds. However, the heavy dose of violence dishes out to them in the garb of entertainment, pollutes young minds and sows seeds of chaos in public life.

Furthermore, the extravagant and sophisticated life styles shown in the films and the mercurial rise of the hero from rags to riches, heighten the aspirations of all and sundry. But there is naturally a wide gap between such aspirations and their fulfillment. Hence, the great frustrations pervade in society.

The Constitution has provided for the freedom of vocation and expression, but at the same time, the film-makers owe it to the society to ensure that they do not pander to prurient tastes and thereby poison the social psyche in a bid to earn more. Freedom of vocation, expression, conscience or belief is acceptable but the stability and health of a society cannot be ignored. In any case, cinema must take cognizance of human collectivity and its associated values. One does not ask for 'social reform' from cinema, but it should at best eschew depriving the society of what it already has.

Just throwing homilies at the film-makers or the film-viewers will not, however, work. Instead, we will have to act. The best means of creating social awareness and responsibility among the film-makers is to form a discriminating and well informed public opinion. In this respect, the role of film-critics becomes important. They can teach readers and viewers how to discriminate between the good and the bad films. The most important criterion on which they can base their judgement is the social relevance of what is exposed to view in the films.

In a country like India with a high percentage of illiteracy and poverty, cinema has an important role to play. It has unqualified potential to inform and educate people. According to Elia Kazan, the famous film director, "Cinema is the most humanising piece of expression that we have in the world today. It is the hope of the world, where people are shown in all their humanity... . Through it you are made aware of the importance of friendliness and brotherhood of man."

47

WHAT FREEDOM MEANS TO ME

What is freedom? It is a difficult question to answer categorically. Does it mean absolute liberty to do as one pleases? Complete non-restraint to pursue any fancy that strikes one? Is such a free existence possible at all for a human being? Freedom is, indeed, a nebulous concept, laying itself open to several interpretations, even conflicting ones.

There are champions of freedom who vehemently oppose any form of social control. Thoreau at least allows the need of some government – "the best government is the least government" – but there are others who denounce any sort of organisation at all. But given the imperfect nature of human beings, surely, such freedom would degenerate into anarchy and finally to the survival of the fittest in the sense of brute power. It would result in the tyranny of the weak, by the strong; it would mean freedom for the strong and enslavement of the weak.

At the other extreme are those who are thoroughly suspicious of individual freedom. They have such a low opinion of human reason that they cannot allow an individual the right to choose and decide on his or her own. Any deviation from a rigid social average is seen as a threat to society. Social equilibrium is the end all to which individual initiative must, perforce, be sacrificed. But such a society will soon lose its vibrant dynamism, become ponderous and static and finally collapse under the weight of its own rigidity, as did the Greek and Roman civilizations.

The extremes, thus, can harm society. But one may deduce that freedom is a social concept. If human beings lived as isolated entities, the meaning of freedom has no importance. It is because they live in groups, in societies, that the concept of individual freedom needs to be understood.

C.E.M. Joad remarks that the situation of the human being is like that of a pack of porcupines huddling together; but a felt wrapping round each one prevents the quills of one from pricking the other. The felt wrapping is, of course, social control. In the absence of social control, one man's actions may prove uncomfortable to another. On the other hand, if the social control becomes excessive, individual identity is likely to be subsumed under that of a group or community. Freedom, thus, has to steer a careful course between a stifling social tyranny and a bewildering licentiousness.

Freedom, indeed, can be a burden. Enjoyment of freedom requires the use of one's brains, it calls for decision, the willingness and ability to choose between right and wrong, indeed, to contemplate on what is right and wrong. The exercise of freedom and the capacity to perceive its perversions requires of a human being a very high degree of integrity and social consciousness. Erich Fromm in his *Fear of Freedom* correctly argues that with a low level of social consciousness, man has a tendency to misuse freedom by either oppressing his fellowmen or by running away from the exercise of freedom. The practice of freedom involves taking decisions with the full awareness of the responsibility it entails; it implies a readiness to accept the consequences of any such decision.

The conscious exercise of freedom is not easy. One meets with opposition from different sides at different levels and of different degrees. Pursuit of freedom in action and thought requires courage of conviction and then the self-confidence to face even social ostracism. Society does not like individual exercise of freedom. Even a hairstyle or dress somewhat different from that of the majority invites the raised eyebrow, sniggers or derisive comment. If one chooses to think differently from the herd, the consequences may be quite dangerous to such a thinker. Socrates, after all, was executed for choosing to think freely. Galileo was tortured for his freedom of thought. If one wants freedom, one must be ready to pay a price for it.

Yet, in each one of us, there is a hidden rebel. Even eccentricity is a form of defiance, a protest, an expression of resentment against conformity. It is this basic instinct in man that sublimates itself in the form of freedom. Each one of us is a non-conformist in some sense or the other and this shows the urge for freedom.

It is the courageous exercise of freedom that makes human beings question social evils and attempt to change things for the better when one says that freedom should not harm society, it does not mean that society has to be accepted as it is with all its ills. As human consciousness evolves, as awareness and knowledge grow, and if social norms seem to have acquired an oppressive quality, the exercise of freedom to change the system becomes imperative. Throughout history, social change takes place mainly because an individual first manifests the courage to question existent beliefs and practices, break free of them and create better alternatives. That is true freedom.

48

THE RIGHTS AND WRONGS OF FREE EXPRESSION

The first cry of a new-born infant is an expression of its response to the outside world. The desire to express oneself is a corollary to the human capacity for feeling, imagination and thought. The need to give vent to our ideas and feelings is at times so great that we have no hesitation in talking to ourselves, when alone. The consideration of the rights and wrongs of free expression, however, arise only when such expression takes the form of communication – between individuals or among groups.

Communication of ideas has been basic to the very development of society and civilization. Exchange of thoughts contributes in the growth of an individual's personality even as it helps him or her to understand the world around and the society of which he or she is a part, and, perhaps, contribute a little to that society. However, complete freedom of expression has never been entertained in any society; indeed, it is doubtful if it could ever be countenanced given the imperfect nature of human beings.

Freedom of expression relates to two forms of communication: purveying of information which is a major function of the media, and the creative aspect which involves the expression of an individual's imagination or ideas. There is no doubt that free flow of information helps entire nations to progress, and this relates specially to scientific and economic matters. In a democracy, a vigilant press is considered to be an effective watchdog of political behaviour: it plays an important role in both building up and disseminating public opinion. And if a government has national and social interest at all, it will be glad to get a true feedback on its policies and their implementation.

In the presentation of information, however, bias can enter—political, racial or social. The opinion of the controlling authority, be it the government or a private party, often colours even what goes by the name of 'news'. The question of media censorship of material which criticizes the controlling authority or that which does not agree with the declared 'editorial policy' is a part of the complex issue of media autonomy and editorial prerogative. But broadly speaking, the freedom of expression is not an absolute freedom anywhere in the world. Our own Constitution puts 'reasonable restrictions' on it in the interests of sovereignty and integrity of India, security of the state, friendly relations with foreign states, public order, decency or morality, or in relation to contempt of court, defamation or incitement to an offense. A pretty long list of restrictions, one would say, and yet it has not been able to quite define the boundaries; the controversy over free expression rages as furiously as ever.

No sane person would disagree if one requires freedom of expression to stop short of abusing or maligning any person or community. However, it is not quite so easy to set limits on freedom of expression in so far as it conveys subjective ideas, thoughts and views. One's thoughts are free – at least one hopes so – but can all one's thoughts be expressed freely? If one has ideas greatly in variance with what society believes in and cherishes, there is bound to be a conflict between the individual and society. Most people like a smooth routine and cling to old beliefs: it gives them a sense of security; they look with suspicion on anything that might cause a change. And yet change is essential for a society to be dynamic, if it is not to stagnate and be fossilised. It takes a brave individual to speak out – pour fresh ideas and views uncaring of consequences on a personal level.

Ironically enough, religion which today is made an excuse to curb free speech has progressed mainly because individuals have, from time to time, questioned existing norms and tenets. The Buddha, Mahavira, Christ, Prophet Mohammad, Martin Luther, Sankara, Ramanuja, Nanak – all dared to express ideas which were at variance with the then widely prevalent beliefs, and either reformed religion or set up new sects. But their distinguishing trait was that they had something positive to offer, and did not merely indulge in destructive criticism of existent beliefs.

Generally, liberal and progressive opinion all over the world is against attacks on freedom of expression, especially artistic expression. It is averred that a prudish establishment can hardly be expected to be an arbitrator on art and obscenity. Very few people quarrel with the idea that crude vulgarity and unwonted or pointless violence should not find a place in creative work. However, when artistic expression appears to conflict with conventional morality, liberal thinkers would want informed critical opinion from respected persons in the art to guide the restrictions or any censorship. On the whole, people should be free to see a film or read a book and arrive at their own opinion. By the same yardstick, an artist has a right to express his or her viewpoint which has its own validity.

If authorities bowed to the wishes of each and every group to ban this or that work because it hurt some susceptibility or other, there would come a time when little artistic work would be produced, and that little would be insipid and not worth reading or viewing. Of course, every individual or group has a right to protest if it feels injured and it would be within its right to insist that its views too be aired in a suitable media. But it is wrong to insist that its views alone should be given importance and anything opposing it should not be expressed.

In the debate over free expression and restrictions over it, the champions of freedom tend to be seen as 'broadminded'; the other side is supposed to be full for prudes and bigots. However, let us not forget that a bigot is anyone who clings to the idea that his or her group alone can be the arbiter of taste or can decide what is right and what is wrong. Today, we have bigots on both sides – those who champion the cause of absolute free expression under any and every circumstance irrespective of the audience or its likely impact and those who are equally rigid in the view that has a right to question what is held sacred by the 'believers'.

Both sides seem to think that they alone know the answers, and that these are valid for everyone, everywhere and for all times. What we see today is a sharp polarization of attitudes on any issue, each side fiercely attacking the other as wholly wrong and showing supreme intolerance for any view but its own. There is no place for a viewpoint that is neither uncompromisingly for nor uncompromisingly against an issue. Things are viewed as pure black or pure white, and no place is left for grey where even if opposing views do not exactly meet, they could at least talk to each other.

A call for a liberal outlook is not to be confused with license to legitimise any and every point of view – one must guard against fascism and racial and communal ideals on which compromise must be avoided. But even if we cherish certain ideas, and some things are basic to our identity, should we simply be debarred from questioning them? We may love and cherish our parents and friends, but in case they quarrel with others, would it be wrong to want to hear the other's point of view? It need not mean condemning our parents or friends. Similarly, we can raise questions about the limits of concepts like secularism and democracy even while not invalidating them. But when we raise those questions, need the language and tone be acrimonious – the language of combat, rude and offensive?

In an environment of liberal tolerance, there would be freedom of expression for all points of view and room enough for dissent, whether held by fanatics, intellectuals or ordinary man in the street. Religious fundamentalism and intellectual fundamentalism are both examples of rigidity which hamper a healthy exchange of views and ideas. Freedom of expression should ordinarily be circumscribed by self-restraint, just as freedom of movement does not allow one to deliberately step on another's toes. There are times when good sense requires freedom of expression to be checked, even if it goes against the grain of liberal thinking. In a situation where communal elements are waiting for the smallest provocation to set the country aflame, perhaps, artistic criteria and the principle of letting people judge for themselves have sometimes to be set aside.

The prevailing cultural and moral ethos do exercise a restraint on freedom of expression, though one may question whether such restraint is justified. However, for freedom of expression to flourish and contribute towards the improvement of human beings and their milieu and society, there is a need for establishing "competing truths" – for truth has many equally valid facets – but for "open-ended and flexible" conversation. And freedom of expression must be exercised with caution, keeping in mind others' sensitivities, as well as the possibility of vested interests and rabble-rousers taking advantage of the situation. Or the precious freedom may be lost to all of us through misuse and abuse by those very persons and means that are eager to emphasise its importance. The rights and wrongs of free expression are not absolute; what may be right today, or wrong, may not be the same tomorrow. Perspectives change, social values change, free expression of ideas can change those values, and one can only hope the change is for the better.

49

STUDY PRESSURE ON CHILDREN

If there is a question to someone that, "Are you ready to marry off your daughter before she turns eighteen?" The answer will be 'No', because it is not legal and she is not physically and mentally prepared for it." But if there is a question, that "Are you ready to send your daughter to school before she is physically and mentally prepared to start serious studies?" — most of the parents will answer "yes, no issue in it."

It is that time of the year again when we find parents leaving no stone unturned to get their child admitted to the so-called 'top-notch' schools even if it means goading three-years-old cramming irrelevant bits of information for school admission interviews.

However, it is only the lesser evil. Another very harmful practice is going on rampantly in school admissions – schools are admitting underage children to higher classes. This is not even discussed openly as the parents are only very happy to cooperate, unaware of the damages this can cause to the child's overall development. In most of the schools there is a cut off date for admission at the entry level, say, September 30, to count the age of the child. By this date the child should have attained three years of age. This means who are not yet three will not be admitted that year even if they are younger only by a week or even a day. On the sly, schools are admitting such kids too through an indirect route by not admitting that year to the entry level class but taking them in the next higher class next year.

For example, the child can get into nursery without having studied in pre-nursery. Parents are happy because they have saved on the school fees of whole one year and they think the child has saved one year. Schools are happy because they have admitted more children without burdening their entry-level class and without breaking the rule of admitting less than a three-year-old child. The only loser is the child struggling hard to be at par with other kids of his class, who are now well-versed in the basics of alphabet or numbers having practised them for full one year in the previous class.

This focus on teaching 3 to 4-year-olds has become a thing of the past in most of the developed countries where regulations regarding age of the child at school entry level of 6-8 years are strictly enforced. It is a well-researched fact that the child's brain is yet to make the neural connections at this age, which will anatomically enable him to develop the skills and concepts needed to learn. Before a certain age, their hand muscles are not developed to perform fine motor skills. However, in our schools, if we have a casual look at the syllabus of kindergarten, one will be surprised to find that it includes lists of 20 each names of animals, birds, flowers, body parts, modes of transport, days of weeks, months of the year, five-six lines compositions, opposite words, counting in numbers and figures, etc. The child has to mug up all these lists. We as parents and teachers are totally oblivious of the danger that we are putting our children in arduous situation.

What will this underage child do in the classroom? When the child is not able to pick up things as fast as his classmates, he feels like a failure. A child cannot differentiate between effort and reality. When they try hard to learn and fail, they conclude that they are good for nothing and can never accomplish anything. They feel depressed, stressful, lose confidence, resort to cheating, start hating schools and give up on learning, and subsequently give up on their own selves. Thus, the seeds of a problem child and a problem adult have been successfully sown.

In our hurry to give the children a head start in life, we are on the contrary making them handicapped for life emotionally and mentally. By forcing them to read and write in spite of their physical and mental ability, we are breaking their spirit. How many children need to suffer before parents and teachers consider this issue serious enough to be examined and pursued with urgency?

The education system must be systematic, motivating and value additive to students, and convenient and economical for implementation to administration. The success of the education system is quite dependent on sub-modules of teaching scheme. Therefore, the issue should be properly addressed.

50

WHY BAN ENGLISH?

With its 22 officially recognised languages and more than 1,650 languages and dialects, India is, indeed, a unique country. However, while being culturally integrated, the country is nevertheless not united linguistically. English seems to qualify as the only language which has the potential to bind the states. But it is easier said than done. Relentless attacks have been carried out, chiefly by politicians, on the English language and its status in India.

The Hindi-speaking belt is against the use of English primarily due to its being a symbol of British imperialism. While politicians are doing their best to promote Hindi, this so-called Hindi expansionism has met with stiff resistance in the southern states. English-speaking Indians have been accused of using an elitist language, of having alienated themselves from their traditions and roots, and of being west-oriented.

The fact though remains that after Hindi, which is spoken by almost 40 per cent Indian population, the dominant language is English. No regional language can claim even 10 per cent of the Indian population as being its users. English has at least 10 per cent users. Even the number of English dailies and newspapers published in India is second only to Hindi newspapers and dailies. The English-speaking population can boast of the highest literacy rate. The newly emerged and affluent middle class, which is almost 200 million strong, has unabashedly adopted English as its language. Thomas Macaulay's proposal of a class of interpreters between the then British Government and the Indian people resulted in the birth of a privileged class of Indians.

One of the prime reasons of opposition to English has been the authoritative positions occupied in educational institutions, the bureaucracy, the judiciary and the media by those privileged enough to get 'English medium' education. This elite group is increasingly emerging as the determinant group. Synonymous with success and material well-being, the English-speaking Indians are determining the lifestyles and social values. Anyone, be it the politician, bureaucrat or the cultural elite, wanting to reach the national audience automatically turns to English as the medium. English-speaking professionals are also increasingly in demand and with the entry of the multinationals and BPOs in the corporate sector, they have literally the whole world at their feet.

But the opposition is not just one of hate. The English-speaking Indians are rightly criticized in many cases for building up a mythical image of being more modern, cosmopolitan, educated and cultured on ground of their knowledge of English. It will not be surprising if many of them actually turn out to be narrow-minded, communal and conservative. Dominance of English in the judiciary has also been severely criticized for being an impediment in imparting justice to the poor and the deprived. Thankfully, this trend is getting reversed with more and more district courts adopting regional languages for hearing cases and delivering judgements.

At the same time, the importance of English is undeniable with increasingly English being a medium of communication in different parts of the world. English has emerged as the official language of as many as 45 countries. Almost one-third of the world's population has adopted English as its official language. Most of the scientific research is published in English. More than half of all business transactions in Europe are conducted in English. To keep abreast of scientific, technological and economic trends, English is a necessity.

The emerging trend of Indians writing in English has also been severely criticized with the charge that genuine literature can only come to expression in the writer's mother tongue. But in many cases, the concept of a mother tongue has become debatable. Different generations often have different languages. Most Indians invariably learn two or even three languages simultaneously. Often one of these three languages is English.

There is no denying the fact that India is a multi-lingual country. No state in India can claim to have a population speaking only one language. It is probably still the association of English with the colonizers which is the main problem in the acceptance of English. But English is no longer a language being used by Indians in the service of a foreign nation. On the contrary, English has given Indians access to the global community as well as mobility within India. Many regional writers have often shown preference for another regional language than their own mother tongue and consequently adopted it for their expression. English should thus also be acceptable as a language of creativity.

It is necessary to expose unwarranted flagellation of English by politicians for popularity and propaganda. People with English medium education have been accused of corruption and dishonesty by certain politicians. In reality their own children are studying in English-medium schools. Such hypocrisy should be brought to light so that it does not lead people astray.

Scientific and anthropological research has revealed that human beings can easily learn more than one language. The furore over multilingualism is thus baseless. In the circumstances, is there any need for Indian languages to fight English? Bilingualism, even multilingualism, is nothing new for Indians. The Indian languages are rich, culturally strong enough to survive along with English. The need of the hour is that on the one hand, the English-speaking elite should give up their arrogance and on the other hand, the regional Indian language-speaking elite should abandon their inferiority complex and rise above cultural chauvinism.

51

WORLD CIVILISATION TODAY

Civilisation basically connotes 'culture' and 'refinement', the qualities of head and heart of man, which brought him above the state of primitive man. Love, charity, spirit and sacrifice, regard for truth and honesty as well as a sense of responsibility to the State and society are some of the essential characteristics of a civilised person in modern society. It is worthwhile to compare these characteristics of the modern age with those of earlier ages. The modern civilisation attaches great importance to the material comforts of life which were absent in the older civilisation. The term, 'material comforts of life' implies good food, sound health, good clothing, nice shelter, nice company, a high standard of living as well as peace and security with the aid of scientific amenities. Today, these things are considered more important than the aspects related to spiritual pursuits which were intended to lead to the peace and happiness of the soul.

In modern civilisation, the pursuit of material wealth, rather than spiritual, has become an all-engrossing, all-embracing pursuit. Wordsworth called this state of affairs that was fast gripping industrial England in the nineteenth century in his beautiful sonnet "The world is too much". According to him, material wealth is a 'sordid boon' to which we have given 'our hearts away'. 'Earning and spending' have become the all-important occupations of man. Nevertheless, this pursuit of material values of life is considered a healthy activity that leads to the promotion of industries and employment. It leads to the general increase in the national dividend and utilisation of the resources of a country for satisfaction of the various requirements of its citizens. This very 'sordid' pursuit goes to provide for employment to workmen, facilities to businessmen for investment and expansion of productive activities and thereby revenue to the State. In modern civilisation, a factory giving employment to a few thousand people is considered to be a wiser national investment than the setting up of a poor house which may provide merely food and shelter to an equal number. Nehru was right when he called the giant projects taken up for the improvement of living conditions in the post-Independence India as our 'modern temples'. Such 'temples' today provide constructive employment to all able-bodied workers thereby adding to the national resources and exchequer.

The next important characteristic of modern civilisation is the importance given to one's appearance. A person is judged by the clothes he wears, his general demeanour and the connection he has rather than by the intrinsic qualities he may possess. The advanced Western nations have contributed to the increase in promiscuity in the modern society.

We can notice quite a few other characteristics of modern civilisation in the context of our society. Education has come to play a significant role in a person's life; it is no longer the domain of the privileged few. Opportunities are offered to every individual to educate himself and his progeny as ignorance and illiteracy have had their sway over the masses for centuries and their evil effects are too well-known to be bypassed. Elementary education is provided free of cost to all those who are wiling to benefit. Community Health Schemes have added to the general health and well-being of the masses. The death-rate in India today is much lower than what it was before Independence. Hence, we face the problem of population explosion, but this in turn is sought to be cured through Family Planning.

Independence and the advent of modern scientific needs and achievements have contributed to the build-up of higher moral and patriotic character. The people are now conscious of their freedom and are enlarging their outlook by going out of their narrow bounds of caste, creed, religion and community. Time is not far off when national barriers will be a hindrance to the free and creative thinking of the modern man and we shall, indeed, be able to have a wider, more varied and exciting international outlook. There is an urgency in the common man today which impels him to take an active interest in the happenings around him. International co-operation and co-existence is being practised all around. The advanced nations are fast coming to the rescue of their less fortunate brethren, thus fostering common global ties. Modem civilisation has given an impetus to a feeling of fellow sympathy and brotherhood among the various peoples.

With the broadening of outlook, modern civilisation has strengthened the bonds of nationalism and internationalism at the expense of local or family ties. The old joint-family system is giving way. Relationships, except when they are from the direct line, are loosening their grip. The family is now narrowing down and it includes only man, wife and their children. Family planning has led to the thinning of the family, and very seldom do modern parents have more than two or three children, compared to the average of eight to ten children per family a few decades ago. The joint family, that housed together a hundred members within the four walls of a single house and stood firm like a rock against various shocks and setbacks, has been broken up into a number of small families living separately, generally, from hand to mouth and with no support or protection against misfortunes or distress or illness from the members. The solid and strong personalities, which the joint family system produced, are rare to be seen in the modern society, where the head of the small family unit has to fight his way singly, devoid of the strong protection of the united or a large joint family.

Despite these handicaps, modern civilisation may be considered superior to, and better than, the older civilisation in many ways. Even though there is a trend towards individualism, the collective feelings of community, nation and the world as a whole have greatly developed and there is now a great sense of unity. Science and technology have brought human beings together by speedy means of transport and communication, thereby bringing the minds and thinking of human beings closer. Whereas man has gained individual freedom, his common existence has been bound strongly with other human beings. If mankind is able to remove ignorance, illiteracy, want, inequality and injustice, it can also prevent the scourage of future wars, modern civilisation could be something to be proud of. We would have achieved a miracle that has been man's ideal since the millennium. Although India's scientific progress is not yet up to the mark, it can be safely predicted that India is now taking its legitimate place among civilised nations and as one of the important states of the world.

52

SCIENCE AND RELIGION

One of the secrets of man's ascendancy has been his cohesion; he could not have survived without his tribe and the tribe in turn smoothened and perpetuated itself through intrinsic bonds. This gave rise to immense subjective power of the laws that guaranteed cohesion. Nobel Prize-winner biologist Jacques Monod has postulated that such social bonds over vast stretches of time "must have influenced the genetic evolution of the innate categories of the human brain." This evolution "must not only have facilitated acceptance of the tribal law, but created the need for the mystical explanation which gave it a foundation and sovereignty." It is this search for explanation, the profound disquiet which forces us to search for the meaning of existence. It has, created all myths, all religions, all philosophies and science itself.

Thus, science and religion have a common origin in the process of civilisation which distinguished man from the apes. Science enabled man to practise and propagate religion, and religion gave him the conditions, including cohesion, necessary for pursuit of science.

In ancient civilisations, scientific thought flourished hand in glove with religious activities. Discoveries were considered revelations and the scientific knowledge represented the greatness of God. In ancient India scientific enquiry was provoked by the sages themselves. Rishi Charka (2nd century BC) made an exposition of the Ayurveda, the science of causes, symptoms and cures of diseases. Aryabhata (476-499 AD), the Indian astronomer who propounded the revolutionary theory that the earth is round and rotates about its axis, mused that his knowledge owed itself to the grace of God. Arabic mathematician Al Beruni insisted that his experimental work was subject to the moral principles of Islam.

The Greeks, about 2000 years ago, are credited with initiation of systematic investigations and application of Aristotelian logic in their endeavour to understand the universe. These methods gained momentum throughout the middle ages, but reason played subservient to the orthodox religion. Whatever scientific knowledge was gained by man during this period was interpreted in the praise of God. Thus, when in 1543, Vesalius, a Belgian physician, published a book on human anatomy, based on dissections and personal observations, he was driven to wonder at the "handiwork of the Almighty, by means of which the blood flows from the right into the left ventricle through passages that escape human vision." Pursuers of science also avoided topics that might impinge on the realms of religion. For example, in 15th and 16th century scientists totally denied the existence of sex in plants since even a mention of it was considered inappropriate and obscene.

It was under such circumstances prevailing during the early sixteenth century that the Polish-German mathematician and astronomer Copernicus, earned the wrath of society by stating that the earth is not the centre around which the sun, the planets and the stars revolve. This was a serious challenge to cosmological teachings of the medieval church. Religious bigots were further enraged when the double motion of earth (a daily rotation on its own axis and an annual revolution round the sun) was put forth as explanation for the diurnal and annual, were till then considered handiwork of the heavens. A few years later the Italian astronomer Galileo discovered that the planet Jupiter had satellites revolving around it and argued that the sun, and not the earth, was the centre of the solar system. The scientific establishment and the Roman Catholic Church both promptly denounced these findings as "false and opposed to the holy scriptures". Galileo was tortured and forced to retreat in 1633 by pronouncing that all his findings, which were contrary to the holy scriptures, were erroneous and based on hearsay. The Pope even forced closure of a formal academy started by his students in 1656.

Far from slowing down the march of science, the religious fundamentalism of medieval Europe seems to have provided the right setting for the growth of modern science. Hereafter, the divergence between religion and science became sharp and the conflict gradually snowballed into a two-sided 'warfare'. When Newton propounded his laws of attraction of gravity, Leibnitz described them as "subversive of nature, and irreverentiality of revealed religion." Newton held that the majestic works of nature not only attested to his existence but also spoke of his glory. However, he rejected the possibility of control of day-to-day events by God. In 1796, the Scottish naturalist James Hutton adopted the Newtonian view that God always acted through natural laws and dismissed the theory of repeated divine control of events as "undemonstrable, speculative and unnecessary".

In early nineteenth century, Jean Baptiste Lamarck, a French naturalist postulated that the simplest living things have given rise to all others. Charles Darwin meticulously assembled the evidence for evolution and described the principles of natural selection in his *Origin of Species*, published in 1859. The evolutionary theory revealed the earth in terms of enormous antiquity and gradual, continuous change in which the existing planets and animals, including man, have slowly evolved from previously living forms. This directly contradicted the orthodox who believed that the earth was only 6000 years old. The Theory of Genesis states that all basic types of living things, including man, were created by God during a creation week. So careful was Darwin in publishing his book that he could not desist from referring to the 'Creator' in order to please the clergy. Fear and tension reduced him to a physical and mental wreck and it was left to his scientific theory. In a dramatic debate, Bishop Samuel Wilberforce upholding Genesis asked T.H. Huxley, who was enthusiastically defending evolution, whether it was through his grandfather or his grandmother that he claimed descent from ape. Much later, when the theory had gained acceptance, Darwin admitted that he was an orthodox believer himself when young, but disbelief had gradually crept over him "at a slow rate, but was at last complete."

Without the precedence of Copernicus and Galileo, Darwin would have been perhaps helpless in the organic world. However, his work created a far greater impact on the new scientific method upon life, mind and culture. This is largely because Darwin brought a philosophy of transition of plant and animal kingdoms. He said of the species what Galileo had said of the earth and in a comparable manner laid the organic world open to enquiry and explanations. These evolutionary concepts had an unlimited effect on the scientific and academic communities in the subsequent years. In fact, in 1882, Friedrich Nietzsche, an eccentric philosopher, could gather the courage to pronounce that "God is dead". As the twentieth century began, Sigmund Freud, the pioneer of modern psychology, reiterated God's irrelevance with the growth of urbanised, industrialised society. Hux refused to find solace in relationship even when drowned in grief over the death of his son.

The onset of two world wars hastened the speed of scientific progress. After the Second World War there has not only been a build-up of arsenals and nuclear stockpiles, but also a pick-up in the technological innovations which have changed the style and substance of life. As Warren Weavers puts it, science and technology ensure that "we are warmed and cooled, clothed and fed, protected, cured, transported and entertained." However, it is equally apparent that the religious fervour is far from declining. Formal religion is becoming more and more popular, as indicated by increasing attendance in churches, mosques and temples. Even religious fanaticism raises its ugly head again and again, but not against science any more. Is the conflict resolved, then?

The relationship of science and religion today is like that of a divorced couple. They hardly interact or pose any threat to each other's weaknesses and assets. Now a man can be a devout Christian, Hindu or a Muslim and an evolutionist at the same time. Millions, belonging to all religions, successfully juxtapose independent scientific and spiritual viewpoints.

Some even regard science as a purgatory of religion, constantly weeding out that which is wrong. Nevertheless, the controversy that once engulfed society still rages in individuals' minds, particularly those of the scientists.

The dispute whether or not there is a God is now to be resolved at personal level. It is interesting to note that scientists as a group hardly react to religious ideologies, although as individuals they may hold strong religious opinions.

Ironically, in USA there still exists a church lobby which seeks legal intervention to exclude study of evolution in American schools. Having lost at the trial in 1925, the fundamentalists forced several publishers to omit evolution from the school textbooks. A few months before the 100th death anniversary of Darwin in 1982, the fundamentalists raked up the controversy again — this time at Arkansas demanding equal treatment to the evolutionist or creationist viewpoint. However, the Federal Judge ruled it unconstitutional as it would force biology teachers into religion in science classroom. It is equally revealing that the more recent resistance of religious groups of scientific advancements such as heart transplants, test-tube babies and gene splicing has been lukewarm and only symbolical.

It is interesting to note how modern scientists as individuals respond to religion and pray to God. Einstein believed in Spinoza's God, "who reveals himself in the harmony of all beings," and not in a God who concerns himself with the fate and actions of man. India-born Nobel Prize winner in Physics Professor Chandrashekhar Raman was an atheist.

Dr. Har Gobind Khorana, on a visit to New Delhi in October, 1974, a few years after he won the Nobel Prize for unravelling the genetic code that laid the basis for synthesis of 'life in test tube', said that "we all believe in God of some or the other kind." He said, "We need God to sustain us." Interestingly, these sentiments are shared by a large number of Indian scientists who have distinguished themselves in the West. Thus, a scientist can also be religious and believe in God.

On the other hand, Western religious leaders generally opine that the scientific approach has depreciated man. In the words of Francis Gerald Endley: "Astronomy proclaims his microscopic size, biology claims that man had animals at least for first cousins in evolutionary series and chemistry affirms that he is a compound of hydrogen, oxygen, carbon and other elements." In his opinion, "If we add to the theoretical degradation of science the fact that it has supplied the weapons whereby the human race can be liquidated, the indignity is complete."

Several philosophers have also emphasized that science is inadequate as a way of life. It cannot give a truly meaningful explanation of any subject of inquiry. Science is unable to answer the mind's question 'why', which is quite as legitimate as 'what' and 'how'. This is because it eschews both value and causation.

53

MAN AS A RATIONAL ANIMAL!

The 'open-endedness' of man is the wonderful result of the specifically human powers of self-awareness which, as distinct from the powers of life and consciousness, have nothing automatic or mechanical about them. The powers of self-awareness are, essentially, a limitless potentiality not just an actuality. They have to be developed and realised by each individual, if he is to become truly human, that is to say, a person.

A simple inspection of the four great levels of being has led to the recognition of the four elements — matter, life, consciousness and self-awareness. It is this recognition that matters, not the precise association of the four elements with the level of being.

Life is either present or absent — there cannot be a half-presence — and the same goes for consciousness and self-awareness. Difficulties of identification are often exacerbated by the fact that the lower level tends to produce a kind of mimicry or counterfeit of the higher, just as an animated puppet can at times be mistaken for a living person, or a two-dimensional picture can look like three-dimensional reality. But neither the difficulties of identification and demarcation nor the possibilities of deception and error, can be used as arguments against the existence of the four great levels of being, exhibiting the four 'elements', four irreducible mysteries. The progressive movement from passivity to activity, which we observe when reviewing the four levels of being, is indeed striking, but it is not complete. An interesting and instructive aspect of the progression from passivity to activity is the change in the origination of movement.

While at the animal level the motivating cause has to be physically present to be effective, at the level of man there is no such need. The power of self-awareness adds for him another possibility of the origination of movement — will, that is the power to move and act even when there is no physical compulsion, no physical stimulus and no motivating force actually present. The progression from passivity to activity is similar and closely related to the progression from necessity to freedom.

Inner space is created by the powers of life, consciousness and self-awareness; but we have direct and personal experience only of our own 'inner space' and the freedom it affords us. Close observation discloses that most of us, most of the time, behave and act mechanically like a machine. The specifically human power of self-awareness is asleep, and the human being, like an animal, acts, more or less intelligently, solely in response to outside influences. Only when a man makes use of his power of self-awareness, does he attain to the level of a person, to the level of freedom. At that moment he is living, not being lived. There is freedom. There are still numerous forces of necessity, accumulated in the past, which determine his actions; but a small dent is being made, a tiny change of direction is being introduced.

To ask whether the human being has freedom, is like asking whether man is a millionaire. He is not, but can become a millionaire. He can make it his aim to become rich; similarly, he can make it his aim to become free. In his "inner space" he can develop a centre of strength so that the power of his freedom exceeds that of his necessity. It is possible to imagine a perfect being who is always and invariably exercising his power of self-awareness, which is the power of freedom, to the fullest degree, unmoved by any necessity. This would be a Divine Being, an Almighty and sovereign power, a perfect unity. There is, then, a marked and unmistakable progression towards integration.

Man has obviously much more inner unity than any being below him, although integration, as modern psychology recognises, is not guaranteed to him at birth and remains one of his major tasks. As biological system, he is most harmoniously integrated; on the mental plane, integration is less perfect but is capable of considerable improvement through schooling. As a person, however, a being with the power of self-awareness, he is generally so poorly integrated, that he experiences himself as an assembly to many different personalities.

Integration means the creation of an inner unity, a centre of strength and freedom, so that the being ceases to be a mere object, acted upon by outside forces, and becomes a subject, acting from its own 'inner space' into the space outside itself.

The degree of integration, of inner coherence and strength, is closely related to the kind of 'world' that exists for beings at different levels. Inanimate matter has no 'world'. Its total passivity is equivalent to the total emptiness of its world. A plant has a 'world' of its own — a bit of soil, water, air, light and possibly other influence of 'world' limited to its modest biological needs. The world of any one of the higher animals is comparably greater and richer, although still mainly determined by biological needs, as modern animal psychology studies have amply demonstrated. But there is also something more like curiosity which enlarges the animal's world beyond the narrow biological confines.

The world of man, again is comparably greater and richer; indeed, it is asserted in traditional philosophy that man is capable of bringing the whole universe into his experience. What he will actually grasp depends on each person's own level of being. The 'higher' the person, the greater and richer is his or her world. A person, for instance, entirely fixed in the philosophy of materialistism, denying the reality of the 'invisibles' and confining his attention solely to what can be counted, measured and weighed, lives in a very poor world, so poor that he will experience it as a meaningless wasteland unfit for human habitation.

54

NATIONALISM VS. INTERNATIONALISM

According to Carleton, a nation is "any group of persons who speak a common language, who cherish common historical traditions and who constitute or think they constitute a distinct cultural society in which among other factors, religion and politics may have played important though not necessarily continuous roles."

Nationality is somewhat different from a nation. 'Nation' implies political independence; while 'nationality' is a non-political concept. A nationality has no territorial limitations. It can exist in different sovereign states or countries. It carries a feeling of psychological affinities and cultural homogeneity. Nationality means a group of people who are emotionally and psychologically bound together by common historical ties. Lord Bryce defines nationality as "a population held together by certain ties, as for example, language and literature, ideas, customs and traditions, in such a way as to feel in itself a coherent unity distinct from other populations similarly held together by like ties of their own." The subjective sentiments and feelings which create unity are common between a nation and a nationality; however, a nation has the characteristics of political unity and sovereignty, which are not essential in a nationality. A nationality may develop into a nation as and when it acquires sovereignty in a given area. A nationality has an individuality of its own and may demand the right of self-determination if it feels confident of its strong national sentiments and carries a special spirit of oneness, or common consciousness or unity founded on political, historical, racial, religious, linguistic and other factors that go to make a State.

The term nationalism is different for both nation and nationality. Nationalism is the spiritual force which holds a nation in a defined territory together for the maintenance of its general and special rights against arbitrary powers within the State and preservation of its independence against aggression from outside. It implies spirit of unity or common consciousness among the people which brings and holds them together, and which makes them achieve common objectives or suffer and even sacrifice their lives in the interests of security of the nation. Nationalism further means a man's spiritual attachment to one's country. People who carry the feeling of nationalism are deeply attached to their nation in the same way as they may be attached to their religion. The country is frequently addressed and loved as 'motherland' or 'fatherland'.

The factors which help the growth of nationalism may be common geographical, historical, political, cultural, racial, religious, economic and linguistic interests which contribute to development and which create, promote and sustain national feelings. The most important factor of national feeling is geographical unity. It is this unity which exhibits and promotes the pride of possession of a common land, which may be worshipped as a 'motherland' or 'fatherland'. Without a sense of pride for a coveted 'homeland', it becomes difficult to develop real national feelings. Geographical unity arouses common interests in many walks of national life — economic, political, social, cultural and educational. These problems open up new variegated areas of mutual understanding and co-operation among the people. People who live together on a common land for a considerably long period devise new ways of living, working and developing common aims, ideals and aspirations.

One significant factor that generates, promotes and vitalises smoother national feeling, is the common historical tradition of the people on "memories of suffering endured, and victories won in common, expressed in songs and legends, in the dear names of great personalities that seem to embody in themselves the character and ideals of the nation, in the names also of sacred places wherein national memory is enshrined."

Nationalism has also common cultural traits signifying unity of ideas and ideals. Unity of culture is based on common customs and traditions, common manners and folklore and common tastes in art and literature. The overall impact is one of a certain dominant view with its common rights and responsibilities to usher in a better standard of life for the fellow citizens.

Common race is also a unifying force. It binds the hearts of the people owing to common ancestry.

It helps greatly in promoting and sustaining the national spirit. Among many nationalities like the Jews, the Poles and the Irish, religion has been the mainspring of national survival. But in modern States toleration of many religions prevails as religious fanaticism very often negates the growth of nationalism. Religious beliefs have become a personal affair. In the USA, Russia, India and Britain, it hardly touches the national life of the people. In India, secularisation of nationality is letting people enjoy their respective religious beliefs and practices without hindrance.

Common economic interest is the most potent factor contributing to the promotion of nationalism. The desire to raise the standard of living and to make life comfortable, interesting and useful, enables the citizens, without consideration of race, caste, creed or religion to help the State in improving the economy of the country in all directions. Looking after his personal economic interests, each individual strives his best to increase production in agriculture and industry and facilitate trade and commerce. Members of varying religious denominations work shoulder to shoulder to fulfil their common economic interests. This greatly helps in binding the people together in the web of nationalism.

Language also plays a vital role in binding people together and creating consciousness among them as a nation. A common language enables the people to project common ideals, sentiments and feelings, set up the common standards of morality, manners and justice and to conserve historical traditions so as to generate a common national psychology.

Nationalism is conceived as a positive feature because of the following reasons:

(a) It fosters love for one's own motherland or fatherland.
(b) It removes the sense of selfishness, narrowness. The nation thus makes progress in every direction.
(c) It inspires deeds of heroism and sacrifice among the people for the achievement of common ideals.
(d) It fosters a healthy spirit of fellow-feeling among people and tends to develop in them a strong desire to improve their own lot and that of their brethren living in the country.
(e) It helps to preserve 'unity amidst diversity' by integrating diverse elements into a common nation through processes of assimilation.
(f) It enables the people to present a united front at the time of need to defend national sovereignty.

There is also a negative side to nationalism. It becomes occasionally visible with its ugly manifestations, when it takes the form of 'aggressive nationalism'. Aggressive nationalism is never healthy as it generates intolerance and hatred for other nations. There is evidence in history to show that it was the aggressive national spirit among the French and the Germans which was responsible for frequent wars between the two nations. Aggressive nationalism is always a threat to the welfare of other nations.

We may sum up the concept of nationalism with Alfred De Grazia's observation: "Nationalism combines love of country and suspiciousness of foreigners. Love of country comes from shared values, and suspiciousness of foreigners comes from the belief that foreigners do not share such values in the same strength. The first shared value is the love of familiar places — the neighbourhood, the land, the homes, the valleys and the mountains, all of the surroundings that one loves because they have been part of oneself from infancy."

It is the process of harmonization and unification of various structural components of the nation. Integration involves acceptance of certain values by most sections of the population as common, which different institutions and agencies in the society tend to preserve and promote.

The objective of integration is maintenance of a harmonious and active relationship between these structural components. It always keeps the nation going and also imparts a meaning and purpose to the life of the individuals so that they feel conscious of being a part of a comprehensible and harmonious national existence. Family sanction, sex relations, care of the children, protection and education and recreation of family members, adherence to religious institutions, all help to develop a sense of relationship with spiritual tones and devotion to national concepts.

Modern nations are open to different races, sects, tribes and beliefs. They provide for secularisation of different groups and their ultimate integration.

Integration is the consequence of differentiation and specialisation. Modern states have unity in diversity — a term which Jawaharlal Nehru used with reference to India.

Now let us compare nationalism with internationalism.

Goldsmith defines internationalism as the feeling that an individual carries of not only being a citizen of his State but also that of the whole universe. Internationalism is thus a concept which demands of the various nations of the world to give up their conflicting and antagonistic separate nationalist ambitions and designs, and co-operate with one another in all fields of activity, thereby to preserve peace in the world. Internationalism demands that no nation in the world should be content with its own good alone but should aim at a policy of 'live and help others to live'. It should be the policy of every nation to co-ordinate its own good with that of others. Our love should not be restricted to the territorial borders of the State of which we are members, but should be so extended as to embrace the whole world.

There is nothing inconsistent if an individual loves his motherland or fatherland and also loves the whole of mankind. In fact, the people of his own country constitute only a part of mankind. Therefore, love of one's own nation does not at all mean hatred for other nations. While each nation and its citizens strive for coming up to advancement in social and economic fields, at the same time there is no reason to feel jealous of other nations if they progress in the same direction at the same or better speed.

Sound nationalism at the present stage of human development at least, is in many ways a prelude to sound internationalism. A great scholar has rightly put it: "Nationality is the necessary link between man and humanity."

Internationalism seeks to reconcile national interests with the larger interests of other peoples. If nations carry a balanced outlook and a healthy regard for the rights and interests of other peoples, there would grow fitful international co-operation. Internationalism is a system of thought designed to promote peaceful co-operation.

Whatever promotes intercourse between various peoples is a contribution to internationalism. Intermittent wars occasionally shake the idea and often put the clock back.

The organisation of fruitful international co-operation requires firstly the foundation of a common set of principles of harmonising and balancing of diverse national interests. The feeling of international co-operation needs to be translated into institutional framework like that of the United Nations. It is only by working together that suspicion and distrust can be overcome and an atmosphere of mutual understanding created.

Humanity seems to be moving towards a world confederation. But the journey is slow and steady. It is only by removing causes of tension between nations that the ways and means of creating some sort of a world federation can be explored.

Nationalism and internationalism used to be considered as conflicting concepts in traditional politics but modern political scientists regard them as mutually compatible and complementary concepts.

55

SOCIETY, INDIVIDUAL AND THE STATE

Society is an ever-changing complex system. It is the web of social relationships. According to Maclver and Page, "Society is a system of usages and procedures, of authority and mutual aid, and many groupings and divisions of control of human behaviour and of liberties."

Let us think of some other features of society. Society exists only where social beings behave with each other in ways determined by their recognition of each other. Society also involves likenesses and differences. It is not only confined to men but also to animals. Thus, wherever there is likeness (or difference), there is society. Aristotle once said: "Man is a social animal." He further said that the person incapable of sharing a common life is "either a beast or a god." For normal humanity, one must have social relationships to make life worth living.

However, the use of the world society, when applied to a limited area or locality, has come to be known as a combination of social beings tied by a web of relationships of one kind or the other. In this sense, society is a group of people organised for the realisation of certain common objectives — political, economic, religious, educational, etc. The aim of every individual is to enrich his life but he is incapable of realising his best self without the cooperation of other citizens. As worker, for instance, left to himself cannot succeed in obtaining from the employer better conditions of service whereas if he organises himself with other workers into a trade union, he can increase his bargaining power. Therefore, a group of people generally organise themselves into various private associations such as the trade unions, religious organisations, etc. in order to achieve common objectives.

Society is different from the State, as the State is one of the institutions of society. The State is a group of people organised firstly for law and order and then for other common activities. Originally, State was brought into existence, in the language of Aristotle, for the sake of life and it was allowed to continue its existence for the sake of better life. Therefore, in the beginning it was essentially a police State, the essential function of which was to maintain law and order and to protect the territory from external aggression. Society, therefore, may be considered to be genus (a large entity) and State may be considered to be a species (a smaller entity).

Since very early times, man is known to have lived in society. Even when he was not so civilised, he lived in the company of his fellow beings whether his society started with his family tribe, group or a combination of them.

Plato said that society is essential for life, while Aristotle improved on this expression by saying that society is essential for good life. Without society, it is impossible for humans to have the basic necessities like food, clothing and shelter. Society was needed even by the primitive people. Their dependence on society went on gradually increasing with time so that they, in due course, gave up their nomadic life and started living a family life.

State is a political institution of society that looks after the material and spiritual interests of its individuals. Each nation today adopts what is called a 'constitution' for its nationals. Sometimes called the Basic Law of Society, the constitution describes the fundamental responsibilities of the State with regard to the functioning of the society as a whole. It establishes the form of governments at the centre, in the regions, districts and villages, in the country for its governance. It also prescribes the outlines of power and privileges of different wings (executive, legislature and judiciary) of the government together with the mutual relationships among them. It also enumerates the basic objectives which shall govern the formulation of policies and programmes of the State for the good of the individuals. The constitution also lays down the basic rules to regulate the behaviour of individuals among themselves and towards the State and society.

These rules very often put limitations on the liberty of the individual so as to prevent him from harming the interests of other individuals for the selfish gain either by exploitation, economic or otherwise, or causing material or physical injury to others.

In return for this restraint on his liberty, the State gives to the individual numerous facilities of citizenship. These facilities include the right to vote and elect political leaders at different levels, enjoy the social benefits of corporate living like the amenities of cheap drinking water, street sanitation, electricity, roads, public transportation, security of life, medical care, etc. and the right to individual belongings and also working opportunity.

In recent decades the State has greatly expanded its role to serve its citizens with more and more material and spiritual benefits arising from mutual cooperation. This has made the life of individual, and thereby of societies, more comfortable, interesting and powerful.

In recent societies, the idea of social atomism has come up. According to atomists, a social atom is an indivisible unit of society and the whole society is made up of living organisms.

Maclver has rightly said: "Our essential theoretical understanding of individual and society is understanding of relationship — a relationship involving those processes in constantly changing pattern of social life."

Maclver has also defined society as a system of usages and procedures, of authority and mutual aid, of many groupings and divisions, of control of human behaviour and of liberty. This everchanging complex system is called society. It involves the web of social relationships which always keep changing.

Gidding has defined society as "the union itself, the organisation, the sum of family relations in which associated individuals are bound together."

A society is organised both in its structure and functions. It consists not only in the mutual interactions and inter-relations of individuals but also in the structure formed by these relations. The essential factors which make up a society are:

(i) Without reciprocal awareness there can be no social relationship and, therefore, no society. A social relationship thus rests on consciousness of the kind.

(ii) In early societies kith and kin represented a sense of likeness but in modern societies, the conditions of likeness have broadened out to the principle of community, nationality or the whole world. Human relationships will be impossible without some understanding of each other and that understanding depends on the likeness, which each sees in the other.

Reciprocal recognition also gives rise to differences among members of society. In fact, it is a variation of the sense of likeness. Likeness and difference coexist side by side. If a society were made up of humans all alike and uniform, it will not have strong bonds of socialities. If there were no differences among men, their relationships would be limited and unchanging.

56

LIBERTY IN THE MODERN WORLD

There are two types of obligations for the State to follow from the modern conception of liberty. First, in the competition between individuals and groups engaged in the pursuit of their own interests, the State has to function as an umpire to ensure that no one gets an unfair advantage over others. Secondly, the conditions under which men pursue their goals are always undergoing change, therefore, the rules governing their activities are constantly in need of revision.

No society, that is not stagnant, can expect to escape this manifold process of environmental change and the modification of laws and social conventions in response to it. The second group of functions of the State follows from this fact. It is to ensure that no group in society distorts, with the power of its wealth or numbers, the operation of this process to suit its own interests. The State should, on the contrary, ensure that if the process of change is informed, the spirit of liberty would bear on it.

Finally, liberty is indispensable for social stability in modern times. So long as men believed in the divine origin of temporal power, the absence of liberty did not appear to them as a denial of something to which they were legitimately entitled. However, with the rise of the secular view of life, the moral basis of authoritarianism was undermined for good. A government that now denies liberty to its subjects, even if it be in the name of other values such as social justice, equality and the like, inevitably finds that they soon begin to clamour for both the promised benefits and the liberty they lost as the advance price of the liberty which means not merely a loss of dignity and self-respect but also of the opportunity to fight for the aims for which liberty was sacrificed.

Contrary to the widely prevalent misconception, this does not mean an attitude of *laissez faire* on the part of the State.

Even Mill, whose formulation of the negative concept of liberty still remains the most eloquent, recognised the need for State action "as soon as any part of a person's conduct affects prejudicially the interests of others." All protective legislation, such as the regulation of factory hours and all ennobling legislation, for example, removing untouchability, would be justified under this principle. With the growing concentration of power in fewer and smaller centres as a consequence of the progressive integration of economic life, the obstacles to liberty have become all-pervasive and stronger than in the nineteenth century. State action, therefore, in the interests of liberty, especially of the weaker sections of the society, becomes necessary on a larger scale now than was imagined by Mill.

However, the State itself is a Leviathan, with a tendency to devour those whom it would seek to protect. The problem in the modern world is, thus, not merely that of defining the limits of the authority of the State or of society over the individual as Mill formulated it. It also includes the much more complex task of discovering the types of action that the State ought or ought not to undertake for creating the conditions in which liberty can flourish in a given type of society. It is obvious that what the State may do in England or in the United States without damaging liberty may stifle growth in a less developed society. Equally, it is possible that what the State may safely leave to non-official agencies in an advanced society, may in others have to be done under its own auspices. Again, what may be appropriate for the State to do at one stage of a developing society may cease to be so after a certain level of development has been reached. And yet by that time the policies of the State may have created certain vested interests which could make policy revision extremely difficult, if not altogether impossible, without exacting a heavy price in terms of human and material loss.

That, this is not a mere hypothetical possibility, has been amply demonstrated by the experience of the former Soviet Union and a number of other countries during recent decades. Nor is it very surprising that this should have been so, for the leadership in an underdeveloped society, is itself likely to be culturally and intellectually underdeveloped and, to that extent, incapable of ensuring that the means shall not defeat the end. The task mentioned above, therefore, becomes all the more difficult in so far as it bears on the cultural factors precisely for those societies for which it is desperately important.

This is not to suggest that there is no solution. Indeed, Mill himself enunciated a guiding principle for determining the type of action that government should take. Such action, he says, should foster initiative and permit 'variety of experiments'. For, according to him, the purpose of State action is to enable each experimentalist to benefit by the experiments of others, instead of carrying out experiments on its own. The mischief begins when, instead of calling for the activity and power of individuals and groups, it substitutes its own activity and power for others.

According to the philosophy of the classical school, man is a hierarchy of elements, some noble and the others base. Of the noble ones, reason represents best his higher self, but the lower self represented by his impulses and desires, is always trying to hold it in constraint by blurring his vision of reality. If, therefore, man is to be 'really' free, the removal of external constraints, imposed by nature and social institutions, is not enough. He has also to be freed from the inner constraints that result from the ascendancy of his lower self over his higher self. Unless this is accomplished, the removal of external constraints may, indeed, lead to what Aristotle called 'licence'.

The notion of 'forcing men to be free' follows from this view of man. Once freedom is given a metaphysical meaning, unrelated to the environment in which man lives and exercises his powers of creation, it is easy to think of compelling him to perceive his own real interests, even if the process involves a certain degree of unhappiness for the time being. Ultimately, when his reason has established its sovereignty over his lower self, he will see that the suffering was a necessary price for the 'real' freedom he has attained.

The conception of freedom implicit in the Communist

thought has little place for liberty. It may comprehend security, social justice, economic equality, the opening of careers to talented ones. But of the freedom to think and to express one's thoughts, the freedom to frame the 'plan of our life to suit our own character', of freedom in short, as ordinary men and women understand it all over the world, there is only little in the concept of positive liberty.

Contact with the West and the pressure of economic development have, no doubt, released the forces of modernisation in many of these societies. However, modernity is understood by them mainly in the technological sense. The culturally liberating role of science, illustrated in the philosophical revolution that the West experienced at the beginning of the modern age, is underplayed, if recognised at all, in their educational systems. Consequently, the forces referred to above are too weak to guarantee the steady growth of liberty in these countries in the face of a native authoritarianism buttressed by the modern State with its machinery of control and repression. In the long run, the spread of education and the needs of sophisticated industrial economy may, as suggested by recent Communist experience, compel the government to relax its grip on the life of the people. In the foreseeable future, however, the odds against liberty will continue to be heavy in a majority of the new States.

India appears to be the sole major exception. Here the democratic tradition is very old, though there have been in different parts of the country a number of movements of social reform which drew their inspiration from an incipient renaissance. It is true that the rise of militant nationalism (Tilak), which itself was preceded by a spurt of cultural revivalism (Vivekananda), prevented this renaissance from culminating into a philosophical revolution. Yet the fact that these developments took place in the context of a growing culture contact with the West, through expanding education and participation in the administration, ensured that the process initiated by the work of men like Ram Mohan Roy, Nariman, Phule and Agarkar would not for ever be blocked.

Even when Gandhi came on the scene with his talk of the inner voice and the emphasis on duties rather than rights, his concern for the socially oppressed and the programmes of social reform that he undertook as an integral part of his political work, mitigated to a great extent the obscurantism of his outlook. In the plane of ideas, he confused the issues between tradition and modernity and thereby prevented their crystallisation. But his insistence on the political and cultural enfranchisement of the lowlies of life where the masses would easily understand and respond to its appeal was significant.

The result of the hundred years' evolution concerning the prospects of liberty in India, has thus been rather complex. The old social structure and its philosophical sanctions have been irreparably shaken though they have not yet been replaced by suitable substitutes. However, the establishment of the rule of law, the creation of a secular administration and the progressive association of Indians with it at various levels, the founding of universities and modern system of education, the permitting of the growth of industries — all these, though done in a limited measure and with motives which perhaps were not altogether altruistic, have laid the groundwork of a polity which, in the course of time, may evolve into a genuinely open society. For we have a Press that enjoys, and even under the British enjoyed, a remarkably high degree of freedom. There is a vocal middle class and a network of voluntary associations — opposition parties organisations — many of which do not hesitate to criticise and oppose, sometimes with considerable success, the policies and actions of the government of the day. The ruling party itself is led by men most of whom are committed to a vaguely understood liberal social democracy. It is true that many of them often put expediency above principle in the name of public interest. But no major issue of public opinion asserts itself and the ruling party develops a popular personality. Together, they succeed in compelling the government to respond as soon as it can do so without serious loss of face.

And yet it is not possible to be confident about the future of freedom in India. The defence of its subversion is all of recent origin and only surface deep. The Press is free, but it rarely concerns itself with what Mill called 'social tyranny more formidable than many kinds of political oppression'. The middle class is vocal but it lacks self-confidence and is unaware of its own leading role in the building up of a better world. Trade unions and opposition parties, though numerically weak, are an important force, but they are most concerned with immediate gains and their vision of the future is too narrowly conceived to inspire confidence. Public opinion, capable of asserting itself, and sometimes aggressively so, is aroused only when issues touching deep-seated emotions are involved. That was what happened during the period of the linguistic reorganisation of the States and again, during the period immediately following the debate in NEFA. But it refuses to be moved when the rights of the individual of a weak social group are at stake.

For instance, in 1957 when the movement for Samyukta Maharashtra was at its height, Professor N.R. Pathak, a well-known historian, was not permitted by a mob to deliver a peace message in his public lectures in Mumbai on the Sepoy Mutiny of 1857. The reason was that Pathak's evaluation of the Mutiny went counter to the strong popular sentiment over it at that time. What was shameful about the incident was not merely the behaviour of the mob, but also the silence of the organised intelligentsia and its leaders over its intolerance. In June, 1963 again, during Nehru's visit to Goa, members of the Scheduled Castes were not allowed to enter the famous Mangeshi temple with him, the temple priests came in for criticism and later the temple was thrown open to the Scheduled Castes as a result of local agitation. What was disturbing here was not so much the earlier attitude of the temple management; they had not heard of human rights as the action of the Prime Minister in entering the temple without insisting on a recognition of the Harijans' right to worship God on a footing of equality with the caste Hindus. Gandhi or Vinoba, even in his personal capacity, would have refused to go into the temple alone. That was the least that Nehru as Prime Minister could have done.

The threat to liberty in India thus lies not only in the seductive appeal of communalism; it also lies in her social system, which drove thousands of Harijans to change their religion so that they could live as self-respecting human beings. But not all oppressed groups have an Ambedkar as their leader, and in the absence of such a leader they are likely to be deceived by the protagonists of totalitarianism.

Whether Indian society will develop sufficient momentum in the near future to make the process of democratic liberalisation more real than it has so far done for its culturally weaker groups, time alone can show. One thing is certain: social liberalisation and the integration of the various groups constituting the Indian people into a modern democratic polity will proceed only to the extent that the abortive renaissance of the nineteenth century gathers strength once again and becomes the mainstream of India's cultural life. To that consummation, the intellectuals can make a unique contribution. Whether they measure to the task, will be judged by history. But the judgements of history are slow in coming and we are living in times when the opportunity to rectify mistakes may be denied to us. That fact distinguishes the challenge we face from those that were faced by preceding generations. It also makes the challenges more exciting.

57

URBAN LIFE TODAY

It must not be forgotten that modern technology has not made itself felt uniformly, nor even universally. Some areas — notably Russia, India and the Orient — are still dominantly agricultural, and their cities do not display the characteristics of cities as we know them in the West. Generally speaking, they still follow the ancient pattern of self-sufficient entities drawing their support from, and in turn serving, fairly well-defined areas. The size and character of any city will be determined by the amount of agricultural products and the foodstuff available to support it, and by the nature and extent of the goods and services which the city is equipped to supply to the area from which it draws its sustenance. Underlying all of this, of course, is the existence of adequate transportation facilities. Indeed transportation is implied in the very concept of trade, and no city can grow beyond the limits imposed by the available means of transport.

If any single word could be used to describe the social life of the modern city, it could probably be the "impersonal". Individual desires and choices are dominant and the contacts between one person and another are so brief and specialised that people seldom know even their associates. The city dweller's life is largely governed by the clock, from the time he arises early enough to get to work — perhaps via the 7.30 bus or train, another impersonal obligation — at a specific time. His work-a-day is usually mechanised, or otherwise performed according to quite exacting standards that allow little self-expression. His leisure time is most often spent in reading periodicals and books, or in viewing the latest movie that "everybody" is talking about, or in some other experience that is being shared by perhaps millions of others in hundreds of other cities or towns. Even his direct contact with other individuals — work associates, those who render services to him, or members of his family — are extremely limited and segmented. The office or shop worker seldom sees anything of his fellow workers "after office hours". Man and wife cannot fully share each other's daily experiences or problems, being so completely separated for most of the day. Even parents and children see little of one another from morning till night. And each, in his own way, is using the multiplicity of goods and services offered by the city in highly standardised and impersonal ways.

The mechanisation inherent in the industrialism of the present day has intensified the division of labour. Specialisation has in turn narrowed the occupational interests and functions of the individual to such a sheer massing of people that anything more than a most casual acquaintance even with "night dwellers" is virtually impossible. The term "neighbour" has lost any real meaning in city life. The enormously increased efficiency of transportation facilities has only torn individuals loose from any sustained interest in a given locality, but has made available (and even necessary) a veritable welter of goods and services. The acceleration of exchange has standardised not only the goods offered in trade, but also the personal relationships involved in the exchange. Mass production, in effect, has produced a mass society.

The impersonal mass society, however, affords the individual a degree of freedom which he cannot have in the smaller, more agrarian community. He is no longer circumscribed in his thought and action by individuals with whom he has little in common except physical proximity. The diversity of the urban environment gives him access to a wide variety of social contact from which he can seek out, to a fair degree, others like himself in tastes or interests. There is a mobility, both in the spatial and social sense. One can attend the temple or theatre or museum or social gathering of one's liking; and he can expect a rise or fall in the social and economic scale much more upon his own merit than upon his family standing or lack of it. Similarly, the intricate variety of jobs in the city gives the individual a chance to seek a type of work that will be compatible with his own temperament and training.

Nevertheless, the development of the urban mass society is not without its costs. Mobility brings with it transience. If the individual gains in anonymity, he also loses in identity. The groups with which he is associated are themselves so specialised and unstable that they can give him little recognition and security that everyone normally must have. This is as true in the job experience as in the social life. The loneliness and isolation confronting the individual in the large city is well known; and it is the source of a large portion of the personal disorganisation found among urban inhabitants.

Probably, the most disastrous effect of the urban mass society, has been its influence upon the character of the family. Family life in the city has been robbed of most of its traditional social values. Factories have made the family almost entirely a consuming agency; it is no longer a working unit. Also, the intense use of land in the city has exerted a strong pressure in reducing the size of the family dwelling. The two together produce a severe strain upon the resources of the family; and as might well be expected, the urban birth-rates are notably lower than those of the rural areas. The city still is a consumer of people; it is not yet replenishing the population it draws from the hinterland. Even the time-honoured social functions of family life, religious experience, instruction of the young, recreation sociability, are now to a very large extent centered outside the home. And this itself may well be a contributing factor in the personal disorganisation.

From the existence of the mass society springs the development of secondary group life and controls. The individual living in the city no longer feels the compulsion or the security of association with other individuals in his immediate environment. Neither his family nor his neighbourhood means as much to him as they did formerly in terms of identity and conformity. Urban life has become much too swift-moving, impersonal and fragmented for the informal primary group controls to remain completely adequate.

Consequently, life in the city is marked by dependence on law and a great variety of voluntary secondary groupings to assure a measure of conformity and complacence by the individual. Criticism and opinion are much too slow to assure compliance by the individual in the city; the specific requirements and penalties provided by law are easily understood and applied. And on the less compulsive side, the great variety of voluntary associations — fraternal, religious, recreational, cultural, occupational, political, welfare or community service — afford for the individual a means of satisfying, to some extent, the gregarious needs formerly met within the family and neighbourhood circles.

It is to be noted, however, that this transfer is by no means universal. The family and neighbourhood still are fairly stable in the less transient city areas where individual dwelling units still predominate. And membership in secondary groupings seems to be directly correlated with ascent in the economic scale. Unfortunately, it is in those areas where overcrowding and underprivileged are greatest that these secondary associations are fewest and where crime and delinquency flourish.

The inability of the individual to stand alone in today's world is never so well illustrated as it is by the position he has in urban life. His most personal needs — food, water, clothing, shelter and security — are available to him only by grace of cooperative effort; and each one of them must be of a quality that will be satisfactory by standards assuring health and safety for that individual. In short, there must be "rules of the game", established by authority competent to enforce the rule; and that authority affects the urban individual most intimately at the local or municipal level of government.

The struggle between individual freedom and governmental activity has been going on for centuries, but the modern fisc of urban life has greatly accelerated the movement toward the assumption of more responsibility by government. Thus, cities now provide public educational facilities (in many cases even at the college level), safeguard health, create parks and playgrounds for recreation, provide economic security to the aged and the indigent. Besides, government arranges to ensure various utilities such as water, gas, electricity and transportation system; and even when these services are privately provided, the quality of the service and the charges to be made are closely regulated by government authority. Many of the standards of public service and administration are set up by State or Central Governments; but actually large part of these functions is carried on by the local government.

Such extensive activities on the part of city government necessarily mean that public business is business in a very literal sense. City governments obviously must function through agents so that large number of citizens are employed, from the highly trained technical or professional personnel down to the most unskilled labourer. The municipality not only renders many services "free" to the citizenry (as for example police, health and fire protection), but also sells others at a price set according to the service rendered, as in the case of the utilities. It, likewise, buys large quantities of supplies such as coal, printed material for records, equipment for the maintenance of public buildings and parks, highways, police and fire protection. It contracts for the construction of public buildings such as schools, museums, libraries, administrative halls, police and fire stations, as well as highways and bridges, to say nothing of negotiating for the necessary sites upon which to erect these various structures. And finally, like any other agency, it must pay its way; and the collection of taxes and the financing of civic enterprises make the fiscal operations no small part of the total governmental functions.

58

INDIAN CIVILISATION — ITS ETERNAL FOUNDATIONS

A true happiness is the right terrestrial aim of man, and true happiness lies in the maintenance of a natural harmony with spirit, mind and body. A culture is to be valued to the extent to which it has discovered the right key of this harmony and organised its expressive motives and movements. And a civilisation must be judged by the manner in which all its principles, ideas, forms, ways of living work to bring that harmony out, manage its rhythmic play and secure its continuance for the development of its motives. A civilisation in pursuit of this aim may be predominantly materialist like modern Western culture, predominantly mental and intellectual like the old Greco-Roman or predominantly spiritual like the still persistent culture of India. India's central conception is that of the Eternal, the Spirit here encased in matter, involved and imminent in it and evolving on the material plane by rebirth of the individual up the scale of being, till in mental plane it enters the world of ideas and realm of conscious morality.

This achievement, this victory over subconscious matter develops its lines, enlarges its scope, elevates its levels until the increasing manifestation of the static or spiritual portion of mind enables the individual mental being in man to identify himself with the pure spiritual consciousness beyond mind. India's social system is built upon this conception; her philosophy formulates it; her religion is an aspiration to the spiritual consciousness and its fruits; her art and literature have the same upward look; her whole Dharma or Law of Being is founded upon it. Progress she admits, but this spiritual progress, not the externally self-unfolding process of an always more prosperous and efficient material civilisation. It is her founding of life upon this exalted conception and her urge towards the spiritual and the eternal that constitute the distinct value of her civilisation. And it is her fidelity, with whatever human shortcomings, to this highest ideal that has made her people a nation apart in the world.

But there are other cultures led by a different conception and even an opposite motive. And by the law of struggle, which is the first law of existence in the material universe, varying cultures are bound to come into conflict. A deep-seated urge in Nature compels them to attempt to extend themselves and to destroy, assimilate and replace all disparates of opposites. Conflict is not indeed the last and ideal stage; for that comes when various cultures develop freely, without hatred, misunderstanding or aggression and even with an underlying sense of unity, their separate special motives. But so long as the principle of struggle prevails, one must face the lesser law; it is fatal to disarm in the midst of the battle. The culture which gives up its living separateness, the civilisation which neglects an active self-defence will be swallowed up and the nation which lives by it will lose its soul and perish. Each nation is a *Shakti* or power of the evolving spirit in humanity and lives by the principle which it embodies. India is the *Bharata Shakti*, the living energy of a great spiritual conception, and fidelity to it is the very principle of her existence. For by its virtue alone she has been one of the immortal nations; this alone has been the secret of her amazing persistence and perpetual force of survival and revival.

The principle of struggle has assumed the large historical aspect of an age-long clash and pressure of conflict between Asia and the West. This clash, this mutual pressure, has had its material side, but has borne also its cultural and spiritual aspect. Both materially and spiritually, the West has thrown herself repeatedly upon Asia, Asia too upon the West, to conquer, assimilate and dominate. There has been a constant alternation, a flowing backward and forward of these two sets of power. The whole of Asia always had the spiritual tendency, in more or less intensity, more or less clearness; but in this essential matter India is the quintessence of the Asiatic way of being. Europe too in medieval times had a culture in which by the dominance of the Christian idea — though Christianity was of Asiatic origin — the spiritual motive took the lead; then there was an essential similarity as well as a certain difference. Still the differentiation of cultural temperament has on the whole been constant. Since some centuries the West has become materialist, predatory, aggressive and has lost the harmony of the inner and outer man which is the true meaning of civilisation and the efficient condition of a true progress. Material comfort, material progress, material efficiency have become her gods. The modern Western civilisation which invaded Asia and with all violent attacks on Indian ideals represent, is the effective form of this materialistic culture. India, true to her spiritual motive, has never shared in the physical attacks of Asia upon the West; her method has always been infiltration of the world with her ideas, such as we today see again in progress. But she had been in the last century physically occupied by the West and this physical conquest was necessarily associated with an attempt at cultural conquest; that invasion too had made some progress. Despite this, English rule has enabled India still to retain her identity and social type; it awakened her to herself and at the same time she became conscious of her strength, guarded her against the flood which would otherwise have submerged and broken her civilisation. It is for her now to recover herself, defend her cultural existence against the alien penetration, preserve her distinct spirit, essential principles and characteristics for her own salvation and the total welfare of the human race.

But many questions may arise — and principally whether such a spirit of defence and attack is the right spirit, whether union, harmony, interchange are not our proper temperament for the coming human advance? Is not a unified world-culture the larger way of the future? Can either an exaggeratedly spiritual or an excessively temporal civilisation be the sound condition of human progress and perfection? A happy or just reconciliation would seem to be a better key to a harmony of Spirit, Mind and Body. And there is the question too whether the forms of Indian culture must be preserved intact as well as the spirit? To these queries the reply is to be found in the law of graduality of the spiritual advance of humanity, its need of advancing through three successive stages.

The first stage is the period of conflict and competition which has been ever dominant in the past and still overshadows the present. For ever when the crudest forms of material conflict are mitigated, the conflict itself still survives and the cultural struggle comes into greater prominence. The second step brings the stage of concept. The third and last is marked by the spirit of sacrifice in which, because all is known as the one Self, each gives himself for the good of the others. The second stage has hardly at all commenced for most; the third belongs to the indeterminate future. Individuals have reached the highest stage; the perfected *Sanyasin* the liberated man, the soul that has become one with the Spirit, knows all being as himself and for him all self-defence and attack are needless. For strife does not belong to the law of his seeing, sacrifice and self-giving. But no one has reached that level, and to follow a law or principle involuntarily is not the truth of one's consciousness; it is falsehood and self-destruction. To allow oneself to be killed, like the lamb attacked by the wolf, brings no growth, furthers no development, assures no spiritual merit. Concert or unity may come in good time, but it must be an underlying unity with a free differentiation, not a swallowing up of one by another or an incongruous and inharmonious mixture. Nor can it come before the world is ready for greater things. To lay down one's arms in a state of war is to invite destruction and it can serve no compensating spiritual purpose.

Spiritual and temporal have indeed to be perfectly harmonised, for the spirit works through mind and body. But the purely intellectual or heavily material culture of the kind that the West now favours bears in its heart the seed of death. India, though its urge is towards the Eternal, since that is always the highest, the entirely real, still contains in her own culture and in her own philosophy a supreme reconciliation of the eternal and the temporal and she need not seek it from outside. On the same principle, the form of the interdependence of mind, body and spirit in a harmonious culture is important as well as the pure spirit; for the form is the rhythm of the spirit. It follows that to break up the form is to injure the spirit's self-expression or at least to put it into grave peril. Change of forms there may or will be, but the novel formation must be a new self-expression or self-creation developed from within. It must be the characteristic of the spirit and not servilely borrowed from the embodiments of an alien nature.

Where, then, does India actually stand in this critical hour of her necessity and how far can she be said to be still firmly seated on her eternal foundations? Already she has been largely affected by Western culture; in fact it may be greater, more insistent, more imperatively violent in the future. Asia is re-arising; but that very fact will intensify and is already intensifying the attempt, natural and legitimate, according to the law of competition, of Western civilisation to assimilate Asia, including India.

59

TRADITION AND MODERNITY IN INDIA

The West could harness the modern money ethics to the task of cultivating new attitudes and value complexes in harmony with the needs of an industrialising society at a time when the hold of religion was still strong on the minds of people. Incidentally, this also means that there was then no threat of a secular totalitarian ideology backed by military power waiting to fill in, at the first opportunity that presented itself, the vacuum created by the breakdown of traditional values unaccompanied by the growth of a viable modern tradition. The situation in India today is different from that in the West at the dawn of the modern age. She does not have the advantages that the West then had. Nor, however, does she have many of the handicaps that the West as the pioneer of modernity had to overcome. She can count on the cooperation and assistance of a better understanding of the processes of social change, provided she has the will and the clarity of purpose to relate modern knowledge and techniques to her needs. More importantly still, she has a fairly well-developed tradition of a functioning democracy which, though not indigenous, has been taking root in the cultural soil of the country for over half a century now. The problem that India has to solve is, therefore, in many important respects different from that of the early West, as also from that of most developing societies of the contemporary world.

For example, the confrontation of tradition and modernity in India is not likely to generate such desperate bitterness as it once did in the West or as it is likely to do in many other countries of Asia. One reason has already been stated above: modernity is not altogether new in India. It is more than a hundred years old and has during this period been making steady headway. Secondly, the Hindu tradition itself is not homogenous, as many of its spokesmen and critics often seem to assume. It is true that dominant Hindu tradition represented by Shankara is world negating and, therefore, inherently incompatible with the modern spirit. But there have arisen at different times a number of protestant schools, including the atheistic and life-affirming, one of Charak, which for a number of centuries seems to have posed a serious intellectual challenge to orthodox Hinduism.

The *Upanishads* and the *Mahabharata* contain enough statements to justify the inference that neither the doctrine of transmigration nor even that of a soul independent of the body was universally accepted. Earlier, the *Vedas* themselves, especially the *Rig Veda*, point to a society that was free from most of the inhibitions of later Hinduism. In considering the compatibility of the Hindu religious tradition with the spirit of modernity, one has to be clear as to which particular Hindu tradition one has in mind. If by 'Hindu tradition' is meant the framework of ideas, attitudes and institutions as codified by Manu, one has to recognise frankly that it is so much deadwood today. One must also recognise that it is this tradition that is still dominant in Hindu society, though its crudities are no longer prominent today. Sati has gone, widows remarry now and then, child marriages are on the wane, caste is being increasingly secularised and even Brahmins have started disowning Manu in matters of food and drink. But the values and attitudes and characteristics of this tradition are very much with us. Some of them include simplicity and *aparigraha* (non-possession of worldly goods), detachment, respect for the status and authority that go with power, caste, age or sex, and lack of civic concern. The supreme value of life is, of course, *moksha,* the release from the bonds of *karma* and the cycle of births. All the other values and attitudes that Hinduism commends have to be in harmony with this summum bonum, even if some of them may not be deducible from it. All these are rooted in the religious outlook implied by the dominant Hindu tradition and, far from being useful in the modern age, are proving a drag on the development of the Indian society.

This, however, does not imply a complete break away from the past. No society can do that, nor is it necessary for India. Her past is remarkably rich and varied, capable of providing a starting point for modernity. It may not contain certain elements of the latter, such as the ideas of free will in philosophy, evolution in science, and an open view of status, role and power allocation. But it offers numerous instances of the spirit of free and critical inquiry of the highest intellectual order, determination to pursue truth regardless of where it leads, a positive and secular approach to life and a tradition of abstract thought necessary for the growth of modern knowledge. Admittedly, most of these are not part of the dominant Hindu tradition today. The point, however, is that given the will to modernise herself, India does not have to seek inspiration solely from a culture which is not a part of her own tradition. She can partly get it from her past and establish continuity with it. Indigenous symbols and myths are available, which can make the transition to modernity less traumatic than it would otherwise be.

However, such use of the past presupposes that there already is a body of men who share modern values and are determined to spread them in society. Their inspiration does not come from the past. The past can provide a bridge for the masses to link the present and the future, provided there is some group in society which knows how to select from among its many strands those which would be suitable for the purpose. The pioneers of the Western Renaissance too looked upon the past in the same spirit. They had no contemporary prototype of what they were seeking to create. And such use alone of the past as harnesses it in the service of modernity and does not wish for the impossible, for their approach to the past is characterised more by intellectual and emotional atavism than by critical selectivity. Their modernism does not extend beyond the narrow sphere of their own professional work. This leads to the spectacle of 'a number of people, very efficient and competent physicists, physicians, chemists, engineers and so on, who cling to traditional habits in their private life.' For example, 'when they fall ill they not only call in qualified physicians but also perform *puja* to propitiate the gods, take talisman and consult holy men.' This is explained by the fact that the Hindus 'actually keep two opposing sets of habit patterns in two watertight compartments and keep fitting from one to another.' In this respect, the Hindu mind differs significantly from the Western, which 'will feel and suffer (from) the stress of the contradiction.' The difference is probably due to the fact that the West has an organised church, which for centuries exercised complete control over both thought and practice. Hinduism has no common shrine and leaves a wide margin for deviation in thought, provided one is conformist in practice; this is but a small step to the types of practice described above.

The problem with the other groups is at a different level. Their conservatism is more often grounded in immediate self-interest and the ignorance of what modernity really is than in any deliberate preference for the traditional way of life. Thus, their indifference to social reforms, like the abolition of untouchability or the dowry system, is tied up with privilege and pecuniary gain in the present and their inability to understand their own long-term interests. But, if a departure from tradition or custom, such as women taking up employment, holds promise of benefits, their response, even in the countryside, is more encouraging than metropolitan intellectuals are likely to imagine. Whenever an imaginative leadership and enough facilities to inspire confidence have been available in recent times, people in the rural areas have shown commendable willingness to adopt new ideas and practices. Those who have watched the response of the agricultural community in Western Maharashtra to programmes of work in the fields of education, agriculture and even family planning would be inclined to believe that the lack of leadership and facilities, not irrational attachment to tradition, is the real problem that advocates of modernity have to solve.

The rise of the right type of leadership is inconceivable so long as an overwhelming majority of Indian intellectuals continue to live in two worlds, the traditional and the modern, at the same time. This would not have mattered much if their traditionalism had confined to the strictly private sphere of life. In point of fact, it is not so, nor would it be possible to keep traditionalism so confined unless it were to be reduced to mere form as in the West. As mentioned earlier, what seems to have happened with most of us is that we have accepted modernity in our professional work alone. In all other spheres of life, not necessarily personal, we continue to be traditional in our values and attitudes unless personal gain is involved. Consequently, the Western liberal institutions — universities, for example, still function largely in an authoritarian way. To take only one illustration, a lecturer in political science in one of the Indian universities, who wished to attend a conference of philosophy, teaches in another town during a vacation had to pretend to be going to his native village in order to avoid obstruction or a black mark from the head of his department. This is, no doubt, an extreme case but it exemplifies very well the authoritarian attitude that governs the organisations and working of the Indian educational system. It points to the failure, for which there is no excuse of this most important agency of modernity in a developing society. Ironically enough, the failure in the post-Independence period is greater than it was under the British rule.

The heart of modernity has to be located in the universities, for the latter cannot be true to themselves, unless they embody what distinguishes modernity from any of the pre-modern traditions, namely, the liberal spirit in its broadest sense and the restless search for truth which is science. Technology and the economic development that make it possible are but a by-product of this 'basic engagement with truth'. This suggests a crucial distinction between modernity and modernisation, which needs to be stressed particularly in the context of developing societies.

Modernity has a wider connotation than modernisation. The latter refers to civilisation and mainly implies a high level of literacy and urbanisation with vertical and geographical mobility, a high per capita income and a sophisticated economy that has gone beyond the take-off stage. Modernity, on the other hand, connotes a certain type of culture whose quality is determined by rationality, the liberal spirit in its broadest sense, plurality of opinion and centres of decision-making, autonomy in the various fields of experience, secular ethics and respect for the private world of the individual.

The main problem, therefore, is not that of devising ways and means for the preservation of what is valuable in tradition. It is rather that of identifying elements such as music, dance, handicrafts and the like. One may also seek to preserve a great deal of the colour and variety in certain aspects of Indian life such as food, dress and festivals. However, this is not enough. It is also necessary to identify the elements that must go if the spirit of modernity is not to be crushed under their weight. This implies an inquiry into the structure and working of each of our major institutions — family, school, university, to name only a few — and an insistent demand for their reform from the standpoint of modernity. What, for instance, should be the lines on which our universities and colleges may be reorganised so as to make them really vital centres of a modern culture? What is involved is values and attitudes and the distribution of power among those who work in these institutions. It is these things which in the final analysis determine the quality of their life, creativity and making even revolt appear as a gesture without meaning. The consequence, as is to be expected, has been the growth of frustration, opportunism and cynicism among those on whose work the transition to modernity depends.

60

TOWARDS A COMPOSITE CULTURE

The Central and State governments in India strive for promotion and dissemination of art and culture through national and regional academies of art, dance, drama, music and letters. Zonal cultural centres have been set up in different regions of the country for projecting, preserving and sustaining the cultural kinship that transcends territorial limits. In addition, the Indira Gandhi National Centre for Arts has been set up at New Delhi as a resource centre and data base, encompassing all arts. All these institutions and the Departments of Art and Culture at the Centre are helped in their objective by the media of mass communication and voluntary agencies. Apart from this, some eminent persons associated with the fine arts are, from time to time, nominated by President to the Rajya Sabha in recognition of their accomplishments made in their respective fields.

Painting: Important traditions of Indian painting include the murals of Ajanta, Ellora and other frescoes, the Buddhist plain leaf manuscripts, the Jain texts, the Deccan, the Mughal, the Rajput and the Kangra schools. The Bengal renaissance and the modern trends bring it to the present. However, the modern trends in Europe and elsewhere have influenced modern Indian painting. Indian folk art and themes have been successfully revived and accepted.

Till the advent of modern trends, architecture and sculpture in India were inspired mainly through the religious motif. The best examples are the temples, mosques, fortresses, palaces, and other monuments which dot the Indian landscape. Massive buildings that have come up after Independence and the formation of some planned cities like Chandigarh have symbolised the beginning of the modern period of Indian architecture. Contemporary Indian sculptors have contributed substantially to the creation of a new awareness of mass, volume and space.

To promote Indian art, both within and outside the country, the government established the Lalit Kala Akademi (National Academy of Fine Arts) in 1954. The Akademi strives to promote this objective through exhibitions, publications, workshops and camps. Every year it holds a national exhibition and every three years, the triennial-Indian exhibition.

The Akademi brings out monographs and portfolios of ancient Indian art, both in English and Hindi, and publishes a bi-annual art journal *Lalit Kala (Contemporary)* in English and *Samakaleen Kala* in Hindi.

The Akademi organises camps, symposia, workshops, seminars and lectures and gives grants to recognised art organisations in the country. It honours eminent artists by electing them as fellows. Every year eminent artists are conferred fellowships. Ten awards of ₹ 10,000 each are given to artists on the occasion of the national exhibition.

The Akademi has permanent artists' studio complex equipped with facilities for training and painting, ceramics, graphics and sculptures at Garhi, New Delhi and Kolkata. It has regional centres at Chennai and Lucknow, where facilities for practical training and work have also been provided. Another regional centre has been established at Bhubaneshwar in memory of Dr. Ananda Coomaraswamy (1877-1947). Here the Akademi organises a lecture annually.

Music: There are two main schools of classical music, namely, Hindustani and Carnatic. Both schools continue to survive mainly through oral tradition being passed on by the teacher to the disciple. This has led to the existence of family traditions called the *gharanas* and the *samprodayas*.

The patronage to music is both State-supported and public. The Sangeet Natak Akademi, All India Radio, Doordarshan, films, voluntary organisations and cultural associations are the main agencies that have brought about a nationwide awareness and appreciation of music.

In recent years, there has been a great revival of interest in folk and tribal music, which has been staged in various cities. Growing in popularity is another category of music, which has come to be known as 'light music'. It is mostly produced for films and auditoriums.

Dance: Dance in India has an unbroken tradition of over 2,000 years. Its themes are derived from mythology, legends and classical literature. There are two main divisions of Indian dance, namely, classical and folk. Classical dance forms are — Bharatnatyam, Kathakali, Kathak, Manipuri, Kuchipudi and Odissi which are largely based on religious topics. Bharatnatyam has roots in Tamil Nadu. Kathakali is the dance-drama of Kerala. Kathak is the principal classical dance of north India and was revitalised as a result of the fusion of Mughal culture with Indian culture. Manipuri dance prevails in the eastern region while Kuchipudi mainly concerns Andhra Pradesh. Its themes are called from the epics, the *Ramayana* and *Mahabharata*. Odissi from Orissa, once practised as a temple dance, is today widely interpreted by artists. The folk and tribal dances of India are of numerous patterns.

Both the classical and folk dances of India owe their present popularity to institutions like the Sangeet Natak Akademi and various training institutes and cultural organisations in different parts of the country. They impart training in different forms of dances. The advanced study and training in different forms of dance and music is carried out by specialised organisations.

Theatre: Theatre in India is as old as music and dance. The classical theatre survives only in few parts of the country. The folk theatre can be seen in its regional variants practically in every linguistic region. There is also the professional theatre, which is mainly city-oriented. Besides, a rich tradition of puppet theatre is found in various parts of the country. Among the many forms prevalent are the puppets, rod puppets, glove puppets and leather puppets (shadow theatre).

There are several semi-professional and amateur theatre groups active in many big cities, performing plays in Indian languages and English.

The Sangeet Natak Akademi, the national academy of music, dance and drama was set up in 1953 for the furtherance of the performing arts of India, a task in which it cooperates with its counterparts in the States and voluntary organisations. Through sponsorship, research and dissemination, it seeks and enhances public appreciation of music, dance and drama, together with a quickened exchange of ideas and techniques for the common gain of Indian performing arts. As part of its coordinating and promotion activities, it holds seminars and festivals, presents awards to outstanding performing artists, gives financial assistance for theatre productions, extends financial help to traditional teachers and grants scholarships to students. It operates a scheme of inter-state exchange of troupes to promote national integration through dissemination of culture. It also supports regional festivals to bring rare art forms of the region to the fore and to promote cultural integration.

In view of the many theatrical, musical and dance forms prevalent in the country, the Akademi has set up a special unit for surveying and documenting them. Its disc and tape library has the largest collection of Indian classical, folk and tribal music and dance and theatre items. The Akademi is running two institutions, for imparting training in dance. These are the Kathak Kendra, New Delhi, and the Jawaharlal Nehru Manipur Dance Academy, Imphal. It has been helping in resurgence of the puppet theatre in the country. It runs a scheme under which subsidy is given for publication of books in various Indian languages and English on music, dance and drama. It honours outstanding performing artists and schools by conferring annual awards.

The National School of Drama, a premier theatre institution, was established in 1959 by the Sangeet Natak Akademi. In 1975, the school was registered as an autonomous institution, fully financed by the Government. It imparts training in dramatics and is propagating theatre in the country. The school has been teaching the theory and practice of drama in a scientific way to talented and enthusiastic young students. It has directly and indirectly played a constructive role in improving the overall standard of plays being produced and techniques being used thereof. It has also gone to the regions for organising theatre workshops and children's theatre training courses so as to make available training facilities to local theatre enthusiasts and to facilitate training of its students in folk, traditional and regional theatre forms. Under its three-year training programmes, it awards scholarships to deserving students and contributes to the development of Indian theatre by training actors, directors and stage technicians. It is conducting a three-year diploma course and provides advanced theatre training in dramatic literature, acting, stage-craft and production.

The All India Radio and Doordarshan have been contributing to bring about an awareness and appreciation of Indian music — classical, light classical, folk and tribal. It has many national programmes to propagate music. The Vividh Bharati Service of All India Radio broadcasts popular film and light music.

61

EDUCATION FOR MODERNISATION

When we speak of universal education as one of the characteristics of highly modernised societies and as one of the special problems of latecomers to modernisation, we mean to attain a minimum universal or nearly universal literacy. Contrary to our general belief, the great change in history with regard to literacy rate was not a consequence of the invention of printing. It is true that China and Japan probably had higher literacy rates than any other non-modernised peoples, but it is extremely doubtful that literacy rate exceeded 30 per cent of the population concerned either before or after printing was invented. The discovery of printing in Europe many centuries later in the fifteenth century did not lead to anything approaching universal literacy. Indeed, it is extremely doubtful that literacy rate reached or exceeded 30 per cent in European settings until well into the nineteenth century. Printing has its relevance no doubt, and one would not wish to cite it, but modernisation is a more crucial variable in predicting high rate of literacy. Other things being equal, the more highly modernised a people, the higher will be their literacy rate.

We use literacy as a synonym for a whole set of learning. Leaning to write is regarded as the obverse of learning to read, but we also expect a universal literacy with regard to such fields as arithmetic and even, oddly enough, some of the general facts and myths of the history and civics of the peoples concerned. All of these become part of the basic — that is, that which they share or accept to share with other members of their society as opposed to the specialised or intermediate learning of modernised people. Other things being equal, the less modernised a people, the less will be the absolute amount of their basic learning, and the less will be the development of their intermediate or specialised learning. With modernisation, the acceleration of development of specialised learning is so enormously great that we are sometimes forced into ignoring the enormous increase in basic learning. Some realisation of this, as it applies today, is implicit in the joking we do about the "New Math". It is not just a joke. A level of mathematical sophistication extending increasingly to the use of computers is a part of basic learning for our children, though it was not for us.

In considering the enormous increase in basic education, no one can afford to overlook the levelling effect of participation in it. When only the elite learn to read, and perhaps, it is one characteristic by which you can identify the elite. Nowadays, you can't tell the Joneses from the Astors that way. One of the greatest "democratising" forces in the history of the world has been the sharing of a common curriculum. Beyond the basic common curriculum of learning to walk and to talk is to eat and to sleep and control bodily functions and interact with other human beings. The common curriculum for all humankind has never been so great as it has become with modernisation. Moreover, never before in history has it exhibited a tendency to become continuously greater all the time. The expansion of basic knowledge is in a sense even more spectacular, though usually ignored, than the proliferation of the specialised knowledge that rests on it. The most spectacular part of all icebergs is the part you never see unless you dive deep.

It is difficult even to discuss universal education as we think of it without referring directly or indirectly to the use of schools as the device to handle education. For non-modernised people in schools, as we think of them, are restricted almost entirely to small portions of the elite. Even for the elite, much of the schooling was provided by individual tutors and the like rather than by schools as we think of them. Schools represent a special organisational device focussed on education. Schools stand in immediate and stark contrast to one of the greatest universals of the non-modernised experience. The universal is that for the non-modernised, the overwhelming proportion of all education for all individuals has taken place in family contexts, not just in the first three years or so of life, but throughout the life cycle of the individual. As modernisation continues, however, it becomes overwhelmingly likely that the vast majority of all that will be considered education will take place in non-family settings as schools.

The break is especially dramatic and traumatic for latecomers who are not yet accustomed, if they are young, to learning things of great importance from people who are not older members of their own families. Furthermore, and no less strategic, the older individuals are not used to having their young learn things of great importance from individuals who are not members of their own families and who are not under their tutelage and control. The overwhelming majority of all of the young, especially of the non-modernised peoples, spend the vast majority of all of their time, including their learning time, in family contexts or those closely associated with family contexts. With modernisation all spend an increasing proportion of their time in schools. What happens to them is regarded as critical both by them and by others. Even the most negative critics of our schools regard what happens there as critical even when they hold it not to be "relevant".

The general exposure of any substantial proportion of the population to education in terms of schools is something that no people have experienced much longer than a hundred years. Probably, most of the world's population has not had much experience with it for as much as half a century. As long as families or some closely related organisational contexts such as neighbourhood groups, clans and so forth, are the fact that learning takes place there simply reinforces the general relevance of such settings, to the extent that schools replace a part of that. Some of the relevance of such contexts is destroyed, but it cannot be automatically replaced by the school context. For the vast majority of people the family context is, after all, a continuing one. Even in our own lives where we string schooling out quite long, the schools are, practically for everybody, specifically a transitional context — a training or preparatory context. A school is not a general living context except for those in the process of training. This may be one of the reasons why people who remain perpetually in school contexts, as do university faculties, have from many points of view a childish aura about them. It may also explain why life in school at any level — even when the great majority of all those of appropriate age experience it — it somehow is still generally regarded as something apart from the "real world".

Today, we not only take universal education for granted and education in terms of schools for granted; we also take higher education for granted. Some years ago, in 1935 something in excess of 70 per cent of US children completed secondary school and more than 55 per cent of those went on to some form of higher education. US has reached a situation in which 50 per cent of its children go in for some form of higher education. There is practically none who does not expect and want that percentage to increase. As has been true of secondary school education before, the college education is sure to become a part of the basic education of our people. Japan is the second country to follow. Such advanced schooling is not compatible with high rate of productivity in other respects on the part of the students during their school years. Unless we find a different way of combining activities with schooling, we shall continue to live with the fact that only extremely affluent societies can afford to keep any substantial proportion of their young out of other productive pursuits for their first twenty to twenty-two years of life. To put it in another way, only the members of highly affluent societies can make higher education universal.

In most non-modernised settings, even to have aspired to higher education may be a mark of distinction. In a setting in which it is a matter of pride to point out that one has failed the entrance examination to the college, those who have had any experience of higher education are, indeed, too elite to accept positions, which, though beneath their elite distinction, are well beyond them in experience. To place them in the kind of bureaucratic positions justified by academic snobbery is to place them in positions for which they are ill-prepared and hence it guarantees troubles for the bureaucracy. To refuse them such positions is to guarantee a highly disgruntled and articulate elite.

In this respect, the experience of armed forces is highly opposite. After all, armed forces, when they are not fighting, are essentially in training and educational contexts. An enormous number of armed forces in history have hit upon the following device. Given the best recruits attainable, whether by universal conscription or by voluntary procedures, those who show aptitude as privates are sent to military schools (or special courses); if they succeed at military schools, they are made cadets; if they are good, they are sent to national academy schools; if they are good at sergeant schools, they are made sergeants; and so on until, following Peter's Principle, they have been demoted to the level of their incompetence. What one does without anybody's having thought it out very well is to adjust the level and nature of advanced training to the level of relevant experience in so far as that can be determined. There is absolutely no reason why this cannot be done in non-military contexts. Given the values and requirements of most of the latecomers, college degrees should not be regarded even as an initial ideal in civilian governmental contexts. Young people who have the required basic education could be taken in and sent along for further schooling as their experience and achievements warrant. That would be one way of getting a closer relationship between experience and relevant higher education than is presently obtainable. It is feared that a major obstacle in doing this may be that the military do it and, therefore, it is automatically considered inalienably military and hence improper for civilian contexts.

There is another factor having to do with higher education that is of some importance. Universities are curious organisations with a long history. In general, only three things have ever been done well in university contexts (and the members of most universities have probably not succeeded in doing those three very well). Those three things are the preservation of knowledge, the transmission of knowledge, and the discovery of new knowledge. The service of universities to the large community must, if the universities are to be viable, consist primarily of performances along some combination of these three lines.

For a good number of years, most of us have been cynical about how good a job is done in terms of the transmission of knowledge. No major proportion of the general public has even been terribly interested in the preservation of knowledge. So, in recent times perhaps, the most striking feature of universities has been their contribution to the discovery of new knowledge. This is in and by itself a special development. Throughout most of their histories, universities have been primarily important for their contribution to the preservation and transmission of knowledge. As the modernisation process developed, two curious things took place. On the one hand, continual increases of basic and specialised knowledge became increasingly critical for survival, let alone the good life and, on the other hand, the overwhelming organisational focus for the discovery of new knowledge came to be the university or a university-simulated organisation. Prior to the twentieth century, the universities even in the West were not the main settings through which contributions to knowledge were developed.

By a series of historical accidents, the United States has become the overwhelming repository of world university resources, especially with regard to contributions to knowledge at the frontiers of discovery. Universities are delicately poised and curiously tolerated organisations. For a whole series of reasons, the temptations for latecomers to develop them quickly, and for the modernised as well as the non-modernised to attempt to use universities for purposes other than the three roles mentioned above, especially to use them as primarily political devices, are certain to be very great, indeed both from within and from without the university. Such attempts will never accomplish the purposes they are intended to serve over any extended period, but they may easily result in the destruction of the universities. If that happens generally in the modernised world, we shall have to look to other contexts for the discovery of needed new knowledge, just as those countries which have not developed universities must do now.

62

CENTRE-STATE RELATIONS IN INDIA

The Union Parliament enjoys exclusive powers to legislate on subjects mentioned in the Union List. It contains subjects like defence, foreign affairs, currency, union duties, etc. The States enjoy exclusive power to legislate on the subjects enumerated in the State List. This list contains subjects like public order and police, local government, public health and sanitation, agriculture, education, etc. Both the Centre and the State Governments can legislate on the subjects mentioned in the Concurrent List, which contains subjects like criminal law and procedure, marriage, contracts, social insurance, economic and social planning, etc. However, if a law of the Union Government and that of a State Government in respect of any subject in the Concurrent List comes into conflict, the Union law prevails over the State law. The residuary powers, that is the powers which are not covered by any of the three lists, vest in the Union Government. In a typical federation like India, only specified powers are vested in the States.

The above distribution of powers shows that the Centre has been made stronger by the Constitution than the States. This fact has been criticised by political reformers in the States.

In certain circumstances, the Union Government can exercise control even over the subjects in the State List. For example, under Article 154 (2) (b) of the Constitution, the Parliament is authorised to entrust any work to officials subordinate to the State Governor. No sanction of the State Legislature or Executive is essential for assignment of such functions.

Under Article 169(1), the Parliament has been authorised to establish or abolish State Legislative Council in any State, provided the legislature of the State concerned passes a resolution to this effect. In other federations like Switzerland, Australia and America, the States are fully independent regarding the constitution of their State legislatures.

Under Article 249 of the Constitution, if the Rajya Sabha passes a resolution by a two-thirds majority that a particular subject in the State List is of national importance, the Parliament can legislate on such a subject. Such a resolution of the Rajya Sabha remains in force for a period of one year and can be extended by one year by means of a subsequent resolution.

During the proclamation of Emergency made by the President of India, on account of internal disturbance or external aggression, the Parliament acquires the authority to make laws on all the subjects mentioned in the State List. However, all such laws made by the Parliament become ineffective six months after the Proclamation of Emergency ceases to operate.

In case of Emergency due to the failure of the constitutional machinery in any State, the President of India can authorise Parliament to exercise the powers of the State legislature. All such laws cease to operate six months after the Proclamation of Emergency comes to an end.

For the implementation of treaties, international agreements and conventions, the Parliament has the power to legislate on any subject and the normal distribution does not stand in its way. Any law passed by the Parliament for this purpose cannot be invalidated on the ground that it relates to a subject mentioned in the State List.

The Parliament can legislate on any other subject in the State List if legislatures of two or more States pass a resolution to this effect and authorise the Parliament to make a law thereon.

It is thus clear that the Indian federation is not a partnership among equals. The Union is certainly superior to the States and at times the States are absolutely at the mercy of the Union.

Certain bills passed by the State legislature have to be reserved for the approval of the President of India before they can become operative. For example, under Article 31(3), the laws pertaining to acquisition of property are not valid till the President accords his approval. Explaining the reasons for the incorporation of this provision in the Constitution, Granville Austin points out that it was included in the Constitution at the instance of Sardar Patel so that the President may be able to stay any law which appears to him to be unreasonable. This provision has been severely criticised by the committee set up by Tamil Nadu Government. This committee felt that the State Government must be left free to legislate on certain matters with a view to effect social and economic changes in the life of the people.

The Governor of the State has also been empowered under Article 200 of the Constitution to reserve any bill for the approval of the President. The President has been authorised to reject any such bill and return the same to the State government. The President is not bound to sign such a bill even if the State legislature repasses the same bill and transmits it to the President. Another point which deserves attention is that no time limit is prescribed for approval of a bill referred to the President. This simply means that the President can kill a bill referred to him by not taking any action on it. Even if the President rejects a bill referred to him by the State legislature, he is not bound to assign the reasons for his decision. Thus, "in theory as well as in practice, the operation of the State Legislative process is subordinate to the supremacy of the Union Executive."

Under the Indian Constitution, the Governor of a State is authorised to issue ordinances, when the State legislature is not in session. Though it is expected that the Governor will issue such ordinance only with the approval of the State Council of Ministers, but under certain circumstances, he can issue these ordinances only with the prior approval of the President of India. At least in the following three conditions, he can issue such ordinance but with the prior approval of the President of India.

(a) If the ordinance deals with a subject regarding which laws can be introduced in the State legislature only with the prior approval of the President.

(b) If a bill has been reserved for the opinion of the President, an ordinance on the same subject can be issued with the prior approval of the President.

(c) Ordinance on a subject on which a law passed by the State legislature is not valid without the approval of the President.

It is thus clear that though the Centre and the States have been assigned independent legislative spheres, the Centre reserves the right to interfere in the subjects reserved for the States.

As for administrative relations, the executive power of the Union extends only to those matters which are mentioned in the Union List and over which the Parliament has legislative powers. In addition, the Union can exercise administrative control over the State through the following methods.

Articles 256 of the Constitution specifies the respective obligations of the Union and the State Government and lays down that "The executive power of every State shall be so exercised as to ensure compliance with the laws made by the Parliament and any existing laws which apply in that State and the executive power of the Union shall extend to the giving of such direction to the State as may appear to the Government of India to be necessary for that purpose. Thus, this Article clearly provides that the executive authority of the State shall be so exercised that the laws made by the Parliament and the existing laws of the States are properly enforced. If the State government fails to enforce the laws passed by the Parliament within its jurisdiction, the Union Government can issue directions to the State Government to do so under Articles 246 of the Constitution."

Article 257 (I) lays down that "The executive power of every State shall be so exercised as not to impede or prejudice the exercise of the executive power of the Union, and the executive power of the Union shall extend to the giving of such directions to a State as may appear to the Government of India to be necessary for that purpose." Thus, within the sphere covered by the State List, the Union Government can give directions to the State Governments.

The Union Government can also give directions to the States regarding the construction and maintenance of means of communications declared to be of national or military importance. The Union Government can also give directions to the States regarding the measures to be taken for the protection of railways within the boundaries of the State. However, the excess expenses incurred by the State Government on this account are paid by the Government of the Union. In case there is any dispute about the quantum of the payment, it is decided by the arbitrator appointed by the Chief Justice of India.

In case the State Government fails to carry out any of the directions of the Union Government, the President has been empowered by Article 365 of the Constitution to hold that a situation has arisen in which the Government of the State cannot be carried on in accordance with the provisions of the Constitution. In other words, if the State fails to carry out the orders or directions of the Union, the President's rule may be imposed on the State. In such eventuality, the President shall assume to himself all or any of the functions of the State Government.

The President, with the consent of the State Government, can entrust to the officers of the State Government any function in respect of any subject over which the executive power of the Union extends. Thus, the States may be converted into agents of the Union Government. However, any extra cost incurred by the States for carrying out such an obligation is to be paid by the Union.

The presence of All India Services like the Indian Administrative Service, the Indian Police Service, etc. further makes the authority of the Central Government dominant over the States. The members of these All India Services are appointed by the President of India on the basis of competitive examination held by the Union Public Service Commission.

The Constitution also makes provision for the creation of new All India Services by the Parliament. The Parliament can create a new All India Service if the Rajya Sabha passes a resolution by a majority of two-thirds of its members present and voting, that it is necessary in the national interest to do so.

The Constitution vests the President with the power to establish an Inter-State Council, to bring about coordination between States. Article 263 which deals with the Inter-State Council says: "If at any time it appears to the President that the public interests would be served by the establishment of a Council charged with the duty of:

(a) inquiring into and advising upon disputes which have arisen between States;
(b) investigating and discussing subjects in which some or all of the States, or the Union and one or more States, have a common interest; or
(c) making recommendations upon any such subject and, in particular, recommendations for the better coordination of policy and action with respect to that subject, it shall be lawful for the President by order to establish such a Council, and to define the nature of duties to be performed by it and its organisation and procedure.

In other words, the Inter-State Council can be set up by the President to inquire into the disputes among States and to make recommendations thereon.

63

FINANCIAL RELATIONS BETWEEN THE UNION AND THE STATES

Often the federation and the units have tried to raise revenue by taxing the same sources such as income tax. In theory, it may look right, but in practice it creates inconvenience. The federation thinks that the States stood in its way of enhanced taxation, while the States look upon the federation as a hindrance and feel they are subjected to double or excessive taxation. There is constant challenge by the States to the authority of the federation to impose a particular tax. At the same time, the federation, too, resorts to the same process against the States. Individual citizens, too, challenge the authority of either the federation or the State whenever it suits their interests.

The result is an enormous amount of litigation. The Indian Constitution lays down a broad scheme for the distribution of revenue resources between the Union and the States. But it has left the task of detailed allocation to the Finance Commission to be set up by the President every five years.

The basic principles that guide the allocation of resources between the federation and the units are efficiency, adequacy and suitability. It is, indeed, difficult to achieve all the three and at the same time, constitutional, natural and economic considerations that stand in the way. Even if a certain system might suggest itself as the most acceptable, it would not satisfy the claims and counter-claims of the various states. Hence, the Constitution has attempted a compromise. According to this, the subject is divided into two parts, namely, (1) the allocation of revenues between the Union and the States, and (2) the distribution of grants-in-aid. The following list shows the respective sources of revenue for the Union and the States:

Union Sources

1. Corporation tax.
2. Currency, coinage and legal tender, foreign exchange.
3. Duties of excise on tobacco and certain goods manufactured or produced in India.
4. Duties of customs including export duties.
5. Estate duty in respect of property other than agricultural land.
6. Fees in respect of any of the matters in the Union List, but not including any fees taken in any court.
7. Foreign loans.
8. Lotteries organised by the Government of India or the Government of a State.
9. Post Office Savings Bank.
10. Posts and telegraphs, telephones, wireless broadcasting and other like forms of communication.
11. Property of the Union.
12. Public debt of the Union.
13. Railways.
14. Rate of stamp duty in respect of Bills of Exchange, Cheques, Promissory Notes, etc.
15. Reserve Bank of India.
16. Taxes on income other than agricultural income.
17. Taxes on the capital value of the assets exclusive of agricultural land of individuals and companies.
18. Taxes other than stamp duties on transactions in stock exchanges and future markets.
19. Taxes on the sale or purchase of newspapers and on advertisements published therein.
20. Terminal taxes on goods or passengers, carried by railways, sea or rail.

State Sources

1. Capitation tax.
2. Duties in respect of succession to agricultural land.

3. Duties of exchange on certain goods produced or manufactured in the States, such as alcoholic liquids, opium, etc.
4. Estate duty in respect of agricultural land.
5. Fees in respect of any of the matters in the State List, but not including fees taken in any court.
6. Land revenue.
7. Rates of stamp duty in respect of documents other than those specified in the Union List.
8. Taxes on agricultural income.
9. Taxes on land and buildings.
10. Taxes on mineral rights, subject to limitations imposed by Parliament relating to mineral development.
11. Taxes on the consumption or sale of electricity.
12. Taxes on the entry of goods into a local area for consumption, use or sale therein.
13. Taxes on the sale and purchase of goods other than newspapers.
14. Taxes on advertisements other than those published in newspapers.
15. Taxes on goods and passengers carried by road or on inland waterways.
16. Taxes on vehicles.
17. Taxes on animals and boats.
18. Taxes on professions, trades, callings and employments.
19. Taxes on luxuries, including taxes on entertainments, amusements, betting and gambling.
20. Tolls.

Taxes levied and collected by the Union but assigned to the States (Article 269)

1. Duties in respect of succession to property other than agricultural land.
2. Estate duty in respect of property other than agricultural land.
3. Taxes on railway fares and freights.

4. Taxes other than stamp duties on transactions in stock exchanges and future markets.
5. Taxes on the sale or purchase of newspapers and on advertisements published therein.
6. Terminal taxes on goods or passengers carried by railways, sea or air.
7. Taxes on the sale or purchase of goods other than newspapers where such sale or purchase takes place in the course of inter-state trade or commerce.

Duties levied by the Union but collected and appropriated by the State (Article 268)

Stamp duties and duties of exchange on medicinal and toilet preparations (those mentioned in the Union List) shall be levied by the Government of India, but shall be collected:

(i) In the case where such duties are leviable within any Union Territory, by the Government of India, and
(ii) In other cases, by the States within which such duties are respectively leviable.

Taxes which are levied and collected by the Union but which may be distributed between the Union and the States (Article 270 and 272)

1. Taxes on income other than agricultural income.
2. Union duties on medicinal and toilet preparations as are mentioned in the Union List and collected by the Government of India.

"Taxes on income" do not include corporation tax. The distribution of income tax proceeds between the Union and the State is made on the basis of the recommendations of the Finance Commission.

Taxes on Professions, Trade, etc. (Article 275): Although the imposition and collection of income tax are within the jurisdiction of the Union, the States are permitted to impose tax on professions, trades, ceilings or employments. Such a tax will not be invalid on the ground that it relates to a tax on income. Taxes on professions, etc. are generally made use of for the benefit of local self-governing institutions such as municipalities, local boards, etc. There is, however, an upper limit of ₹ 2,500 per person per annum prescribed for this tax.

Grant-in-Aid (Article 275): Federalism is not only a unifying but also a levelling-up force. Among the constituent States of the Union are some which are developed and advanced while others are undeveloped or underdeveloped and backward. One of the results expected of a federal union is the opportunity that it should provide for the socially and economically backward units to better their lot. A common method adopted for this purpose is the system of the Union giving grants to the needy States. Article 275 provides for this by empowering Parliament to pay, out of the Consolidated Fund of India, certain sums every year as grants-in-aid of the revenues of such States, to the extent that such assistance is adjudged as necessary. The grants so fixed are based upon the recommendations of the Finance Commission. It is not necessary that every State should get grants-in-aid every year. If, in the opinion of the Finance Commission, a particular State does not need such assistance, Parliament may leave it out while allocating such grants. The Constitution, however, makes it obligatory for the Union Government to pay such grants-in-aid to cover the schemes of development undertaken by a State with the approval of the Union for the purpose of promoting the welfare of the Scheduled Tribes in that State or raising the level of administration of the Scheduled Areas.

Finance Commission (Article 280 and 281): As has been pointed out earlier, the constitutional requirement of setting up a Finance Commission is an original idea. According to this, the President should, within two years from the inauguration of the Constitution and thereafter on the expiry of every fifth year or at such earlier intervals as he thinks necessary, constitute a Finance Commission. The Commission will consist of a chairman and four other members who are all to be appointed by the President. As the Commission has to be constituted at regular intervals, a certain measure of continuity in the work of these Commissions is ensured. And each Commission profits by the work of its predecessors.

According to Article 280, the Finance Commission has to make recommendations to the President on two specific matters and only "any other matter referred to the Commission by the President in the interests of sound finance."

The two specific matters are:

(i) The distribution between the Union and the States of the net proceeds of taxes which are to be, or may be, divided between them and the allocation between the States of the respective shares of such proceeds; and

(ii) The principles which should govern the grants-in-aid of the revenues of the States out of the Consolidated Fund of India.

The President, after considering the recommendations of the Finance Commission with regard to income tax, prescribes by order the percentages and the manner of distribution. Parliament is not directly concerned with the assignment and distribution of income tax.

The importance of the Finance Commission as a constitutional instrument capable of settling many complicated financial problems that affect the relationship of the Union and the States may be seen from the recommendations of the last 13 Commissions. The present system of allocation of finance between the Union and the States is almost entirely the result of these recommendations.

Viewing the Union-State relationship in the financial field as a whole, one finds that it is in harmony with the general nature of the Indian federalism, namely, the tendency for centralisation. The Union Government is financially stabler and stronger than the State Governments. This was necessary to facilitate the planned development of the country as a whole and to check parochial and even separatist tendencies in the economic activities within individual States. As it is, the States are, in view of their limited resources, bound to look up to the Union for financial aid for most, if not all, development projects. Naturally, they will have to follow the lead of the Union and often even submit to its dictates.

In this connection, the role of the Planning Commission is very significant. It is concerned with the national five-year plans and the mobilisation and allocation of resources for the implementation of those plans. The Planning Commission is not a body established by the Constitution, but by the Union Government. Yet the role of the Commission is decisive in the allocation of finances for development purposes. And this places the States in a position of financial dependence on the Commission for the five-year plans.

This is not a happy situation from the point of view of the States. Perhaps, in the initial stages of development of India as a new politically independent country, this was necessary both to ensure the unity of the nation and the balanced development of the different regions. But during the last fifty-five years, the pattern of Indian economy has undergone a considerable change. The States today feel that if they have to pursue their developmental objectives satisfactorily, they should have greater financial resources. And this is possible only if either the Centre gives them a large share of the Central revenues or allows them to have more taxation powers, if necessary, through constitutional amendment. It is not likely that the Centre would agree with either of these demands readily. But there is an indication to believe that these demands are bound to gather momentum and strength in the years to come.

Financial relations between the Union and the States, especially in a developing economy, cannot remain static for long. Adjustments will have to be made in the light of the changing pattern of the economy. Legislative enactments on taxation cannot be made for all times to come. After all, the relationship between the Central and State Governments in a federal system is a dynamic one; and the problems arising out of this relationship cannot be solved once for all any more than the problems of life itself.

64

HISTORY OF ECONOMIC PLANNING

Planning in India is undertaken by the Planning Commission. Planning is largely done to bring about a change in the standard of living of people. Planning ensures efficient utilisation of the country's resources for improving the quality of life of the people. Till 2011-12 there have been 11 five-year plans— the twelfth being currently underway. These plans have helped improve the quality of life of the people of India.

The First Five-Year Plan (1951-1956) had a two-fold objective to correct the disequilibrium in the economy caused by the Second World War and partition of the country, and to initiate simultaneously a process of all-round balanced development which would ensure a rising national income and a steady improvement in the living standards over a period of time. The plan accorded highest priority to agriculture, including irrigation and power projects.

The Second Five-Year Plan (1956-1961) sought to promote a pattern of development which was ultimately to lead to the establishment of a socialistic pattern of society in India. In particular, it stressed that the benefits of economic development should accrue more to the relatively less privileged sections of society and there should be a progressive reduction in the concentration of incomes, wealth and economic power. The plan aimed at 25 per cent increase in national income, rapid industrialisation with particular emphasis on the development of basic and heavy industries, large expansion of employment opportunities and reduction of inequalities in income.

The Third Five-Year Plan (1961-1966) aimed at securing a market advance towards self-sustaining growth. The objectives of the plan were to secure an increase in the national income, to achieve self-sufficiency in foodgrains and increase in agricultural production, to expand basic industries like steel, chemicals, fuel and power, and to establish machine-building capacity to utilise fully the manpower resources of the country and ensure substantial expansion in employment opportunities and to establish progressively greater equality of opportunity and bring about reduction in disparities of income and wealth.

The finalisation of the fourth plan was delayed due to the situation created by the Indo-Pakistan conflict, two successive years of severe drought, devaluation of the currency, rise in the prices and erosion of resources available for plan purposes. However, three annual plans between 1966 and 1968 were formulated.

The Fourth Five Year Plan (1969-1974) aimed at accelerating the tempo of development in conditions of stability and at reducing fluctuations in agricultural production as well as the impact of uncertainties of foreign aid. It aimed at raising the standard of the people through programmes which, at the same time, were designed to promote equality and social justice. The plan laid particular emphasis on improving the conditions of the less privileged and weaker sections of the society.

The Fifth Five-Year Plan (1974-1979) was formulated at a time when the economy was facing severe inflationary pressures. The major objectives of the plan were to achieve self-reliance and to adopt measures for raising the consumption standards of the people living below the poverty line. The Plan was ended one year ahead with the close of the annual plan 1977-78 and work was initiated for a new plan for the next five years with new priorities and programmes. The new concept of continuous long-term plan called 'rolling programme' was formulated but this had to be given up and the original pattern of five-year plan was restored.

The Sixth Five-Year Plan (1980-1985): Having terminated the fifth plan a year ahead of its scheduled operation, the Janata Government at the Centre launched the sixth plan in 1978-79. However, this plan was once again disbanded with the new Government taking charge at the Centre and a revised sixth plan was formulated. This revised plan, published in

1981, was effective from the year 1980 onwards and covered a period up to the end of 1985.

The removal of poverty was the foremost objective of the sixth five-year plan, even though it was recognised that with the given magnitude of the problem, it could not be accomplished in a short span of five years.

The sixth plan envisaged a public sector outlay of ₹ 97,500 crores during 1980-85. Of the public sector outlay of ₹ 97,500 crores, ₹ 12,539 crore were provided for agriculture and allied activities and ₹ 12,160 crores for irrigation and flood control. These two taken together made a total outlay of ₹ 24,699 crores for the agricultural sector of the economy which was a little more than 25 per cent of the total envisaged public sector outlay of the sixth plan.

The public sector outlay over the sixth plan period amounted to ₹ 1,10,821 crores (at current prices) as against the envisaged outlay of ₹ 97,500 crores at 1979-80 prices.

The plan, in spite of all odds against it, was a tremendous success. The economy attained a growth rate of 5.3 per cent as against the 5.2 per cent laid down in the plan. Production targets were largely achieved in the fields of foodgrains and oilseeds. However, the realised rate of 5.5 per cent growth rate in the industrial sector was much below the plan target of seven per cent. Success was also striking in the realm of poverty alleviation. In brief, the sixth plan made a fairly convincing success in strengthening the impulses of growth.

The Seventh Five-Year Plan (1985-1990): The Seventh Plan, which came to a close on March 31, 1990, is estimated to have achieved a GDP growth of 5.6 per cent per annum as against the target growth rate of five per cent envisaged under the Plan. Though the GDP growth rate fluctuated from year to year, being just five per cent in 1985-86 and below four per cent in 1986-87 and 1987-88, the impressive growth rate of 10.4 per cent recorded in 1988-89 and 5.2 per cent growth in 1989-90 enabled the plan to exceed its growth rate envisaged for the five-year period.

The Seventh Plan envisaged public sector outlay of ₹ 1,80,000 crores at 1984-85 prices. The actual expenditure over the first four years of the Plan and the revised outlay for the last year, add up to a total expenditure of ₹ 2,20,216.3 crores which was over 23 per cent higher than the envisaged outlay. Even after allowing for the price rise over the period, it was evident that the pace of planned expenditure was, by and large, satisfactory.

The financing pattern of the planned expenditure was different from the Plan projections. The main areas of concern related to shortfalls in the surpluses of public enterprises, steep rise in Centre's non-Plan expenditure and the increasing reliance on deficit financing. Among the items of non-plan expenditure, defence, interest payments on public debt and subsidies on food and fertilisers accounted for nearly one-third to three-fourths of the revenue receipts of the Central Government over those years of the Seventh Plan.

Of the total public sector outlay of ₹ 2,20,216 crores, 91.4 per cent (₹ 2,08,478 crore) were raised through domestic sources while foreign aid contributed ₹ 19,719 crores, i.e., 8.6 per cent of the total public sector outlay. Performance was most disappointing in the case of balance from current revenues which were negative. Deficit financing during the Seventh Plan was estimated to have been of the order of ₹ 34,132 crores as against ₹ 14,000 crores envisaged under the Plan.

The ratio of gross domestic saving as a percentage of the GDP at current market prices improved marginally from 20.4 per cent in 1984-85 to 21.7 per cent in 1989-90 as against the target of 24.5 per cent envisaged under the Plan. There was also only a marginal improvement in the ratio of gross capital formation from 22.8 per cent in 1984-85 to 24.1 per cent in 1989-90 as against the target of 25.9 per cent for the Seventh Plan.

The Eighth Five-Year Plan (1992-1997): The Seventh Plan ended on March 31,1990. In the normal course the Eighth Plan should have begun on April 2, 1990. However, due to some unavoidable circumstances including the changes in party in power at the Centre, the Plan document could not be finalised. It was only when the Government under P.V. Narasimha Rao assumed office that the Plan was finalised and implemented with effect from April 1, 1992. The duration of the Eighth Plan is thus from April, 1992 to March 31, 1997. The Eighth Plan sought to give priority to the following set of six objectives:

(i) Generation of adequate employment to achieve near full employment level by the turn of the century;

(ii) Containment of population growth through active people's cooperation and an effective scheme of incentives and disincentives;

(iii) Universalisation of elementary education and complete eradication of illiteracy among the people of the age group of 15 to 35 years;

(iv) Provision of safe drinking water and primary health care facilities, including immunisation to the entire population and complete elimination of scavenging;

(v) Growth and diversification of agriculture to achieve self-sufficiency in food and generate surpluses for exports; and

(vi) Strengthening the infrastructure (energy, transport, communication and irrigation) in order to support growth process on a substainable scale.

The Eighth Plan concentrated on these objectives keeping in view the need for (a) continuous reliance on domestic resources for financing investment, (b) increasing the technical capabilities for the development of science and technology (c) modernisation and competitive efficiency so that the Indian economy can keep pace with and take advantage of the global developments.

The Eighth Plan aimed at achieving a growth rate of 5.6 per cent annum in Gross Domestic Product (GDP) over the five-year period 1992-1997. This growth target was set against the backdrop of 5.8 per cent GDP growth rate achieved during the

Seventh Plan period 1985-1990. In view of this encouraging performance of Seventh Plan, some people advocated for a six per cent growth target. But due to resource crunch that the public sector was facing, the growth target had been fixed at 5.6 per cent.

The Eighth Plan envisaged a total outlay of ₹ 7,98,000 crores in both public and private sectors taken together, of which public sector outlay would be ₹ 4,34,100 crores. This means that the share of public sector in total Plan outlay under the Eighth Plan would be 45.2 per cent as against 52.9 per cent in the Sixth and 47.8 per cent in the Seventh Plan. Of the total public sector outlay of ₹ 4,34,100 crores, ₹ 3,61,000 crores would be public sector investment and ₹ 73,100 crores current outlay, i.e., outlay of recurring and non-investment nature.

The energy sector received the largest share in the outlay followed by the transport sector. Taken together, these two sectors accounted for about 40 per cent of the public sector outlay in the Eighth Plan. Share of agriculture had been put at about 12.7 per cent, which combined with about 8 per cent share of rural development claims over one-fifth of the public sector outlay. In fact, the share of outlay for rural development in the Eighth Plan was larger than any other preceding Plan and thus signified the emphasis of rural development and poverty alleviation that the Plan sought to place on it in the context of overall development of the economy. Industry sector had been allocated around 11 per cent of the total public sector outlay.

The Ninth Five-Year Plan (1997-2002): The main targets of the Ninth Five-Year Plan were speedy industrialisation, human development, full-scale employment, poverty reduction and self-reliance on domestic resources. The main objectives of the Ninth Five-Year Plan were :

- To prioritise agriculture with emphasis on rural development.
- Generation of employment opportunities and promotion of poverty alleviation.

- Price stabilisation to accelerate the growth rate of the economy.
- To ensure food and nutritional security.
- To provide infrastructural facilities like education for all, safe drinking water, primary health care, transport, energy.
- To check the population growth.
- To promote social issues like women empowerment, protection of benefits of certain groups of society.
- To create liberal market to promote private investments.

The Tenth Five-Year Plan (2002-07): The Tenth Five-Year Plan targeted to make India's economy as the fastest growing economy with focus to raise the growth rate to 10%, besides reduction in poverty rate and increase in the literacy rate. The plan also attempted to create an investor-friendly market to achieve the growth rate and also sought active participation of the private sector. Its objectives included the reduction of poverty by 5 percentage points by 2007, increase in forest cover by 25 per cent by 2007, and access to potable drinking water to all villages of India.

The Eleventh Five-Year Plan (2007-2012): The main objectives of the Eleventh Five-Year Plan are :

- To accelerate GDP growth to 10%.
- To reduce educated unemployment to 5%.
- To reduce infant mortality to 28 and maternal mortality ratio to 1 per 1000 live births and total fertility rate to 2.1 in the health sector.
- To create 70 million new work opportunities.
- To ensure electricity connection and safe drinking water to all villages and increase forest cover by 5%.
- To raise the sex ratio for age group 0-6 to 935 by 2011-12 and to 950 by 2016-17.

Thus, planning in India has helped achieve growth in different spheres of life. Today, Indian economy is one of the fastest growing economy of the world with a consistent growth rate of 8-10%. Certainly, this shows the success of planning in India.

65

PUBLIC SECTOR ENTERPRISES IN INDIA

Public sector is considered a powerful engine of economic development. It is an important instrument of self-reliance. The growth and expansion of public sector has, no doubt, led to a considerable growth in various sectors of our economy. We are today self-sufficient in food production and our industrial base has been considerably strengthened and diversified both in the basic and core sector as also in the other areas of manufacture.

However, despite these achievements, an analysis of the rate of growth over these years indicates that our progress has been rather slow in comparison to many other developing countries of the world. In 1950, India's industrial sector, for example, was bigger than Taiwan's or South Korea's. The share of our exports in world markets was higher than that of China, South Korea, Singapore, Indonesia or Malaysia. The level of poverty in these countries was equal to or more than what prevailed in our country. Over the years, all these countries have passed us by. They export much more than what we do. Their industry is more competitive than ours. They have a higher level of foreign exchange reserves than us and, barring China, all these nations have succeeded in eradicating poverty and achieved the status of "middle income nations". Their per capita incomes are, at least, twice as high as ours. Their people are more educated, have better health facilities and enjoy a quality of life superior to that available to an average Indian.

What went wrong? When we look closely, we find that the tardy rate of our growth is the outcome of a deeper structural malady that overtook our economy ever since we embarked on the path of planned economic growth. Controls on production, licensing restrictions, along with high protective walls fostered monopolistic trends within our industry and made it import-intensive and inward-looking. Lack of competition ensured that there was no pressure for change, the technological resolutions that had spread from the advanced nations to our Asian neighbours had passed us by. Our companies produced goods of poor quality that could be sold only in the domestic market and had little acceptability abroad. Most large companies including those in the public sector imported more than they exported. Given our reliance on imports of petroleum and other bulk produces, the high levels of foreign exchange consumption of our industrial sector ensured that we incurred large trade deficits on a recurring basis. This increased our vulnerability to external shocks; our foreign account collapsed whenever oil price shot up abroad, as happened in 1979-80 and again in 1990. The problem got accentuated over the period, as, to finance these rising deficits, we had to increasingly resort to costly foreign commercial borrowings, since the climate for cheaper concessional aid had turned adverse. This led to an accumulation of a huge foreign debt and the consequent rise in debt service payment further weakened our balance of payments.

There is no gainsaying the fact that public sector, which was supposed to act as a lever to lift our economy out of the grave economic malaise fostered on us by the centuries of colonial rule, failed miserably to come up to our expectations.

The country had decided to create a sector, where it would be able to develop an industrial base, which, being free from exploitation, achieved faster growth and acquired a commanding height in the economy. It was not only to generate resources for development. However, for long it has been felt that these objectives had remained largely unfulfilled. It is no secret that we have not been able to provide productive employment to an overwhelming majority of employable people and disparities in income and wealth have further increased.

In terms of performance to be judged by indicators such as productivity, profitability, capacity utilisation, etc., our public sector presents a gloomy picture.

As regards capacity utilisation, it has never exceeded 55 per cent in as many as 93 SLEPs (Central Level Public Enterprises).

Despite their impressive role, public sector enterprises in India suffer from several problems and shortcomings. Some of these are described below :

Investment decisions in many public enterprises are not based upon proper evaluation of demand and supply, cost benefit analysis and technical feasibility. Lack of a precise criterion and flaws in planning have caused undue delays and inflated costs of projects. Many projects in the public sector have not been finished within the time schedule.

Due to inefficient financial planning, lack of effective financial control and easy availability of money from the government, several public enterprises suffer from over-capitalisation. The Administrative Reforms Commission found that several public enterprises, such as Heavy Engineering Corporation, Hindustan Aeronautics and Indian Drugs and Pharmaceuticals Ltd. were over-capitalised. This resulted in high capital-output ratio and wastage of scarce capital resources.

Manpower planning is not effective due to which several public enterprises like Bhilai Steel have excess manpower. Recruitment is not based on sound labour projections. This leads to inefficient utilisation of manpower.

One of the major problems of the public sector has been low utilisation of installed capacity. In the absence of definite targets of production, effective production planning and control and proper assessment of future needs, many undertakings have failed to make full use of their fixed assets. In some cases, productivity is low due to poor materials management or ineffective inventory control.

The inefficiency of public enterprises is largely attributed to poor management. Managerial efficiency and effectiveness have been low due to inept management, too much centralisation, uninspiring leadership and lack of personal stake. Political interference in day-to-day affairs, rigid bureaucratic control and ineffective delegation of authority hamper initiative, flexibility and quick decisions. Besides, due to lack of proper training, use of bureaucratic practices have also contributed to the inefficiency of public sector. Motivations and morale of both executives and workers are low due to the lack of appropriate incentives.

Despite all these, public enterprises have played significant role in realising the goals set according to constitutional ideals, such as too much concentration of economic power in private hands, increasing people's participation in economic development of the country, creating a socialistic pattern of society, a few among others. Above all, its greatest contribution is in attainment of national self-reliance.

66

ADVENT OF ECONOMIC LIBERALISATION

The year 1991 witnessed a change in the economic policy with the introduction of liberalisation and decontrols. Industrial Policy Resolution of 1991 threw open several more areas to the private sector. The controls were relaxed and general liberalisation of the system was attempted with the general globalisation of the economy.

Planning Commission is the apex organisation responsible for executing several plans of development all over the country. While the Finance Commissions, the statutory constitutional bodies, have been relegated to the secondary position of distributing revenues of non-plan and non-developmental funds, the Planning Commission, an extra-constitutional agency has assumed a prominent role in the economic development of the county, as most of the development funds are released by it to the State Governments. As per the Constitution, economic and social planning is the concurrent legislative power, but the Planning Commission was set up by the resolution of the Cabinet in 1950, with the Prime Minister as its chairman. The prime responsibility given to the Planning Commission was effective implementation of Five-Year Plans. Also described as the "economic cabinet of the country" by some critics, Planning Commission has assumed a very important place in Indian economy. The process of liberalisation aims at reduction of controls and regulations, relaxation of Foreign Exchange and Regulation Act (FERA), freer trade with no trade barriers and free flow of foreign investments.

Planning Commission basically has a regulatory function in which the activities and schemes of development are monitored. The process of liberalisation of economic system is likely to alter its existing role considerably. In a deregulated economy, the planning assumes the role of virtual indicative planning. Even the planning departments of State governments also undergo considerable change from the traditional role. Indian Plans are already distinct from "regimentation plans" of the former Soviet Union and were termed as "democratic plans". During the past over four decades of planning, the market forces have largely guided the decisions of the planning process. Today, there is a recognition that in many areas of activity, development can best be ensured by freeing them from unnecessary controls and regulations. Under the changed and liberalised scenario, it is not a choice between the market mechanism and planning, but the challenge is to properly dovetail the two in such a manner that they become complementary to each other. As the process of liberalisation gains momentum, the role of planning in India is likely to undergo further changes.

When the planning was conceived in India and the Planning Commission was set up in 1950, the role envisaged for planning was quite comprehensive. During the planning era, public sector expanded with a wide-ranging influence on the economic life of the country. The controls and regulations which were the dire need after Independence to protect the domestic infant industries in the country were stretched to such limits that these activities dampened people's initiatives and their sense of responsibility. India claimed that it followed the "democratic planning" witnessed in the erstwhile USSR, but no tendencies of extreme centralisation came to be seen in the Indian context. As the developmental funds are controlled and regulated by the Commission for the Union as well as the States, its importance has grown out of proportion. The priorities of local needs in the far flung areas of the States are also determined in New Delhi. The public sector performance has not come up to the mark and the advent to private sector in almost all areas of the economy in a big way has rendered the concept of public sector redundant in the modern day context. The role of resource allocation, hitherto considered the most important function of Planning Commission, is also required to be re-defined.

Thus, under the changed circumstances, the entire role of Planning Commission is required to be re-defined. The prevailing multi-agency approach also needs to be amended to provide coordinated policy formulation in an integrated approach. Such an approach can lead to better results at lower costs and lesser loss of time. The local planning agencies at District, Block or even Panchayat level need to be strengthened. These agencies have to play increasingly greater role to ascertain the local developmental needs and to decide about the resource allocation at local level.

In addition, planning has to assume a different role by promoting the private sector, as against its traditional role of guarding and encouraging the public sector. The process of liberalisation and decontrols has encouraged a large number of private investors, both domestic as well as foreign, to invest in the Indian economy on a large scale. The Government has already carried out disinvestment from the public sector enterprises, which is an indication of the Government's renewed confidence in the private sector. Under such a situation, the role of Planning Commission has to transform towards broad indicative planning rather than strictly regulatory one.

In a developing country like ours, where a large proportion of population lives below the poverty line, social sector is utterly under-developed. Industry is in the process of developing and other facilities require active Government support for development. Thus, Government role in overall planning cannot be over-emphasized. Active Government involvement in creating infrastructures like schools, hospitals, institutions of excellence and scientific research is very essential. The country has to plan and structure the system of education to cultivate necessary calibre, skills and value systems. This effort will have to be substantially supported by the private sector. But the planning process cannot be allowed to be left to the private sector entirely, as our private sector is not yet fully equipped to handle the entire range of needs of the country, particularly of the poorer and weaker sections. Performance of Indian planning has been laudable in the field of poverty alleviation and upliftment of the down-trodden. In the field of eradication of poverty and upliftment of the poorer sections by ensuring social justice, planning will have to continue to play a major role. Another area, where planning has an important role to play, is the balanced regional development. If this objective is left to the market forces, most concentration of new industries will be around the industrially developed areas, and backward and interior areas poor in infrastructure, will be completely left out. Planning process has to ensure the flow of financial resources and investment in the desired pockets by making special provisions for tribal areas, hilly areas and other backward areas.

Similarly, the role of the public sector in certain areas cannot be undermined. Despite the need for privatising some of the public sector enterprises, the public sector has to continue playing a very special role in the field of communication, transport, energy, irrigation and defence production. The areas like environment, forest, civil and police administration, management of rare minerals, land and water resources have to be managed by government agencies and need constant and detailed planning.

67

STRATEGIES FOR POVERTY ALLEVIATION IN INDIA

Poverty is defined in terms of income, expenditure and nutritional value. Poverty line is drawn on the basis of barest minimum desirable nutritional standards of calorie intake. Even when defined in these modest terms, nearly half of India's population is estimated to be deprived of this basic minimum. People below the poverty line comprise largely those whose consumption is very low and who have little physical resources of production. Quite often they are located in the climatically unfavourable regions with extremely low and fluctuating levels of production, income and meagre avenues of the gainful employment.

In the post-global era, India economy is consistently growing at a faster rate of nearly 10 per cent per annum and it has become the fourth largest economy in the world. The benefits of this growth are undoubtedly being reaped by a significant proportion of the population across the country including the lower strata of the society. According to the National Sample Survey results, people living below the poverty line have dramatically come down during the post-economic reforms era. However, about 25 per cent of the population still falls below the poverty line.

There are various factors responsible for the uneven development of society. Modern economy is technology-driven and not labour-intensive. High volume of high quality goods are produced with fewer labour hands. In other words, modern economy is not generating employment in the ratio of people looking for job. One-fourth of India's population is still illiterate; and even among literate, a good number of people do not have the employable skills of the modern economy. The economic system is not tuned to the changing economic scenario. Besides, dwindling cultivable land and declining profitability in agriculture are pushing the rural unemployed to the cities, leading to the increase in the pool of unskilled workforce.

It is, therefore, quite clear that economic reform has though brought prosperity to the country, its benefits are not evenly distributed. Even there are people who are unable to participate in the economic development process and are totally deprived of the benefits. Such programmes need government's intervention so as to ensure that they are not left behind the development process and may be equally benefitted from the development process. They need welfare measures in the form of poverty alleviation programmes so that they may survive if not prosper in this era of economic reform.

Consistent with the objective of poverty alleviation, a number of general as well as specific programmes were implemented for improving the living conditions of the poor during various five-year plans. These programmes have been broadly classified into self-employment programmes, wage employment programmes, food safety programmes and social security programmes. However, in spite of these efforts, the problem of poverty continued to elude any solution. The government, apart from relying on the overall higher rate of growth of the economy, sought to alleviate poverty through some specific measures. A new scheme, the Integrated Rural Development Programme (IRDP), was incorporated for alleviating poverty and deprivation among the rural masses. The main objective of the IRDP is to raise the level of living of the poorest families in the rural areas above the poverty line on a lasting basis by giving them income generating assets and access to credit and other inputs. It is aimed at evolving, on the one hand, an operationally integrated strategy at increasing productivity and production in agriculture and other sectors, and, on the other, improving resource position and income level of vulnerable sections of population. The programme now covers all the 5,011 blocks in the country.

With a view to providing technical skills to rural youths to enable them to take up self-employment in agriculture, rural industries, services and business activities in the rural areas, the scheme of Training Rural Youth for Self-Employment (TRYSEM) was also started.

Another scheme, viz. National Rural Employment Programme (NREP) — aimed at poverty alleviation in rural areas, was launched in October 1980. Under this scheme, besides generating employment opportunities, subsidised wheat and rice was provided to the workers.

Another scheme, viz. Rural Landless Employment Guarantee Programme (RLEGP) was introduced with a view to providing guarantee of employment to at least one member of every landless household up to 100 days in a year and for creating durable assets for strengthening the infrastructure to meet the growing requirements of the rural economy.

With effect from April 1989, these special employment programmes, viz. NREP and RLEGP have been merged with a new scheme called Jawahar Rozgar Yojna (JRY). This is an employment guarantee scheme which seeks to provide employment to at least one member of each rural family below the poverty line. The cost of the JRY is borne by the Centre and the States on 80:20 basis.

A scheme, called Self Employment for Educated Unemployed Youth (SEEUY) was introduced by the Government to create self-employment opportunities and encouraging the educated unemployed youth to undertake self-employment ventures in industry, service and business sectors. Under the scheme, loans are given on concessional terms.

Another scheme, called Self-Employment Programme for Urban Poor (SEPUP), has been initiated during the subsequent plan period for providing self-employment opportunities to the urban poor. The programme covers all the cities and towns of the country not covered under the IRDP.

For alleviating urban poverty, Nehru Rozgar Yojna (NRY) has been designed to provide employment to urban unemployed and under-employed poor. The scheme has two components, viz. (a) Scheme for Urban Micro Enterprises (SUME) wherein families are provided assistance for setting up small enterprises and, thus, generate self-employment and (b) Scheme for Urban Wage Employment (SUWE) and Scheme of Housing and Shelter Upgradation (SHASU) under which wage employment is generated.

The JRY was revised and relaunched in April 1999 and was named as Jawahar Gram Samirdhi Yojna (JGSY). The main objective was creating economic assets and infrastructure in the village with the creation of employment being the primary objective. However, the programme failed to meet the expected target.

Another wage employment programme, namely, Employment Assurance Scheme (EAS) was launched but the solutions to the problems have still eluded. Hence, all these fragmented efforts of poverty alleviation were combined to launch a new programme, namely, Sampoorna Gramin Rozgar Yojna (SGRY), in which all the previous programmes were merged. This new programme has three-fold objective—generation of employment for the rural people, creation of community assets and infrastructure, and ensuring food and nutrition security for the rural poor.

The wage employment programmes failed to meet the target of poverty alleviation, though to some extent they contributed in bringing down the percentage of population from poverty.

However, government also launched food security programme so as to help the poor in meeting the basic need of food. Hence, Public Distribution System (PDS) was launched. The PDS was in fact originally a universal public distribution system (UPDS). Though it was not conceived as anti-poverty programme, it was initiated to provide a means to distribute foodgrains to the people. It turned out to be a significant poverty alleviation programme of the government in the post-economic reform era. It directly acted as safety net for the very poor. But the programme suffered poor implementation, besides other problems.

In the post-economic reform era, government also launched various social security programmes largely for those who are at the bottom of the BPL facing destitution and desertion. This includes National Social Assistance Programme (NSAP) which has programmes for different weaker segment of the society, such as elderly, women, etc.

Though statistics show that poverty is declining in India, but much remains to be done. Poverty is more of social marginalisation of an individual, household or group in the community, rather than inadequacy of income to fulfil the basic needs. Indeed, inadequate income is, therefore, one of the factors of marginalisation, but not the only factor responsible. The goal of poverty alleviation programmes should aim at largely increasing the income level of individual group but bringing the marginalised group section to the mainstream of the development process of the country. The country cannot claim economic growth when a section of the society is marginalised to the periphery of the society. Hence, poverty alleviation programmes should address the issue of poverty from broader perspectives.

68

RURAL DEVELOPMENT SCHEMES IN INDIA

To ameliorate the conditions of under-privileged people, many schemes, such as Community Development Agency (CDA), Marginal Farmers and Agricultural Labour (MFAL), Drought Prone Area Development Programmes (DPDAP) were started by the Government. However, it was realised that despite all these programmes, the majority of the rural population continued to remain in the grip of grinding poverty. Thus, with a view to improving the economic and social life of the 'poorest of the poor' living in the rural areas, a new development strategy was designed, which is known as Integrated Rural Development Programme or IRDP. Conceived in March 1976, the IRDP was initially launched in 1978-79 in 2,300 blocks, and was extended to all the 5,011 blocks of the country with effect from October 2, 1980.

The main objective of the Integrated Rural Development Programme is to improve the economic and social conditions of the poorest section of rural society. It aims at raising their levels of living and bringing them above the poverty line on a lasting basis by giving them income generating assets, credit facilities and other inputs.

The families eligible for assistance under this programme are those whose annual family income is less than ₹ 4,800 per year. It also includes cultivating families, where the size of operational holding is less than five acres of land. Among these families, the poorest ones are provided assistance in the initial stages and the remaining ones are covered gradually. The final selection of the poorest families is done at a meeting of the Panchayat gram sabha. The selected poor families are provided job opportunities in the form of self-employment. For this, they are given credit, subsidies, etc. to purchase income-yielding assets and are also provided with other required inputs and market support.

Special attention is being paid to rural women under the IRDP. There is a special component of the programme for organising rural women for productive activities on a group basis. The identified poor rural women are offered training and provided with suitable assets for increasing their family incomes.

A national scheme for Training of Rural Youth for Self-Employment (TRYSEM) was launched by the Central Government on August 25, 1979. The aim of this scheme is to equip the rural youth with necessary skills and technical knowledge with a view to enabling them to seek self-employment. Under this scheme, only those persons in the age group of 18 to 35 years, who belong to the target poverty groups of small and marginal farmers, agricultural labourers, rural artisans and others below the poverty line, are eligible for training. TRYSEM, as a part of IRDP, aims at training two lakh rural youth every year at an average rate of 40 youth per block. Over 2.8 lakh rural youth were trained under TRYSEM during 1992-93. The target for 1993-94 was to train 3.5 lakh rural youth for self-employment. Besides training, the scheme envisages organisational and operational linkage with other institutions so that credit, marketing, raw material supplies, etc. may be provided to the trainees at the appropriate time.

Land, in rural areas, continues to be regarded as an important asset, a significant resource of production and widely accepted measure of social strength. Thus, for improving the socio-economic status of the poor landless labourers, who constitute the hard core of rural poverty groups, it is necessary that the surplus land made available through implementing land ceiling laws, be distributed expeditiously among the landless poor. Though land ceiling laws have been enacted and are being implemented in all the States except Nagaland, Meghalaya, Arunachal Pradesh and Mizoram, where land is generally held by the community, the progress in acquisition and distribution of surplus land is very slow.

Drought Prone Areas Programme (DRAP): Started in 1973 and being implemented in 947 blocks, spread over 155 districts of 13 states in the country, the DRAP aims at an integrated development of these areas through optimum utilisation of land, water and livestock resources with a view to expanding production, opening up more avenues of employment and increasing incomes of the people inhabiting these areas. The economy of these areas is sought to be insulated from the effects of recurring droughts through diversification of agriculture, and by promoting pasture development, soil management and water conservation.

Launched in 1977-78, the Desert Development Programme (DDP) aims at integrated development of desert areas with a view to providing the local population better incomes and more employment opportunities. The programme covers 227 development blocks in 36 districts in seven States, of which 17 are in hot and arid zones of Rajasthan, Haryana and Gujarat, defined as desert areas by the National Commission on Agriculture. The DDP also covers the cold arid zones comprising two districts in Jammu and Kashmir, and two districts in Himachal Pradesh. Development of forests and grasslands, dunes stabilisation, ground water development, construction of water harvesting structure, rural electrification for energising pumpsets and development of agriculture, horticulture and animal husbandry are some of the major components of the Desert Development Programme.

Bonded labour comprises that class of rural workers which has remained attached to the landlords and other village bigwigs for generations together, working for them for a mere pittance, without ever having a chance to choose or change their masters, thus perpetuating the vestiges of the much maligned and obnoxious slave system of the bygone ages. As such, these people remained tied up to the lowest rungs of the society without any freedom of participation in the process of rural development. Consequently, legislation was passed for abolition of the system of bonded labour and steps were taken to release them from their age-old bondage. The State

Governments were made responsible for identifying and rehabilitating the released bonded labourers. In addition to the on-going beneficiary schemes, a Centrally-sponsored scheme for rehabilitation of freed bonded labour was launched in 1978-79. The scheme provides Central grant of 50 per cent of the total cost on a matching basis, subject to a ceiling of ₹ 2,000 per bonded labourer.

The Minimum Needs Programme (MNP), introduced in the first year of the fifth five-year plan (1974-1978), is aimed at improving the quality of life and providing infrastructural support needed for supporting and supplementing the other beneficiary programmes for helping the rural poor.

The MNP is essentially a programme of investment in infrastructure and human resource development. It seeks to improve the consumption levels, productivity and efficiency of the poor through provision of free or subsidised services according to the internationally accepted norms. The main components of the Minimum Needs Programme are: (i) elementary education, (ii) adult education, (iii) rural health, (iv) rural water supply, (v) rural roads, (vi) rural electrification, (vii) house sites for landless labourers, (viii) environmental improvements of urban slums and (ix) nutrition. Besides these, three more components have been added to the Minimum Needs Programme under the Seventh Five-Year Plan. These are (i) rural domestic cookery energy, (i) public distribution, and (iii) rural sanitation. But MNP seeks to provide these services through public agencies in a time-bound manner. The integration of the Minimum Needs Programme with other beneficiary programmes like the IRDP, TRYSEM, etc. can have a more enduring impact on the alleviation of poverty in rural areas.

Launched in 1989, the Jawahar Rozgar Yojna (JRY) is an employment guarantee programme which seeks to provide employment to at least one member of every rural family living below the poverty line. The scheme is being implemented through the village Panchayats who will be given annual financial assistance. The Centre and the States would bear the cost of the scheme on 80:20 basis. The highlights of the scheme are: (i) at least one member of every rural family living below the poverty line to be given employment for 50-100 days a year at a work place near his or her residence, (ii) 30 per cent of the jobs are to be reserved for the women and (iii) the job creation plans to be developed by the Panchayats in accordance with the rural needs and resource endowments. The JRY will reach in due course all the 440 lakh rural families living below the poverty line. All the existing rural wage employment programmes, such as National Rural Employment Programme (NREP) and Rural Landless Employment Guarantee Programme (RLEGP) have been merged in the JRY. During 1992-93 employment equal to 782.1 million man-days was created under the JRY. The Eighth Plan sought to further strengthen the scheme and use it as an effective instrument of poverty alleviation programme.

Although these schemes have contributed a lot in rural development, yet much remains to be done. An ideal approach should include the governments, panchayats, NGOs and private companies in the development of rural India. This will not only help in reducing the imbalance in urban and rural India, but will also have a multiplier effect on the overall growth of the economy.

V

69

EXPANDING RURAL INDUSTRIES

Rural Industry continues to play a significant role in the expansion of employment, improvement in poductivity and earnings. It also has a major role in poverty reduction in many non-industrialised countries, particularly in India, where over three-fourths of its population live in villages.

Mahatma Gandhi stressed that India was destined to be a rural civilisation but he had not, at any time, mentioned that rural India is to have an agricultural economy. When Britain was ushering in the Industrial Revolution, a large percentage of the rural population in India was deriving income from non-agricultural activities. Even in 1940, as much as 60 per cent of the population was dependent on non-agricultural activities in spite of the devastation caused to India's village industries by the British Rule. The traditional rural industries contributed to the stability of rural economy.

China has made significant advance in rural industrialisation in recent years. The number of rural enterprises has increased tremendously in recent times. The gross product value of rural industries has also registered good growth rate and its contribution is great in the garb of economy. This development provides hope of finding a solution to China's large population and employment problem, and in narrowing the wide gap between the cities and the countryside.

India's rural industries cover its significant informal sector. The term informal sector covers both the micro base of entrepreneurship which spontaneously emerges, as also a micro sector that has been deliberately created as an appendage of large capital. Viewed from this angle, an array of economic activities falling under the rubric 'rural crafts', such as handlooms and handicrafts, can form the compass of rural industries.

Labour intensive small scale rural enterprises generate employment and income, transfer skills, promote regional activity and provide goods and services in rural areas. They are often the primary source of non-farm employment for women and the landless. Forest-based processing enterprises have proved to be among the most relevant. Although the mean size of the labour force engaged per family remains quite small (generally below 5 workers), such enterprises show low capital to labour ratios and provide a major source of cash income for the landless and the poor.

Five-year plans in India have great emphasis on promotion of rural industries for benefiting the rural population. This includes the generation of employment and development of rural infrastructure as well. A large number of people living in rural areas draw their livelihood from rural industry. Thus, planning in India focuses on the promotion and development of rural industry so as to increase productive employment opportunities, by integrating traditional production infrastructure skills and locally available raw material.

Rural industry in India has been growing in aggregate size and increasingly contributing to rural income generation. Recognising that the long-term development of Indian economy depends critically on the effective exploitation of the productive potential of the rural industry, the government established the Ministry of Agro and Rural Industries in September 2001. This was done with the main objective of facilitating coordinated and focused policy formulation and effective implementation of programmes, projects, schemes, etc. for improving skills, upgrading technology, developing supply chain, expanding markets and capacity building of the entrepreneurs at community village level.

Rural industry is divided into three subsets calling for differentiated strategies: The first are the village/household enterprises including khadi and village industries, handloom, handicraft, sericulture and coir which have tremendous potential in terms of utilisation of local resources and skills, and creation of gainful employment with low investment and minimal dislocation. The second pertains to the tiny sector which has shown capability to promote growth and employment generation. Though most of these industries at present come under urban areas, a number of them can be transferred to rural areas providing employment opportunities to local masses. A new sector of food processing is now taking concrete shape and is bound to play an important role in the rural areas in due course of time.

The types of industries that are promoted should be suitable for the specific area or region. With great variation in levels of growth and socio-economic situations, the nature and extent of industrial dispersal and the range of industries to be undertaken in under-industrialised region would vary considerably. For example, a fertile agricultural region might concentrate on food processing and the production of agricultural equipment and inputs; pasture region will present a greater possibility of industries relating to animal husbandry such as dairy products and leather, and coastal regions may concentrate on fishing and exploitation of marine living resources.

Apart from the variation in local needs and the necessity to upgrade local skills and crafts, the nature and pattern of such industrial activities will also cover a wide range such as repairs and servicing of machinery and equipment, labour intensive units such as readymade clothing to meet local needs, processing of perishable and non-perishable local produce, production of simple agricultural equipment, manufacture of building materials, cloth and shoes and production of implements and products for the organised urban industrial sector.

Sustainability of rural industries has become a crucial area of debate in recent times. Marketing was considered a problem rather than an opportunity. This 'problem' was sought to be addressed through enhanced public policy interventions, such as bhandars and common marketing centres organised by the government, marketing federations and cooperatives.

The issue of rural industrialisation, therefore, needs to be viewed from a new angle and on far more scientific lines. The core of a scientific approach is to understand the market opportunities for rural products along with the country's development priorities and to chalk out a strategy where rural industries have an important role to play. It is often presumed that in rural areas, industries form only a subsidiary occupation. Most traditional industries are household-based and family labour-based. However, in an open economy, where materials and technology flow freely and markets are open and global in nature, production at the household level becomes rather difficult. This demands a change in the household organisation of production itself.

The imperatives for innovation demand a coordinated approach that can energise rural entrepreneurs. While the public programmes since Independence have focussed on upgrading technical skills of the rural poor, precious little has been done so far to motivate them into entrepreneurial activities. This is one area which needs to be emphasised in the coming years. Besides, in the changing scenario, rural industries need to have some dynamism relating to technology, product design and organisational structure. Only then India will be able to exploit the full potential of rural industry.

70

POPULATION PROBLEM OF INDIA

Population in itself is not a problem, but lack of basic education and poor economic conditions is. India is the second most populous country in the world, containing one-sixth of the total world population in an area of more than 2.5 per cent of global land. The prevalent high maternal, infant, childhood morbidity and mortality, low life expectancy and high morbidity have been a source of concern for the policy makers since Independence. It is the population growth that neutralises all development, made in different sphereas of life. Thus, population stabilisation is an essential prerequisite for sustainability of development process so that the benefits of economic development result in enhancement of the well-being of the people and improvement in their quality of life.

It is the problems of the increasing number of mouths to be fed that has alarmed people in all parts of the world. Economists are baffled, sociologists are scared, and politicians and administrators are worried. It has created various problems like unemployment, poverty, starvation and illiteracy, besides shelterlessness. And unfortunately, those living in the 'have-not nations — the developing countries of Asia, Africa and Latin America.

India is the first country in the world to formulate a National Family Planning Programme in 1952 with focus to reducing the birth rate to the extent necessary to stabilise the population at a level consistent with growth of national economy. Thus, the key elements of healthcare to woman and children and provision of contraceptive services have been the focus of India's health services right since Independence. This has been followed in successive five-year plans which provide the policy framework and funding for planned development of nationwide healthcare infrastructure and manpower. The family welfare programmes provide additional infrastructure, manpower and drugs, vaccines, contraceptives and other consumables needed for improving health status of women and children and to meet all the felt needs for fertility regulation.

India, a developing country, comes second to China in the world in figures of population. Although, the world is forty times as large as India in area, the world population is only seven times as large as India's. One of every seven persons in the world is an Indian. Obviously, India, like other developing countries, is also experiencing a heavy pressure of population.

The population in India has increased from 236.5 million in 1901 to over 1.22 billion as per census 2011. More than 5,500 babies are born every day. We add to our population about 12 million people every year. Although, it took thousands of years until 1971 for our population to reach 500 million, at the present rate of growth our population will double itself within the next few years.

The main cause of this extraordinary growth in our population is not excessive births. It is rather our victory against death and disease. Our achievements in controlling communicable diseases like malaria, small pox and cholera and in improving health services have steadily brought down the death rate from 27 per 1,000 in 1951 to 16 today, while the birth rate has not come down proportionately. Life expectancy at birth has risen from 32 years in 1950 to 67 years today. Thus, our number is multiplying every day. As a result, there are 20 million births a year and about 8 million deaths, giving an annual increase of about 12 million in our already huge population.

The result of the increasing numbers is obvious — much of our effort to raise the standard of living of our people through successive five-year plans has been nullified.

The growth of population, besides neutralising all developmental efforts, brings distress to the community, to the family and to the individuals. In the words of one of our economists, "To plan when population growth is unchecked, is like building a house where the ground is constantly flooded."

What then needs to be done? The remedy is to reduce the number of births. In order to stabilise the relationship between population and the basic necessities of life, we must bring our birth rate down as quickly as possible.

The national family planning programme was started in a modest way in 1952. Now, India is among one of the foremost countries which takes concrete measures to boost this programme, and we are now in the midst of the world's largest family planning drives.

The importance which the Union Government has attached to birth control is evident from the fact that about ₹ 50 crore — half of the outlay on health in each annual plan— is set apart for family planning. A department of Family Planning (now Family Welfare) functions in the Union Ministry of Health. The Government of India has accorded "top priority" to the programme needed for population control. It has been decided that all our efforts should be made to reduce the birth rate to 25 per thousand as early as possible.

The most important reasons for the contemporary population explosions round the world are tremendous technological changes and spectacular control of disease as a result of scientific research and technological development. In developing countries there is a decrease in the death rate, while there is no decrease in birth rate, leading to population explosion. In the advanced nations of the world, there is a rapid rise in the standard of living. When there is a rise in the standard of living, large number of children cease to become an economic liability, instead they become an economic asset. In the agricultural societies of advanced countries, a large number of children and women also constitute an added economic asset.

Population growth is a stimulant to economic growth up to a point, but afterward it becomes a serious impediment. Larger population provides abundant labour as well as a big market for consumption. When a country is under-populated, it becomes a serious impediment to economic development.

The alarming rate of increase in population, at the rate of about 12 million per year, produces an occasional crisis in food situation, necessitating import of foodgrains, involving large amount of foreign exchange, which otherwise would have been available to promote economic growth. Though the food production may have increased during that period, it is not enough to feed the excess population.

Another consequence of vast growth of population is that it reduces capacity to save and invest. Capital formation is crucial to economic growth but in India most of the resources are used up in supporting the growing and unproductive population so that the family as well as the country continue to live in poverty. One of the major needs of the developing countries is additional investment on highways, railroads, communication systems, power generation, irrigation pumps and so forth. A decline in fertility is essential so that there are fewer dependents per wage-earner, who may then be motivated to save a good proportion of his total income. This is the usual method adopted in Russia and other socialist nations.

Studies have shown how even 50% decline in fertility might favourably affect the total amount of capital investment, the proportion of which could be used for improving productivity rather than for providing for population increase. Only could then there be an increase in income per equivalent adult consumer. If there is no reduction in the size of the family, it is difficult, if not impossible for it, to save in order to increase capital formation. It has been found in studies that high fertility can depress private savings in the way.

Thus, the progress made during the post-Independence era would have been highly significant, but there has been no remarkable dent on poverty since the population has been increasing at the rate of about 12 million per year. Thus, all the gains have been liquidated by population growth.

Ashish Bose, eminent economic analyst, has rightly

commented: "The present reproductive pattern in India is wasteful, uneconomic and highly inimical to the health and wealth of the nation. Further, the size, density, rate of growth and age structure of the population are all unfavourable to economic progress. Our land is limited, capital is scarce and organisation inefficient. Vast industrial and human resources in themselves cannot bring about economic progress. They can only sustain in primitive economy. And this is what actually is happening in India."

In the urban areas again there is a surplus population due to two reasons: excessive increase in population and a steady migration from the rural areas of illiterate and unskilled people. Further, there is a problem of unemployment among the educated people. With the increase in educational facilities, there is a tremendous increase among the matriculates and the liberal arts graduates every year who want only the white-collared jobs; they are not trained to produce goods nor any service.

Gunnar Myrdal, renowned Swedish economist and sociologist, has commented as follows:

"In India Gandhi's thought on population issue acted as a continuous inhibition to wholehearted acceptance of contraception. Even when Gandhi came to acknowledge the necessity of decreasing fertility, he insisted that it should be accomplished through abstinence." "There can be no two opinions on the necessity of birth control. But the only method handed down from ages past is self-control or *Brahmacharya.* It is an infallible sovereign remedy doing good to those who practise it. The union is meant not for pleasure but for bringing forth progeny. And the union is criminal when the desire for progeny is absent," said Mahatma Gandhi. Even some of the leaders like Sushila Nayyar, who later became a minister of health, incharge of family planning, was of the opinion in early 1950 that "The State can never control population whether it be a drive for increasing or lowering the birth rate."

In certain segments of the country, especially rural areas, bearing and rearing of children is looked upon as an investment. They offer a measure of security which in illness and old age and all too frequently begin to lighten their parents' work while still in early childhood. The fact that married women work less often outside the home make even the smaller children less of a burden. Moreover, with the relative prevalence of the joint or extended family system, the responsibility for bringing up children and the direct burden of looking after them should be assumed not to rest exclusively on the individual parents. This should weaken the motivation for limiting the births, both because of the awareness that other members of the extended family can be relied on to share the burden and because any couples which exclusively limit their offspring may as a direct result be called upon to make a larger contribution to the support of the children of other family members.

While parents and teachers play the most important role in moulding the attitudes and values of the children under their care, the society generally plays no small part in fashioning their modes and codes of behaviour.

In large metropolitan cities like Mumbai, Kolkata, Delhi, Chennai, Chandigarh, etc., the strong influence of Western ways of behaviour, greater freedom, and more frequent marriages between persons of different castes, creeds and countries have, to a great extent, broken down the old barriers, traditions and customs, and have resulted in the exposure of young people to a wider range of behaviour than their parents, and certainly their grandparents ever experienced. In such a setting, young people have to make choices at a much younger age, not only with regard to their profession, their friends, their clothes and hair styles, but also with regard to their sexual behaviour.

Thus, the prime objective of any programme for family life, education would be to enable young people to make personal and socially responsible choices about their sexual behaviour and to help them to achieve satisfying and responsible interpersonal relationships through the development of ethical standards.

It is essential for every young person to recognise that the sexuality, with which he or she is endowed, is a power which is to be used with a sense of responsibility, not merely to serve as an instrument to achieve temporary pleasure, but as a means of achieving the deeper happiness, which comes through the establishment of lasting relationships based on mutual love and understanding.

71

HOUSES FOR THE MILLIONS

As India's economy has boomed in recent years, India's predominantly rural population has flocked to the cities hoping to get a slice of the growing prosperity. A massive shortage of affordable housing has left may no choice but to live in makeshift tenements with few basic utilities, as per the country's first report on urban poverty.

Millions of Indians are forced to live in squalid slums, not because they are improverished, but because city planners have failed to build low-cost alternatives, resulting in the problem getting worse, as warned by the report.

The report estimates by 2030, some 50 per cent of Indians will live in cities, up from 28 per cent currently. With the population already touching 1.22 billion (2011 Census data), the challenge is huge. Already, about one-quarter of city dwellers are living "in slums amidst squalor, crime, disease and tension," the report said.

The Indian government has approved an ambitious scheme to provide affordable housing to millions of slum dwellers. The scheme aims to check proliferation of slums. The scheme is named Rajiv Awas Yojana (RAY) after former prime minister Rajiv Gandhi.

Housing projects would provide residents properly constructed homes, linked to basic infrastructure like sewage, electricity and running water.

Under the scheme, the federal government will provide financial assistance to states willing to assign property rights to slum dwellers. The money would be used to build low-cost houses and improve the basic civic services in the slums.

The plan is expected to benefit 32 million people in 250 cities and aims to give property rights to the owners of the houses built under the scheme. The first phase of the scheme has been approved at a cabinet meeting, chaired by Prime Minister Manmohan Singh.

The government has also announced setting up a $222 m (£ 137 m) fund to faciliate lending to urban poor for housing purposes.

The objective behind the government's new housing policy is to choose its role from a builder of houses, to be the main agency which should organise facilities required for house building. Also, the policy recognises the role of non-government and community organisations in assisting the underprivileged sections of society to secure adequate and affordable shelter. Clearly, under the compulsions of the liberalised economic policy and, bearing in mind the scandals surrounding the houses the DDA built in Delhi, the Centre is transferring the job of funding housing projects to non-government bodies and private organisations. Action is to be taken to increase institutional finance and NRI investments in housing. Fiscal concessions have been proposed with regard to custom and excise duty which, according to the Union Housing Ministry, should encourage entrepreneurs to set up manufacturing units for the production of low-cost building materials by utilising agro-industrial wastes. In the new dispensation, which amounts to privatisation of the housing section, the government is retaining for itself only a supervisory role. It is too early to say what impact this shift in the housing policy would have on the quality of houses to be constructed.

It is essential to ensure accountability of the builders in the private sector who unlike government or quasi-official organisations are sometimes difficult to trace after a mishap. Another requirement is that the dwelling units should be affordable, without compromising quality. The policy would lose meaning if it fails to take into account the growing demand for new houses. Growing urbanisation and expanded housing estates lead to new problems. While planning the housing problems that come with them, like transport, shopping, schools, medical facilities, open grounds and recreation, should be taken care of under a comprehensive housing policy.

Government and other agencies need to work in proper coordination so as to ensure houses to those without shelter with all the basic amenities without compromising the quality. But the biggest challenge is to provide basic services to the urban poor and slum dwellers without letting the elite capture the benefits. Government needs to be sincere in implementation and then realising the vision of housing for all would not be difficult and they will have their dream homes.

72

SHOULD THERE BE SEX EDUCATION IN SCHOOLS?

For the last nearly two decades the children in India are increasingly being exposed to the world through the expansion of the electronic media. In this process, particularly with the growth of foreign satellite channels, they are exposed to cruder versions of sex along with violence and crimes related to it. In view of these emerging trends, sex education in its psychic and social bearings is of such importance that it can hardly be ignored. But, paradoxically, children are still brought up in ignorance of facts that are vital to them or, worse still, adopt the faulty attitudes of the adults who surround them. Undoubtedly, the refusal to incorporate sex education will result in further damage to their spirit of inquiry. Considering that the foundation of a child's character is laid during his or her school days, a faulty upbringing may be responsible for the development of various forms of sexual deviations later.

Although AIDS in India began relatively late, its spread is alarming. Moreover, despite the non-availability of comprehensive data on the spread of sexually transmitted diseases (STDs) among the country's youth, there is evidence that a substantial number of young people in India are having unprotected sex. There is no denying that the ongoing AIDS awareness campaign in the country has been successful to a certain extent. The basic goal should be to produce the next generation of children fully informed about these diseases through sex education.

In a situation where a vast majority of the country's population continues to be ignorant of the ethics of responsible behaviour in human reproduction, it is only natural that various social taboos such as child marriage, preference for sons and large families have been encouraged and have come to contribute to the perpetuation of birth rates which continue to be very high. Youngsters in particular, who constitute almost 40 per cent of the country's total population, suffer from inaccurate information and misconception regarding sexuality. A study conducted some time back in Bhubaneswar suggested that out of 256 postgraduate students surveyed, a majority of them were not fully aware of the concept of family planning and different birth control measures.

To undermine the importance of sex education, a fallacy has been created by its opponents that the biology course in school can serve the purpose of instruction in sex. It is a misleading approach since in most cases teachers have not been found efficient in imparting education related to the reproductive system even in plants and animals. Most of the teachers feel awkward and children sense this. This is not surprising since most teachers themselves were brought up avoiding open references to the sexual process.

It has also been argued that at the present stage of socio-economic development, population education may be an appropriate alternative to sex education. In some schools, initiatives have already been taken in this direction. Nevertheless, population education primarily deals with size, distribution and composition of population. It does not aim at giving any insight into the totality of issues connected with sexual behaviour. Treating it as an alternative to sex education would, therefore, be incorrect.

A child's desire to know where babies come from is not a sign of perverted sexuality, but a desire to discover an important fact. It is as natural as his desire to know where the sun goes when it drops below the horizon. And the answer should be given as simply and as readily as possible. The child will then learn and assimilate what he wants to know, and what he needs to understand long before he has reached adulthood.

Given the opposition that sex education is facing in the country, the main challenge lies in advocating it as a discipline integrated with other school subjects. It must be drawn into some general philosophy of education and learning. For this, we have to get rid of all the ridiculous ideas which surround it. The government is especially expected to play an active role by doing away with the prejudice against sex education.

Here it is important to mention that a recent International Conference on Population and Development held in Cairo, while recognising equal rights for women and men in the family and at all levels, set before all governments three immediate goals: education, specially for girls; reduction in infant and maternal mortality; and universal access to family planning and health services for women. However, during the deliberations on these issues, it was made clear that in the coming years sexual health, reproductive rights, responsible sexual behaviour and family planning are going to be the major themes of discussion on population and sustainable development.

73

BANKING IN INDIA

Banking in India dates back to the last decades of the 18th century. The first banks were The General Bank of India, which started in 1786, and Bank of Hindustan, which started in 1790 but they no longer exist. The oldest bank in existence in India is the State Bank of India, which originated in the name of Bank of Calcutta in June 1806, but almost immediately became the Bank of Bengal. This was one of three presidency banks, the other two being the Bank of Bombay and the Bank of Madras, all three of which were established under charters from the British East India Company. For many years, the Presidency banks acted as quasi-central banks, as did their successors. The three banks merged in 1921 to form the Imperial Bank of India, which became the State Bank of India after Independence.

The State Bank of India is the largest commercial bank in the country and is among the 100 topmost banks in the world. The State Bank has five subsidiary banks attached to it. These are:

(i) Bank of Bikaner and Jaipur,
(ii) State Bank of Hyderabad,
(iii) State Bank of Mysore,
(iv) State Bank of Patiala,
(vi) State Bank of Travancore.

Earlier, the State Bank of India had seven associate banks that constituted the State Bank Group. The other two associate banks— State Bank of Saurashtra and State Bank of Indore— were merged with the State Bank of India in August 2008 and June 2009, respectively.

Besides these public sector banks, which control over 90 per cent of the banking activity in the country, there are non-nationalised scheduled banks and non-scheduled banks. A bank which has capital and reserves of over ₹ 5 lakh is called a scheduled bank and those which have capital and reserves less than this limit prescribed by the RBI Act, are categorised as non-scheduled banks.

Currenty, India has 88 scheduled commercial banks— 27 public sector banks (that is, with the Government of India holding stakes), 31 private banks (these do not have government stakes) and 38 foreign banks. They have a combined network of over 53,000 branches and 17,000 ATMs.

With an increase in the range of financial activities in the Indian banking sector, there are different types of banks that cater to specific requirements of the customers. Today, we have banks catering to customers through personalised services and banks that offer specific services. Typically, banks can be classified on the basis of their activities, such as business and investment.

In post-economic reform era banking sector has undergone considerable change. Now there are a number of private banks apart from the nationalised banks. The following are the main types of banks in India:

Privately Owned: These banks operate on a purely profit basis. Also called new generation banks, these are controlled by the state governments of their respective countries. While they are known to offer quick, easy and convenient options for customers, they are not considered as reliable and committed to growing the wealth of their customers as nationalised banks.

Publicly Owned: These banks are operated and controlled by the government. These banks actively maintain a huge number of operations that constitute the country's liquidity in the banking sector. They are considered safe, reliable and committed to the customers and the regulations formulated by the Reserve Bank of India.

These banks handle a number of tasks pertaining to the banking sector. Publicly owned banks also determine the interest rates that other banks in the country offer.

Regional Rural Banks (RRBs): With a view to improve the flow of credit to the rural sector of the economy, a number of Regional Rural Banks have been set up in the areas where commercial and cooperative banking facilities were lacking. These banks cater to the credit requirements of the weaker sections, small marginal farmers, landless labourers, village artisans and petty businessmen in the rural areas. These banks mainly focused to agro-sector. The total number of RRBs stands at 82 as at the end of March 2010 following the process of their amalgamation initiated by the government in 2005. The total number of RRBs has reduced from 196 to 82 as on March 31, 2010.

Cooperative Banks : The cooperative banks in India started functioning almost 100 years ago. These banks constitute an important part of the Indian financial system. The cooperative banks were specifically set up to cater to the needs of the rural population. These banks are also popular in urban areas. In fact, some cooperative banks in India are more forward looking than many of the state and private sector banks. Issues such as agricultural credit and other related topics are taken care of by the cooperative banks. Though the cooperative movement originated in the West, but the importance assumed by such banks in India is rarely paralleled anywhere else in the world. The cooperative banks in India play an important role in rural financing. The businesses of cooperative banks in the urban areas also have increased phenomenally in recent years due to the sharp increase in the number of primary cooperative banks.

Cooperative banks in India are registered under the Cooperative Societies Act. The cooperative banks are also regulated by the RBI. They are governed by the Banking Regulations Act, 1949 and Banking Laws (Cooperative Societies) Act, 1965.

The significant growth of cooperative banks in India is attributed largely to their better local reach, personal interaction with customers and, above all, customer satisfaction.

National Bank for Agriculture and Rural Development (NABARD): In the field of rural credit and agricultural development, establishment of NABARD is a major event. This Bank was established in July 1982 as an apex body with the responsibility for overall development, policy planning and financial support for agricultural and rural development. The NABARD provides credit to rural sector through cooperative banks, commercial banks, regional rural banks and other financial institutions set up to finance rural development. The Bank ensures coordination in operations of various institutions engaged in the field of rural credit.

Export-Import Bank of India: Recognising the importance of exports in India's development programmes, the Government of India set up Export-Import Bank of India in January 1982 as a statutory corporation wholly owned by the Union Government. The main objectives of the Export-Import Bank (EXIM Bank) are to ensure an integrated and coordinated approach in solving the problems of exporters, providing special attention to capital goods exports and export of technical services; and to tap domestic and overseas markets for resources, undertaking development and financing activities in the area of exports.

The EXIM Bank provides financial assistance to the exporters and importers and acts as the principal financial institution for coordinating the working of other institutions engaged in financing exports and imports. It also provides refinance facilities to commercial banks and financial institutions against their export-import financing activities.

Reserve Bank of India: The Reserve Bank of India, which is the central bank of this country, was established on April 1, 1935. It was originally started as a shareholders' bank with a share capital of ₹ 5 crore divided into shares of ₹ 100 each fully paid-up. But since January 1949 the Reserve Bank has been nationalised and it is now a purely State concern. The Government of India holds the entire share capital of the Bank which has been acquired for payment of compensation to the shareholders.

Functions and Powers: The Reserve Bank of India, as the Central Bank of the country, performs the following functions:

1. *It is the issuer bank:* The bank has the sole right of issuing paper notes in India. While issue of one rupee notes, coins and subsidiary coins is done by the Ministry of Finance, Government of India, the RBI undertakes their distribution on behalf of the Government.

2. *It acts as banker to Government:* It has been entrusted with the task of receiving all money on behalf of the Government as also with the task of making payments on their behalf. It performs these functions through the State Bank of India, which works as its agent at places where it has no office of its own. In addition, the Bank is the adviser to the Government on all financial matters.

3. *It is bankers' bank:* Being the apex bank, it acts as the banker to other banks. All scheduled banks have to keep a certain percentage of their time and demand liabilities with the Reserve Bank. The scheduled banks have also to submit weekly returns of their business to the Reserve Bank.

4. *It regulates the flow of credit:* The RBI formulates and administers monetary policy and regulates the volume and flow of the credit created by the commercial banks. It operates general credit control measures through changing the bank rate or through open market operations. It also uses selective credit control measures to regulate the flow of credit in some specific lines of activity.

5. *The RBI exercises supervisory powers over the commercial banks:* Every bank has to get a licence from the RBI to do banking business in India, and this licence can be suspended or cancelled if the banks fail to fulfil certain stipulated conditions. For opening new branches, the banks have to seek permission of the RBI. The RBI has the power to inspect the banks and seek any information from them.

6. *It maintains the external values of the rupee:* Since March 1947, India is a member of the International Monetary Fund. It has, therefore, to maintain its rate of exchange at the level

which it has declared to this fund. The Reserve Bank takes suitable measures to maintain the value of the rupee at this declared level.

As a central bank, certain restrictions have been imposed on the Reserve Bank. It is not to compete with the commercial banks. It is not allowed to pay interest on its deposits. It cannot engage directly or indirectly in trade. It cannot also acquire or advance loans against immovable property. It is also prohibited from purchasing its own shares or the shares of any other bank or any company or granting loans on such security.

74

INDIA'S DEFENCE SYSTEM — ARMY, AIR FORCE AND NAVY

India's defence system is an integrated and advanced system. The primary military organisation of India is the Armed Forces which comprises the Army, the Navy and the Air Force. The President of India is the Supreme Commander of the Armed Forces. However, the Indian armed forces include few auxiliary forces such as the Indian Paramilitary Forces, the Indian Coast Guards and the Strategic Forces Command.

Besides, a number of other services also constitute an integral part of Indian defence system. These are: Armoured Corps, Regiment of Artillery, Corps of Engineers, Corps of Signals, Mechanised Infantry, Army Service Corps, Military Nursing Service, Army Medical Corps, Army Dental Corps, Army Ordnance Corps, Corps of Electrical and Mechanical Engineers, Remount and Veterinary Corps, Military Farms Service, Army Education Corps, Intelligence Corps, Corps of Military Police, Judge, Advocates General Department, Army Physical Training Corps, Pioneer Corps, Army Postal Service Corps and Defence Security Corps. In addition, the Army has its own Recruiting Organisation, Record Offices, Depots, Boys Establishments, Selection Centres and Training Institutions.

The **Army** is organised into six commands, viz. Southern, Eastern, Western, Central, Northern and Training. Each command is under a General Officer Commanding-in-Chief who holds the rank of Lieutenant General. A General Officer Commanding-in-Chief is the commander of demarcated geographical area and has both field and static formations under his command. The major field formations are Corps Division and Brigade commanded by a General Officer Commanding of the rank of Lieutenant General, a General Officer Commanding of the rank of Major General and Brigadier, respectively. The major static formations are Areas,

Independent Sub-Areas and Sub-Areas. An Area is commanded by a General Officer Commanding of the rank of Major General and an independent Area by a Brigadier.

The **Air Force** is organised both on functional as well as geographical basis. There are five operational commands. These are: Western Air Command, South-Western Air Command, Central Air Command, Eastern Air Command and Southern Air Command. In addition, Maintenance Command and Training Command are two functional commands.

Today, the Air Force consists of an array of modern aircraft. Its fleet includes fighter bombers, air superiority fighters, interceptors, transport and logistic aircraft and helicopters. The fighter force comprises Hunters and Ajeets which are older generation aircraft, and MiG-21 variants, MiG-23s, MiG-25s, MiG-27s and Jaguar which represent the modern generation strike aircraft. MiG-29s and Mirage-2000 provide the Air Force with a present generation air defence aircraft. The ageing-light bomber, Canberra is presently used in ancillary roles. The transport fleet consists of IL-76s, AN-32s, Boeing-737 and indigenously produced HS748. Domier-228 has replaced the otter aircraft and is manufactured under licence by the HAL. The helicopter fleet has been modernised through acquisition of M-I8s, MM-7s and MI-26s. In addition, the force has been supplemented with MI-25s and MI-35s which are used as attack helicopters. MI-25 helicopter has done yeoman service for the IPKF on some fronts. Chetak/Cheetah helicopters are manufactured by HAL for the Air Force. They are used as airborne Forward Air Controller (FAC), Anti-Tank Guided Missile (ATGM) carrier and for search and rescue operations.

HPT-32 manufactured by HAL is used as the basic trainer aircraft. HJT-16 (Kiran) and Police Iskara aircrafts are used as trainers in the applied stage of training. HS748 is used as transport aircraft trainer. The Air Force MI-8 helicopters are specially modified to undertake tasks in Antarctica. MI-17 and Chetak are used for high-altitude operations. They provide logistics support to ground forces.

The **Indian Navy** is a well balanced three dimensional force consisting of sophisticated missiles capable warships, two aircraft carriers, minesweepers, advanced submarines and the latest aircraft in its inventory. Many of the warships are of indigenous design and have been constructed in Indian shipyards. These ships compare well with the ships of similar capability constructed by the advanced countries. The Naval forces are maintained and supported by modern dockyard facilities encompassing state-of-the-art technology. At present, it has two major naval bases at Mumbai and Visakhapatnam.

The Navy is responsible for defence and security of India's maritime interests and assets, both in times of war and peace. The Chief of the Naval Staff at the Naval Headquarters, New Delhi, is assisted by four Principal Staff Officers, namely, the Vice Chief of Naval Staff, Chief of Personnel, Chief of Material and Deputy Chief of Naval Staff.

The Navy has three commands, i.e., Western, Eastern and Southern, with their headquarters located at Mumbai, Visakhapatnam and Cochin (Kochi), respectively. Each command is headed by a Flag Officer Commanding-in-Chief in the rank of Vice Admiral. Western Command and Eastern Command have under them operational fleets, i.e., Western and Eastern Fleets comprising warships, submarines, aircraft and other support ships. Southern Naval Command is responsible for all training activities of the Indian Navy.

Recruitment to the Army is carried out through 12 zonal recruiting offices, 70 branch recruiting offices and 46 regimental/corps training centres, spread all over the country. Application system of recruitment continues to form the basis for recruitment in the Army. To adequately reach out to the candidates of rural and remote areas and to broaden the base of recruitment, recruitment *Melas* at the scale of one to two per recruitment zones per year are being held since January 1992. To enable quick disposal of large number of applications received by zonal recruiting offices, automation has been resorted to as a pilot project at the recruiting office, Delhi Cantonment. Six more zonal recruiting offices are being equipped with computers for automation in the near future.

Recruitment of airmen to Indian Air Force is done through the Central Airmen Selection Board located at the Air Force Station, New Delhi. There are 13 selection centres under this Board and they make necessary arrangements in the conduct of selection tests and final enrollment. After calling the applications through advertisements in national/regional dailies and through mass media, a written test on an all India basis is held and the all India merit list is drawn up with the help of computers.

Recruitment of sailors in the Navy and other ranks to the Army is carried out through network of 71 recruiting offices covering the entire country. The application system has been introduced from 1988 with a view to ensuring fair screening and eliminating touts and agents. According to this system, candidates are not required to personally visit recruiting offices. They can send their applications through post to the Zonal Recruiting Office concerned. Screening of applications and issue of call letters is done by the Zonal Recruiting Officer after considering the educational qualifications, additional qualifications (driving, typing, etc.) and achievements in NCC, games, etc. The screening of candidates, who are issued call letters, is carried out through a written examination, aptitude tests, medical tests, etc. The entire recruitment process is carried out by a team and completed on a fixed time schedule.

In January 1992, the Government approved the induction of women in the following branches: (i) Army Postal Service: (ii) Judge Advocates General Department; (iii) Army Education Corps; (iv) Army Ordnance Corps (Central Ammunition Depots and Materials Management) and (v) Army Service Corps (Food Scientists Catering Officers).

Government has recently approved the induction of women in additional branches of the Army, viz. Corps of Signals, Intelligence Corps, Corps of Engineers, Corps of Electrical and Mechanical Engineering and Regiment of Artillery.

Government had earlier approved induction of women in selected branches of Air Force and Navy also. In pursuance of these decisions, the selection process was commenced and a good number of women cadets have already completed their training at INS Madurai and have joined the Navy as officers. In the Air Force tens of women cadets have completed their training of Air Force Academy at Hyderabad and in the Army about 50 women cadets, who had been undergoing training at the Officers Training Academy (OTA) at Chennai since September 1992, have since passed out.

Selection for Commissioned Officers in the Armed Forces is done on an all-India basis through a written examination conducted by the Union Public Service Commission. In addition, selection of technical graduates for entry into certain technical corps/branches of Army is done through Army Headquarters and Services Selection Boards (SSBs).

Sainik Schools: Sainik Schools prepare boys academically and physically for entry into National Defence Academy. There are 18 sainik schools in the country, one in each State, except in Nagaland, Meghalaya, Tripura, Sikkim, Arunachal Pradesh, Mizoram and Goa. These schools are affiliated to the Central Board of Secondary Education and follow the 10+2 pattern of education.

Admission is made to class VI on the basis of an all-India entrance examination held every year in February, in which boys in the age group of 10-11 years are eligible to appear. Since its inception a total of 4,529 boys from these schools were selected for admission to the National Defence Academy, Naval Academy, Armed Forces Medical College, etc.

Rashtriya Indian Military College: Education on public school lines is imparted at Rashtriya Indian Military College (RIMC) principally for boys who subsequently desire to join the National Defence Academy, with a view to obtaining commission in the Armed Forces. The intake is at class VII. The college runs classes from 8th to 10+2. Selection for the RIMC is through a written-cum-viva voce examination conducted through State governments. Seats for the various States are reserved on the basis of population and allotted subject to availability of vacancies. The intake into the RIMC is bi-annual.

National Defence Academy: National Defence Academy (NDA) at Khadakvasla is a joint services training institution which imparts academic as well as service training. The syllabus of the Academy has been approved by the Jawaharlal Nehru University for the grant of BA/BSc degree at the time of passing out from the Academy. The first course commenced training on the revised syllabi in January 1989. After passing out NDA, the cadets go to their respective service academies for further training, before being commissioned as officers in the Armed Forces.

Indian Military Academy: Indian Military Academy (IMA) at Dehradun caters for the training of Gentlemen Cadets (GCs) for commission into the Army. Gentlemen Cadets join the IMA through the following modes of entry: (a) on passing out from NDA; (b) on graduation from the Army Cadet College, which is a wing of the IMA itself; (c) direct entry graduate cadets who join on qualifying a Union Public Service Commission examination and selection through the Services Selection Board and (d) technical graduates.

Officers Training Academy: Officers Training Academy (OTA) at Chennai trains cadets for Short Service Commission in the Army. OTA holds a 44-week course for graduates who qualify in the examination conducted by the Union Public Service Commission and the Services Selection Boards and who are between 19 and 25 years of age on the first day of the month in which the course starts. The Academy also runs Regimental Commission courses and Permanent Commission (Special List) course for the grant of commission to selected JCOs/NCOs.

The principal training units/establishments for the general service officers and men of the Navy are located at Cochin (Kochi). These units impart training in gunnery, navigation, anti-submarine warfare, communication, aviation, etc. Other major training establishments are Naval Academy, Goa, where basic training is given to Naval cadets and direct entry officers of all branches; INS Chilka, Orissa, where basic training is imparted to sailors and artificers; INS Shivaji, Lonavala, where basic engineering training of technical officers, specialised training for all engineering branch officers, sailors and artificers, NBCD training to all personnel is given; INS Valsura, Jamnagar, where specialised training for electrical branch officers and sailors is given; INS Satavahana, Visakhapatnam where specialised training in submarine cadre is given; INS Hamla, Marve, Malad, Mumbai, where specialised training is imparted to officers and sailors of logistics cadre, INS Kunjali, Mumbai, where regulating branch training and MT driving training is undertaken; INS Asvini (INM), Mumbai, where medical assistants' training is given, INS Agrani, Coimbatore, where management and leadership training is given to senior sailors; College of Naval Warfare, Mumbai, where Higher Command Courses are conducted and INS Garuda, Cochin (Kochi) and INS Hansa, Goa, where specialised training in aviation branch for both technical and non-technical personnel including flying training is imparted; Navy Shipwright School, Visakhapatnam, where specialised training in shipwright branch is imparted.

Air Force trainees are inducted from four sources, viz. National Defence Academy, ex-airmen, National Cadet Corps and direct entry selection by UPSC. The inductions are for both permanent as well as short service commissions. However, these are also granted to the flying (pilots) branch and for helicopter pilots from September 1990. SSC courses have also been introduced in the ground duties administrative branches for fighter controllers and ATC officers and the first such course commenced in April, 1992. All non-NDA trainees undergo pre-course training at Air Force Station, Begumpet (Secunderabad), before commencing the basic stage of flying training. The basic stage of flying training (stage I) for pilots is imparted at the Air Force Academy, Hyderabad, followed by advanced flying training (stage II) at Air Force Station, Hakimpet, Andhra Pradesh. Wings and Commissions are conferred on successful completion of stage II of flying training.

Thereafter, the trainees are bifurcated for applied stage (stage III) of training, viz. fighter stream at Hunter and MIG operational conversion units; transport stream at Air Force Station, Yelahanka, Karnataka and helicopter stream at the Helicopter Training School, Hakimpet.

Ordnance Factories: 30 ordnance factories spread all over India operate a wide-range of technologies and product-mix. Some of the important products are field guns, anti-aircraft guns, mortars, various small arms and ammunitions for weapons and guns, rockets, projectiles pro-technics, bombs, grenades, mines, demolition and depth charges, infantry combat vehicles, battle tanks, self-propelled guns, transport trucks and patrol vehicles. High-altitude and combat clothing, optical and fire control instruments, engineering equipment, supply dropping equipment including parachutes, rubberised items, various knitted and woven items like blankets, war equipment and a wide-range of general stores are produced by them.

75

SHOULD MILITARY EDUCATION BE MADE COMPULSORY?

The world in the modern era is fast resolving itself into rival camps, armed to the teeth with the threatening, complicated and deadly weapons of destruction. Nearly each and every country looks suspiciously at other countries and is afraid of some hostile designs against itself.

Almost all governments across the globe spend a huge portion of their resources to maintain their military forces so that they are always ready for war. Hence, a trained and well-equipped army is unavoidable even for a country like India, which proclaims its faith in the Gandhian cult of non-violence and universal peace. The question arises— should military services be made compulsory?

Should the country go in for conscription?

It is now widely accepted that preparedness for war is the best guarantee for peace. Everyone has the right to defend his country. In this view, military training should be made compulsory for all, and every one should be called up for military service. Conscription is sure to provide a permanent army which is always ready to take the field at a moment's notice. In the last war, Germany had a conscripted army. On the other hand, in England and America, recruitment was on a voluntary basis. Consequently, it took the latter countries several years to attain the efficiency of Germany.

Merits and Demerits of Compulsory Military Education

Compulsory military education helps make the youth of a country disciplined, dutiful, patriotic and physically fit. They know how to obey and how to command. They play a key role in building up a nation. Young men, trained in military discipline, become efficient workers in peacetime too.

Every coin has two sides — bright side and the dark side. Compulsory military education is no exception. Such a system might well be a standing invitation to war. Furthermore, a nation will not willingly allow conscription where the people are the masters, where the people own the material resources of the country. For a discontented people, trained in war, might in the end recoil upon the warmongers or in military upheavals.

War strategies and warfare these days are much more different from those which were prevailing in the ancient times. A large infantry was an asset in olden times and the soldiers were frequently used as cannon fodders. Nonetheless, modern war is a mechanized war. These days countries are reducing their standing army and replacing it by high-powered missiles and a huge air force. Therefore, to go in for conscription now seems to be outmoded.

It is expected that the horrors of war will mend man's desire for military conquest. However, in the world, as at present constituted, where newspapers incite a militant disposition daily, a conscripted army is of utmost importance for civil defence at least, for putting down internal disorder and militant terrorism. Conscription does make a nation fit and well-organised, not necessarily for attack but certainly for self-defence and a sense of security.

Essentials of Military Education

In the times gone by, only a short course of drilling and training in the use of elementary weapons was sufficient. Hence, the NCC training was made compulsory in colleges to build up services for the second line of defence. However, success in modern warfare depends much more on weapons and skill than on sheer number as was in the days past.

With the growing mechanisation of weapons and the possibility of manipulating them from a long distance, that is remote control device, there is a need to recruit a huge army from scientists and technicians who are trained to wage long-distance warfare.

Now-a-days, war has become a push-button affair. You have just to push a button to destroy a large army. In such conditions, the employment of huge armies cannot be considered a wise affair.

In the countries like India, which is forced to encounter a proxy war in the Northern border of Kashmir and eastern border of Assam and attached states and whose cities are on the target of terrorists and militants, new and effective strategies and techniques of warfare are unavoidable. Some big powers, hostile to India, are blatantly aiding and abetting Pakistan against India. Therefore, Indian army has to remain in a high state of preparedness.

So, military training has to be efficiently conducted in India and a large peacekeeping army is also necessary.

76

ROLE OF MEDIA IN A DEMOCRACY

Introduction

Democracy is a system of government in which all the people of a country, who have attained a certain age, are free to vote to elect their representatives. Thus, democracy is actually the rule of the public itself. The people themselves decide how to govern themselves. Media that actually works like a coordinator between the people and the government has been playing a vital role since its origin.

Role of Media

Media plays a vital role in framing a healthy democracy. It is the backbone of a democracy. It lets us know various social, political and economical activities taking place around the world. It is like a mirror which shows us or strives to show us the bare truth and harsh realities of life. It is the media which reminds politicians about their promises which they had made at the time of elections. This reminder compels politicians to be up to their promises in order to remain in power. News channels on the TV during elections help people, especially illiterates, in electing the right candidates to power.

Television and radio have made a significant achievement in educating rural masses in making them aware of all the events in their language. Coverage of exploitative malpractices of village heads and moneylenders has helped in taking stringent actions against them by attracting government attention. Media plays a very important role in exposing loopholes in the democratic system, which ultimately helps government in filling the vacuums of loopholes and making a system more accountable, responsive and citizen-friendly. A democracy without media can be compared with a vehicle without wheels. In the age of information technology, we are bombarded with information. We get the pulse of the world events with just a click of mouse. The flow of information has increased manifolds. The perfect blend of technology and human resources (journalist) has not left a single stone unturned in unearthing rampant corruption in politics and society. We all are well aware of whatever is happening across the globe. Thanks to technology that has brought a kind of revolution in journalism.

Demerits of Media

No doubt, media is very important and plays crucial role in a democracy. However, it also has its limitations and dark sides. Excessive coverage or hype of sensitive news by media has led to communal riots at times. The illiterates are more prone to provocations than the literates. Constant repetition of news, especially sensational news on news channels, breeds apathy and insensitivity. For instance, in Dhananjoy Chatterjee case, the overloaded hype led to death of quite a few children who imitated the hanging procedure which was repeatedly shown in most of the TV news channels. There is a plethora of such demerits. Media should take utmost care in airing or publishing such sensational news. Commercialisation has led to a stiff competition in media. Everyone is trying hard and employing every possible strategy to outdo others. Print media has gone one step further in publishing articles, cover stories and so forth on sex. According to media experts, who are glued to TV news channels, which have cropped up swiftly in the recent past, these types of articles, cover stories, etc. are cheap means of alluring a specific range of readers.

Conclusion

No one is perfect in this world and so is the media. There is still a lot of scope for improvements by which media can raise up to the aspirations of the people. A democracy cannot be thought of without active and honest media. Media is like a watchdog in a democracy that keeps government active. From being just an informer, it has become an integral part of our life. With the passage of time, it is growing over more matured and more responsible entity. The present media revolution has helped people in making informed decisions and this has led to the beginning of a new era in democracy.

77

IMPORANCE OF SPORTS AND GAMES

Games and sports are very vital for the overall development of a person. Their importance is being increasingly recognised in India from both the educational and social points of view. They are being encouraged more and more in schools, colleges and universities. In fact, they have become an essential part of the curricula. Time was when only a few students, who were fond of certain sports like football, hockey, cricket or tennis, were offered special facilities. But now regular programmes are drawn up in all educational institutions to persuade as many students as possible, regardless of special aptitudes, to participate in games and not merely watch matches occasionally to cheer up their favourite teams and attend the prize distribution functions at the end of a sports season.

According to the educationalists and others, it is in the interest of society as a whole that adequate facilities should be provided, depending upon the availability of funds, for games and sports for the country's youth including both the boys and the girls. Sports foster friendship and amity. Nor does the belief that those who take part in sports or games would be not good at studies and that each year their absence from the class or shortage of lectures would be condoned as they can either attend to their studies or be on the playing field holds good. It is felt necessary that apart from some exceptional cases of students having extraordinary talent and skill in certain games, or the students who are expected to be high on the merit list in university examinations, most other students should play one or the other game, not necessarily for gaining distinctions but for the sake of sports.

Several factors are required to be taken into consideration in this connection. First, physical fitness is of the utmost importance for everyone. Participation in games and sports invariably ensures good health, fitness and generally freedom from ailments of various types which find easy victims among people who take no physical exercises and are either lazy, indolent or desk-bound or are book worms and keep studying all the time under the mistaken concept that they can win success in life by studying all the time and concentrating on the development of their mental faculties. They are more or less of the opinion that brains matter, not brawn, and also that spending hours on the playfield is a waste of time. However, such students, sooner or later, find that unless the human body is kept in smooth trim and in an overall fit condition, even the brain will refuse to cooperate after some time. It is an accepted fact that good physical health is of vital importance if one desires to get proficiency in studies and for gaining distinctions in examinations. One who possesses an unhealthy body has more chances to lose. Physical exercise is very essential and sports whether it is cricket, hockey or football offer good physical exercise.

Secondly, regular participation in sports is very essential to get a healthy channel for the diversion of energies. If students and other youth participate in sports regularly, their constructive sublimation is sure; misdirection of youthful vigour is much less and the tendency to indulge in indiscipline and mischief is controlled; disruptive activities of various kinds are curbed. Young people have surplus energy. If this is fruitfully utilised, the foundations are laid for a healthy society where people are fully aware of the need for discipline, co-operative effort, team spirit, the cult of sportsmanship, of joint devotion to the achievement of a common aim in collaboration with others. Sports and games inculcate in them the quality to cultivate the virtue of working together. They learn not only being good winners but also good losers. Two teams playing a game cannot win simultaneously and ups and downs are common. The losers must learn to their defeat sportingly. The right spirit can be learnt on the playgrounds. There is no point in bearing a grudge against the rivals. Today's losers can be tomorrow's winners, as in society in general and the political arena in particular.

Thirdly, playing games and the spirit of sportsmanship

assist to inculcate lasting values which make for good soldiers, good fighters and good discipline, apart from promoting physical fitness. In British schools and colleges, full importance is given to sports, particularly cricket and football. The result has been the creation of a well-developed, healthy, disciplined and an efficient society in which people know the right proportions in life. They put everything in the right perspective and seldom conduct themselves in an unsporting, ungentlemanly and unbecoming manner. Playing sports and games on the playground instructs people to play the sports of life in the right spirit, which is what matters most, not victory or defeat.

When the government encourages sports and games, provides playgrounds, necessary equipment and other facilities, rewards outstanding sportsmen, the society is benefitted in many a way. The crime graph dips indicating that the incidences of general crimes decrease, because the right spirit and the right approach to things is developed on the playground. Sport, it has been said, is not only a manifestation of animal energy of surplus strength to develop more strength; it is, in addition, a safe and complete outlet for the aggressive spirit in people.

In genuine sports, the aim is to play the game in a fair and acceptable manner according to the rules of which every player is supposed to be fully aware. Those who violate the rules, play foul or exceed the permissible limits, or indulge in unfair tactics are pulled up by the refree or the umpire. Anyone who refuses to mend his ways or repeatedly violates the rules is ordered to quit the field and is replaced by another player. Such rules are useful to inculcate the habit of honouring the judge and of observing the rules.

It is now obvious that society is sure to get benefit if its members play the game according to the prescribed rules. Those who flout the rules or laws and become anti-social elements are hauled up by the forces responsible for maintaining law and order. The executive authorities enforce the laws and the judiciary punishes those whose guilt is duly established. Sportsmen generally tend to become good citizens, and society is thus the ultimate beneficiary.

While most people admit the importance of sports in a healthy and developed society and under a good government, there has also been much criticism of the craze, enthusiasm and fervour displayed by people of all ages, especially some of the country's youth whenever cricket matches are played in India or abroad and wherever India is one of the participants. Work virtually comes to a stop in offices, factories, schools and colleges. Everyone starts listening to cricket commentaries, forge his or her work and duty. All their attention is concentrated on the ball-by-ball commentaries. At wayside shops, in trains and buses, on ships and in aircraft, it is the same story during the cricket season— people listening to radio commentaries or watching cricket matches on TV.

However, this is not what we mean by sport and sportsmanship. The right word for this habit is craze. It does not develop any of the traits which sports and games inculcate— discipline and playing the game in the right spirit.

According to some experts there is a close link between sports and a country's industrial development and the general progress of society. That is why, it is contended, most of the gold medals at the Olympics are generally bagged by the advanced countries including the USA, Russia and Germany.

Is there a link between performance in sports and a country's military might?

Militarily, China is the most powerful country in the East, but Japan, which matches the USA in industrial advancement, does very well in sports despite its small size. India is a large country, and given the proper incentives and the necessary facilities, this country's sportsmen should do well on the sports field, but whether it is the climatic factor or the lack of adequate nutrition and of incentives, they do not compete favourably with the players of the USA, Russia, Germany and Australia.

Whatever the case, the relatively poor performance of our athletes in international competitions does not weaken the case for encouraging sports which help to lay the foundations of a healthy society.

78

FOREIGN DIRECT INVESTMENT IN INDIA

The fast and rapidly developing economy of India in most of its sectors has made it one of the mot popular places in the whole world for Foreign Direct Investment. India's ever-expanding markets, liberalisation of trade policies, advancement in technology and telecommunication, and loosening of diverse foreign investment restrictions, have further made India the apple of investors' eye for most productive, profitable and secure foreign investment. A recent survey carried out by the United Nations Conference on Trade and Development (UNCTAD) shows that India has obviously emerged out as the second most popular and preferable destination in the whole world for highly profitable foreign direct investment. China enjoys the first rank in this regard.

In recent years, the investors from US, UK, Singapore, Mauritius and so forth have made the bulk of the foreign direct investment in Indian business sectors of infrastructure, telecommunication, information technology, computer hardware and software, and hospitality services. Global Jurix, one of the leading full-fledged legal organisations of India with global repute, has been helping companies, business corporations, organisations and other potential investors all around the world, in making foreign direct investment in Indian business sectors in various ways.

FDI Law Practice India

There are a variety of ways in which foreign direct investment in Indian business sectors can easily be made through the Governmental and Automatic Routes. Nonetheless, the joint ventures are the most popular and preferred forms of making investment in Indian industry. At present, Telecommunications, Hospitality sector, Infrastructure (Power,

Steel, Railways, etc.), Education, Retail sector, Real Estate, Biotechnology, Petroleum and Petroleum Products, Alternative Energy, etc. are considered to be the most lucrative business for FDI in our country. Foreign investors from all classes and categories can get help from Global Jurix for getting highly lucrative and secure FDI in India.

They can get help in following regards :

- Corporate and Commercial Law services
- Establishment of Joint Ventures
- Company Formation and Company Law services
- Setting up Subsidiaries
- Drafting all requisite Contracts, Agreements and other Documents
- For making all Mandatory Compliances
- Project Finance
- Tax Planning
- Private Equity
- Dispute Resolution
- And, other legal services for FDI in India.

Reasons of Making FDI

You know that Foreign Direct Investment (FDI) denotes the direct investment into the production of a country by a foreign company, either by buying a company in the country or by expanding operations of an existing business in the country. There are several reasons why foreign direct investment is made such as to take benefit of cheaper wages in the country, special investment privileges such as exemptions provided by the country as an incentive to get tariff-free access to the markets of the country or the region. Foreign direct investment is in contradiction to portfolio investment that is a passive investment in the securities of another country.

As a part of the national accounts of a country, FDI denotes to the net inflows of investment to obtain a lasting management interest in an enterprise being operated in an economy other than that of the investor. It is the total of equity capital, other long-term capital and short-term capital as shown in the balance of payments. It involves participation in management, joint venture, transfer of technology as well as expertise. There are two types of FDI: inward foreign direct investment and outward foreign direct investment, which result in a net FDI inflow (positive or negative) and "stock of foreign direct investment", which is the cumulative number for a given period. Direct investment does not include investment through purchase of shares.

79

JAN LOK PAL BILL

The Jan Lok Pal Bill or the Citizen's Ombudsman Bill is a draft anti-corruption bill. Drawn up by civil society activists, this bill seeks the appointment of a Jan Lok Pal. The Jan Lok Pal would be an independent body and would investigate corruption cases, complete the investigation within a year and envisages trial in the case getting over in the next one year. The Jan Lok Pal Bill was drafted by Justice Santosh Hegde, Prashant Bhushan and Arvind Kejriwal. It envisages a system where a corrupt person found guilty would go to jail within two years of the complaint being made and his ill-gotten wealth being confiscated. It also offers power to the Jan Lok Pal to prosecute politicians and bureaucrats without government permission. Retired IPS officer Kiran Bedi, Sri Sri Ravi Shankar, Anna Hazare and Mallika Sarabhai are also part of the movement, called India Against Corruption.

Major Features of the Jan Lok Pal Bill:

The Jan Lok Pal Bill has been one of the most discussed topics in the recent time. Let us go through its major features which have been mentioned below:

1. The bill provisions that an institution called Lok Pal at the Centre and Lokayukta in each State will be set up.
2. Just as the Supreme Court and the Election Commission, both the Lok Pal and Lokayukta will be completely independent of the governments. Their investigations cannot be influenced by any minister or bureaucrat.
3. Cases against corrupt people will not linger on for years anymore. It is because investigations in any case will have to be completed in one year. The trial of the case should be accomplished in next one year so that the corrupt politician, officer or judge is sent to jail within two years.
4. The loss caused by the corrupt person to the government should essentially be recovered at the time of conviction.

5. The Jan Lok Pal Bill is very beneficial to the common people. It facilitates that if any work of any citizen is not done in the prescribed time in any government office, Lok Pal will impose financial penalty on the guilty officers which will be given as compensation to the complainant.

When can you Approach the Lok Pal?

Common people can approach Lok Pal to get solution of their problems if any of their work concerning any government office is not resolved within a fixed period of time. For example, if your ration card or passport or voter card is not being made or if police is not registering your case or any other work is not being done in prescribed time, you may approach the Lok Pal. He will have to get it done in a month's time. Besides, you can also report any case of corruption to Lok Pal such as ration being siphoned off, poor quality roads being constructed or Panchayat funds being not utilised properly. In all such cases, Lok Pal is required to accomplish necessary investigations within a year and it would be mandatory to complete the trial within the next one year. Thus, the guilty would be behind the bars within two years.

Who will Appoint the Lok Pal Members?

The Jan Lok Pal Bill ensures that the Lok Pal members should not be appointed by the government so that they can work honestly, impartially and without any pressure. It provisions that its members are selected by judges, citizens and constitutional authorities and not by politicians, through a completely transparent and participatory process.

The whole functioning of Lok Pal/Lokayukta will be thoroughly transparent. Any complaint against any officer of Lok Pal shall be investigated and the guilty officer will be dismissed within two months.

Presently, we have Chief Vigilance Commissioner (CVC), departmental vigilance and anti-corruption branch of Central Bureau of Investigation (CBI) as anti-corruption agencies. In the Jan Lok Pal Bill, these agencies will be merged into Lok Pal. Lok Pal will have thorough powers and machinery to independently investigate and prosecute any officer, judge or politician.

The Lok Pal would ensure full protection to those who are being victimised for raising their voice against corruption.